New Bridges

1res

PROGRAMME 2011

W0352309

Sous la direction de François GUARY
et Marie FORT-COUDERC

par

Marie FORT-COUDERC
Professeur certifié

Gaël MANESCAU
Professeur certifié

Sylvie PERSEC
Professeur agrégé

Serge TRIPODI
Professeur agrégé

Avec la participation de
Joyce BOURJAULT
Professeur agrégé

James WALTERS
Professeur agrégé

Avec la collaboration de
Patricia VRINAT-HINDLE
Professeur agrégé

Nathan

Cover photos

Background picture: Kord.com/Eyedea.
From top to bottom and from left to right: Brooklyn, Brighton Beach, Russian quarter of New York, known as Little Odessa, 2009: © Caroline Maufroid/La Collection (detail); Urban youth hanging out in the Lower East Side of New York City: © Karen E. Evans/Plainpicture (detail); Road 66 sign: © Steve Snowden/ShutterStock; South Africa: Demonstration to celebrate the release of Nelson Mandela, February 11th 1990: © Gérald Buthaud/ANA (detail); The Spiderman balloon moves down Central Park West marking the start of the Macy's Thanksgiving Day Parade in New York, November 26th 2009: © Finbarr O'Reilly/Reuters (detail).

Édition : Josiane Attucci-Jan

Iconographie : Sophie Suberbère

Conception de la couverture : Denis Hoch

Conception de la maquette : Frédéric Jély

Cartographie, graphiques et illustrations : AFDEC (p. 141), Graphito (p. 145) ; Laurent Blondel ; Amélie Veaux (p. 12), Philippe Tastet (p. 110, 118)

FSC MIXTE Papier issu de sources responsables FSC® C022030

Le papier de cet ouvrage est composé de fibres naturelles, renouvelables, fabriquées à partir de bois provenant de forêts gérées de manière responsable.

Aux élèves de Premières

Bienvenue dans *New Bridges 1res* et dans la première année du cycle terminal du lycée.

Il s'agit pour vous, au cours de ces deux années du cycle terminal, de développer votre autonomie dans la pratique de l'anglais et de passer du niveau seuil B1, que vous avez acquis en fin de classe de seconde, au niveau avancé B2, que vous devrez avoir atteint en fin de classe de terminale. *New Bridges 1res* a été conçu pour vous aider à franchir progressivement les différentes étapes de cet apprentissage et atteindre le niveau B1+ à la fin de la classe de première.

Vous trouverez dans ce manuel :

■ Une tâche finale à accomplir à l'issue de chaque unité

La tâche finale est annoncée en début d'unité : il s'agit d'une mise en situation de communication autour d'un scénario dont vous serez – seul, à deux ou en groupe – l'acteur ou les acteurs. Deux activités langagières seront mises en jeu pour la réalisation de cette tâche. Tout au long de l'unité, des entraînements à partir de supports variés ainsi que des micro-tâches vous guideront vers cette tâche finale.

■ Dans chaque unité, une activité langagière dominante et un entraînement dans les quatre autres activités langagières, qui faciliteront le travail en groupes de compétences

Les pages *Focus on* de chaque unité vous permettront de vous entraîner dans une activité langagière dominante, liée à la réalisation de la tâche finale. Vous trouverez également, au cours de chaque unité, un entraînement dans les autres activités langagières.

Chaque unité vous permettra ainsi d'améliorer vos compétences dans les activités de réception (compréhension de l'oral et compréhension de l'écrit), de production (expression orale en continu et expression écrite) ainsi que dans les activités d'interaction orale.

■ Un enrichissement culturel

Le programme culturel du cycle terminal est centré sur le thème **« Gestes fondateurs et mondes en mouvement »** et structuré autour de quatre notions : Mythes et héros, Espaces et échanges, Lieux et formes du pouvoir et L'idée de progrès. Chaque unité s'articule autour de deux ou trois notions de ce programme et s'appuie sur des supports de toute nature (textes, images, documents audio, extraits de film) qui vous permettront de mieux connaître les sociétés anglo-saxonnes.

Les pages *Spotlight* éclairent la thématique de l'unité à travers le prisme d'un des domaines du programme : Arts, Croyances et représentations, Histoire et géopolitique, Langue et langages, Littérature, Sciences et techniques, Sociologie et économie.

Les pages *Art Quest* sont consacrées à trois formes d'expression artistique : la photographie par le biais de photographies iconiques, l'art contemporain américain et le cinéma en présentant des films liés à l'immigration.

■ La possibilité de vous évaluer par rapport aux niveaux B1 et B2 du Cadre européen commun de référence pour les langues (CECRL)

Les pages *Check your skills* en fin d'unité vous permettront tout au long de l'année de faire régulièrement le point sur votre niveau dans les cinq activités langagières.

Prenez le temps de découvrir votre livre, les deux pages suivantes devraient vous aider à l'utiliser au mieux. N'oubliez pas de consulter les dernières pages du manuel : les *Culture keys*, la Méthodologie et le Précis grammatical. Ce sont des pages de référence qui vous seront utiles tout au long de l'année.

Nous souhaitons vivement que vous soyez à même de tirer le meilleur parti de vos cours et que vous éprouviez beaucoup de plaisir à pratiquer l'anglais avec *New Bridges 1res*.

Les auteurs

Découverte du manuel

OUVERTURE

Découverte de la thématique de l'unité
Présentation de la tâche finale

Expression orale

- ***Keywords*** : lexique essentiel de la thématique

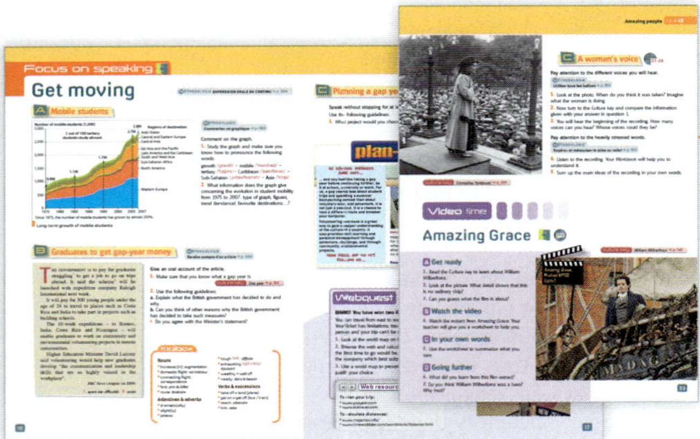

FOCUS ON

Activité langagière dominante de l'unité

- Trois exercices d'entraînement
- Renvois aux pages de Méthodologie traitant de la compétence travaillée
- ***Webquest*** : réalisation de tâches à partir d'une recherche sur Internet ou ***Video time*** : étude d'un document vidéo

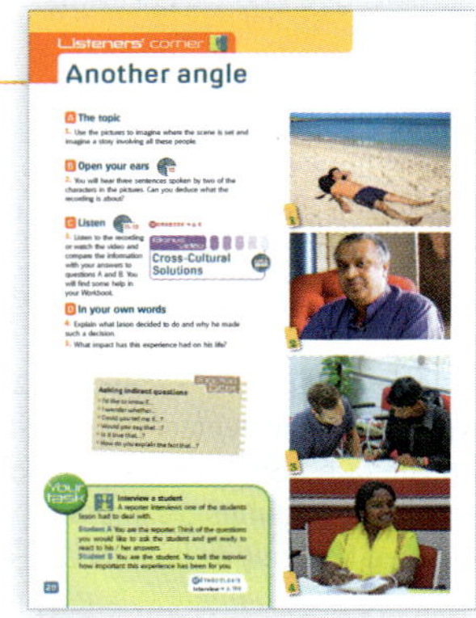

LISTENERS' CORNER

Entraînement guidé
à la compréhension de l'oral

- ***The topic*** : découverte du thème
- ***Open your ears*** : préparation à l'écoute
- ***Listen*** : compréhension de l'oral
- ***In your own words*** : reformulation

SPEAKERS' CORNER

Entraînement guidé à l'expression orale
en continu et à l'interaction orale

- ***Read*** / ***Listen*** / ***Look and speak*** : expression orale
- ***Going further*** : approfondissement

WRITERS' CORNER

Entraînement guidé
à l'expression écrite

- ***Get ready*** : préparation de l'activité
- ***Write…*** : conseils méthodologiques

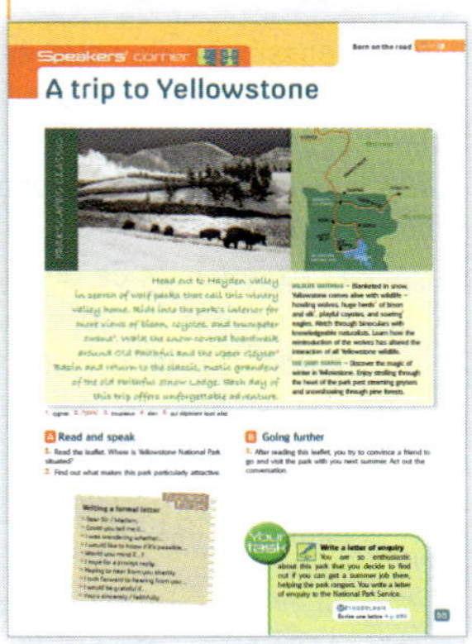

Logos utilisés dans le manuel

- Compréhension de l'oral
- Compréhension de l'écrit
- Expression orale en continu
- Interaction orale
- Expression écrite
- 29 CD de l'élève
- 27 CD pour la classe
- DVD DVD avec les vidéos
- TICE Activités en lien avec les technologies de l'information et de la communication pour l'éducation

Rubriques récurrentes

- toolbox : Lexique pour parler du document
- function box : Structures de communication
- Your task : Activité en lien avec le document

TEXT 1 / TEXT 2

Entraînement guidé à la compréhension d'un texte de fiction ou de presse

- ***Warming up*** : préparation à la lecture
- ***Reading comprehension*** : compréhension écrite
- ***In your own words*** : reformulation
- ***Going further*** : approfondissement
- ***Language training*** : Savoir prononcer, Pratiquer la grammaire, en lien avec le texte

SPOTLIGHT

Enrichissement culturel autour d'un domaine du programme

- Activités à partir de documents divers

FINAL TASK

Une tâche finale organisée autour de deux activités langagières

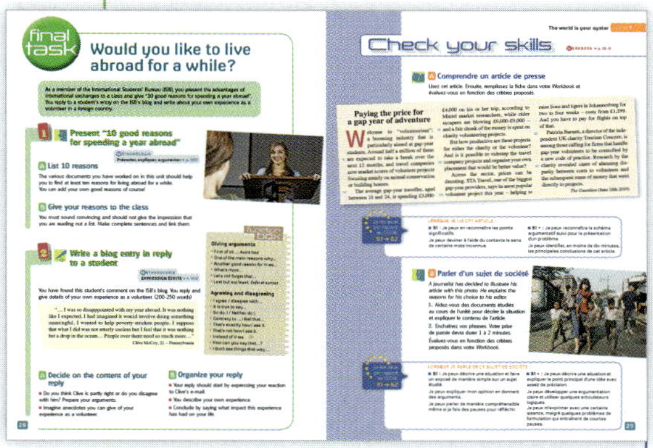

LANGUAGE WORKSHOP

Renforcement de points clés

Grammaire – Grammaire de l'oral – Lexique

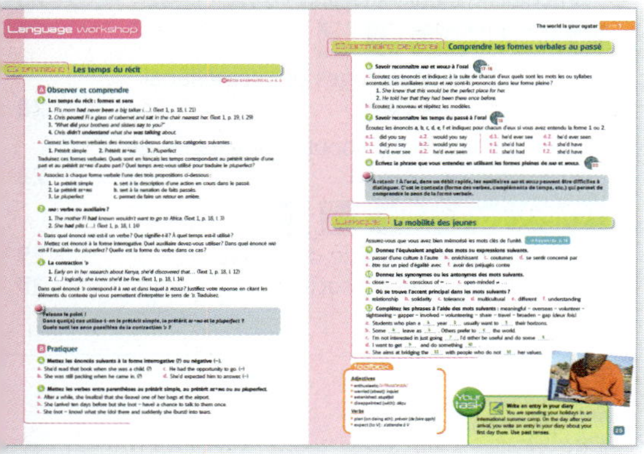

CHECK YOUR SKILLS

Deux activités langagières testées pour s'évaluer

- **Je me situe par rapport au CECRL** : des critères pour s'évaluer par rapport aux niveaux du Cadre européen

sommaire

Breaking the ice

The time capsule

1

Espaces et échanges

L'idée de progrès

The world is your oyster

2

Mythes et héros
L'idée de progrès

Amazing people

Art quest

3

Espaces et échanges
Mythes et héros
L'idée de progrès

Born on the road

4

Espaces et échanges
Mythes et héros

American dreams

Art quest

5

Espaces et échanges
Lieux et formes du pouvoir
L'idée de progrès

Southern voices

Sommaire

Reading

Méthodologie des activités langagières

Précis grammatical

Le groupe verbal

Le groupe nominal

La phrase

À l'issue du cycle terminal des séries générales et technologiques, le niveau de compétence attendu pour la langue vivante 1 est B2, pour la langue vivante 2, B1.

	Compréhension de l'oral	Compréhension de l'écrit	Expression orale en continu	Interaction orale	Expression écrite
B1	**Comprendre les points essentiels d'une intervention énoncée dans un langage clair et standard.** • comprendre ce qui est dit pour réaliser une tâche en situation réelle ou simulée ; • comprendre une information factuelle sur des sujets de la vie quotidienne ou étudiés ; • suivre une conversation en situation réelle ou simulée ; • comprendre les points principaux d'une intervention sur des sujets familiers ou étudiés, y compris des récits courts ; • suivre le plan général d'un exposé court sur un sujet connu ; • comprendre les points principaux de bulletins d'information et de documents enregistrés simples portant sur des sujets connus.	**Comprendre des textes essentiellement rédigés dans une langue courante.** • comprendre des instructions et consignes détaillées ; • comprendre suffisamment pour entretenir une correspondance suivie ; • localiser des informations recherchées ou pertinentes pour s'informer et réaliser une tâche ; • comprendre un enchaînement de faits ; • reconnaître les grandes lignes d'un schéma argumentatif.	**S'exprimer de manière simple sur des sujets variés.** • prendre la parole devant un auditoire, mettre en voix un texte ; • restituer une information avec ses propres mots, éventuellement à partir de notes ; • relater des expériences vécues, en rendre compte (événements, dialogues, texte écrit ou oral) ; • décrire ; • expliquer ; • exprimer des sentiments, une opinion personnelle ; • argumenter pour convaincre.	**Faire face à des situations variées avec une relative aisance à condition que la langue soit standard et clairement articulée.** • engager la conversation et maintenir le contact pour échanger des informations, réagir à des sentiments, exprimer clairement un point de vue ; • prendre part à une discussion pour expliquer, commenter, comparer et opposer ; • interviewer et être interviewé, conduire un entretien préparé et prendre quelques initiatives ; • faire aboutir une requête.	**Rédiger un texte articulé et cohérent, sur des sujets concrets ou abstraits, relatif aux domaines qui lui sont familiers.** • restituer une information avec ses propres mots, paraphraser simplement de courts passages écrits ; • prendre des notes sous forme d'une liste de points ; • rédiger un courrier personnel (incluant des avis sur des sujets abstraits ou culturels) ; • rendre compte d'expériences, de faits et d'événements ; • écrire un court récit, une description, un poème, de brefs essais simples ; • rédiger des messages courts de type informatif ou injonctif.
B2	**Comprendre l'essentiel d'une intervention longue, d'une argumentation complexe énoncée dans un langage standard.** • suivre une grande partie de ce qui est dit dans une longue conversation ; • comprendre la plupart des émissions, reportages et films en langue standard, reconnaître le point de vue et l'attitude du locuteur ; • comprendre l'essentiel d'une conférence, d'un discours ou d'un exposé complexes à condition que le sujet soit assez familier.	**Lire avec un grand degré d'autonomie et utiliser les références convenables de manière sélective.** • identifier rapidement le contenu et la pertinence d'une information, d'un article ou d'un reportage dans une gamme étendue de sujets ; • comprendre un texte littéraire contemporain en prose ; • comprendre des articles et des rapports sur des problèmes contemporains et dans lesquels les auteurs adoptent une position ou un point de vue particuliers.	**S'exprimer de manière organisée sur une gamme étendue de sujets relatifs à ses domaines d'intérêt.** • développer un exposé de manière claire et méthodique en soulignant les éléments significatifs ; • faire une description claire et détaillée sur un sujet connu ou étudié ; • exprimer avec finesse et précision des sentiments, une opinion personnelle ; • développer une argumentation claire, nuancée et enchaîner les arguments avec logique.	**Participer à des conversations avec spontanéité et aisance, avec des locuteurs natifs.** • échanger des informations précises, expliciter, demander des éclaircissements ; • prendre part à une conversation sur des sujets connus ou étudiés : exposer son propre point de vue, évaluer les points de vue d'autrui, émettre des hypothèses ; • interviewer et être interviewé, conduire un entretien avec efficacité et aisance de manière de plus en plus autonome ; • corriger lapsus et erreurs après en avoir pris conscience.	**Écrire des textes clairs et détaillés sur une gamme étendue de sujets relatifs à son domaine d'intérêt.** • résumer un large éventail de textes ; • résumer l'intrigue et la suite des événements d'un film ou d'une pièce ; • écrire des lettres exprimant différents degrés d'émotion, souligner ce qui est important ; • écrire des descriptions élaborées d'événements et d'expériences dans un texte articulé ; • écrire un essai ou un rapport qui développe une argumentation de façon méthodique.

Breaking the ice

The time capsule

►You've found an old trunk in your back yard. You open it an understand it's a time capsule*! You decide to figure out when was buried. After looking at the items inside, you hesitat between the 1960s, 1970s or 1980s.

**A time capsule /'kæpsjuːl/ is a container holding historical recorc or objects representative of current culture that is deposited f preservation until future discovery.*

1

A Speaking

1. Describe the various items sticking out of the trunk and guess how old they are.

2. You have pulled out of the trunk a film poster and a personal photo.

a. Describe the film poster. Do you know when this episode of the famous saga was released?

b. What event are the people on the photo certainly attending? From the way they are dressed, can you guess when the photo was taken?

2

toolbox

Nouns

- platform shoe
- button: *badge*
- floppy disk drive: *lecteur de disquette*
- space opera /'ɒpərə/
- spaceship
- alien /'eɪlɪən/ (noun + adj.)
- robot /'rəʊbɒt/
- laser beam
- sword /sɔːd/: *épée*
- minibus
- flower power
- festival
- headline: *gros titre*
- news item /'aɪtəm/: *information*
- single: *45 tours*

Adjectives

- old-fashioned = outdated
- bulky: *encombrant*
- threatening /'θretnɪŋ/: *menaçant*

Verbs

- attend: *assister*
- announce
- break up = split: *se séparer*
- symbolize
- represent = stand for

B Reading

You've found some newspapers at the bottom of the trunk. Unfortunately it is impossible to read the dates when the papers were issued.

Read these three articles and say what events they refer to. Do you know when the three events approximately took place?

LONDON TIMES
January 31st 19

ULSTER'S BLOODY SUNDAY

THIRTEEN WERE KILLED yesterday as Army paratroopers broke up a banned Civil Rights march in Londonderry. An end to the conflict seemed further away than ever today as

Saint Louis Dispatch
January 27th 19

Pact to end Vietnam war reaches
Cease fire begins today.

AN AGREEMENT TO STOP THE SHOOTING has at last been hammered out at the Paris peace talks. Announcing this in a television broadcast to the American people, President Nixon said

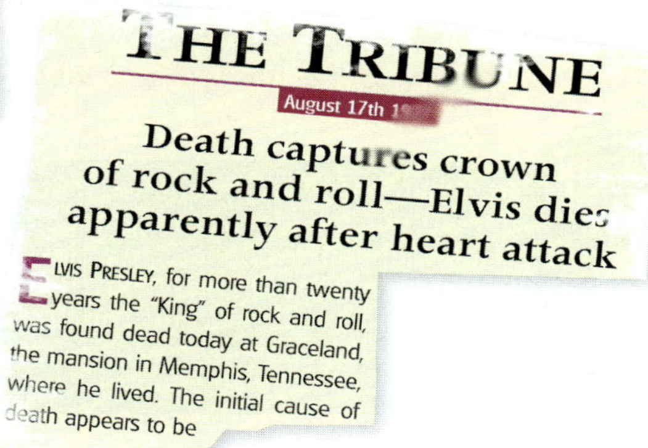
THE TRIBUNE
August 17th 19

Death captures crown of rock and roll—Elvis dies apparently after heart attack

ELVIS PRESLEY, for more than twenty years the "King" of rock and roll, was found dead today at Graceland, the mansion in Memphis, Tennessee, where he lived. The initial cause of death appears to be

C Listening

CD 1 4

Now you pull out the Beatles' single *Let it be* and a cassette.

Listen to the recording and find out:

a. the Beatles' nickname;
b. the problem they had at the time;
c. who wrote the song and which year the record was issued.

D Discussing

1. Compare the results of your investigation with a schoolmate's and decide which decade the trunk was buried.

2. You and your schoolmate have decided to make your own time capsule. Discuss the items representative of the 2010s that you are going to put into the trunk.

E Writing

You have decided to put a note in your time capsule in which you explain why you have chosen to bury these items. Write the note.

Évaluations diagnostiques
Vous venez de vous entraîner dans les cinq activités langagières. Votre professeur va maintenant vous fournir des fiches permettant de vous évaluer et de déterminer à quel niveau du CECRL vous vous situez dans ces cinq activités.

Unit 1

Espaces et échanges

L'idée de progrès

The world is your oyster

Would you like to live abroad for a while?

final task

As a member of the International Students' Bureau, you present the advantages of international exchanges to a class and give "10 good reasons for spending a year abroad". You reply to a student's entry on the ISB's blog and write about your own experience as a volunteer in a foreign country.

Keywords

Nouns
- gap year: *année sabbatique*
- gapper = gap year student
- volunteer (noun / verb): *bénévole*
- volunteering
- relationship
- solidarity
- tolerance
- customs: *coutumes / habitudes*

Adjectives & adverbs
- overseas: *à l'étranger*
- multicultural
- close = intimate /ˈɪntɪmɪt/
- understanding
- open-minded ≠ narrow-minded
- different (from sb)
- aware (of) = conscious (of)
- rewarding: *enrichissant*
- meaningful: *qui a du sens*

Verbs & expressions
- travel the world
- backpack: *voyager avec un sac à dos*
- cross cultures: *passer d'une culture à l'autre*
- go sightseeing /ˈsaɪtsiːɪŋ/: *faire du tourisme*
- feel concerned (about)
- get involved (in sth, with sb): *s'impliquer*
- socialize /ˈsəʊʃəlaɪz/: *fréquenter des gens*
- broaden one's horizons /həˈraɪzns/
- be prejudiced against: *avoir des préjugés contre*
- be on an equal footing with: *être sur un pied d'égalité avec*
- share: *partager*
- bridge a gap: *combler le fossé*

LANGUAGE WORKSHOP → p. 25

Friends beyond borders

"The world is your oyster" means your life lies ahead of you and you will have lots of opportunities to find something of great value.

1. Describe the picture briefly and say in what way it illustrates the expression "The world is your oyster".

2. What opportunities for meeting people all over the world does modern technology open up?

3. What about you? Would you say that the world is your oyster?

toolbox

Nouns

- oyster /ˈɔɪstə/: *huître*
- pearl /pɜːl/: *perle*
- photomontage /ˌfəʊtəʊmɒnˈtɑːʒ/
- identity picture / photo
- mosaic /məʊˈzeɪɪk/
- social network
- flight: *vol*

Adjectives

- convenient
- on-line ≠ off-line
- face-to-face

Verbs & expressions

- stare at: *regarder fixement*
- interact
- enable /ɪˈneɪbl/: *permettre*
- make friends (with)
- be on friendly / good terms (with)
- come from all walks of life: *venir de divers horizons*
- browse the web

Get moving

MÉTHODOLOGIE EXPRESSION ORALE EN CONTINU → p. 153

A Mobile students

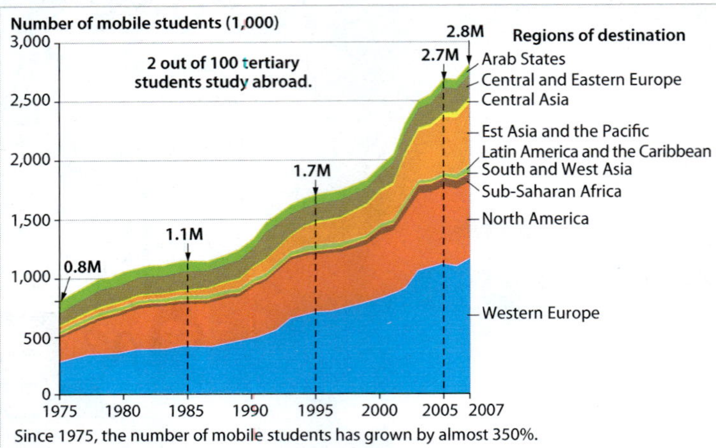

Long-term growth of mobile students

MÉTHODOLOGIE
Commenter un graphique → p. 154

Comment on the graph.

1. Study the graph and make sure you know how to pronounce the following words:

growth /grəʊθ/ – mobile /'məʊbaɪl/ – tertiary /'tɜːʃərɪ/– Caribbean /ˌkærɪ'biːən/ – Sub-Saharan /ˌsʌbsə'hɑːrən/ – Asia /'eɪʒə/

2. What information does the graph give concerning the evolution in student mobility from 1975 to 2007: type of graph, figures, trend *(tendance)*, favourite destinations…?

B Graduates to get gap-year money

MÉTHODOLOGIE
Rendre compte d'un article → p. 153

THE GOVERNMENT is to pay for graduates struggling[1] to get a job to go on trips abroad. It said the scheme[2] will be launched with expedition company Raleigh International next week.

It will pay for 500 young people under the age of 24 to travel to places such as Costa Rica and India to take part in projects such as building schools.

The 10-week expeditions – to Borneo, India, Costa Rica and Nicaragua – will enable graduates to work on community and environmental volunteering projects in remote communities.

Higher Education Minister David Lammy said volunteering would help new graduates develop "the communication and leadership skills that are so highly valued in the workplace".

BBC News (August 1st 2009)

1. *ayant des difficultés* 2. *projet*

Give an oral account of the article.

1. Make sure that you know what a gap year is.

culture key Gap year → p. 139

2. Use the following guidelines:

a. Explain what the British government has decided to do and why.

b. Can you think of other reasons why the British government has decided to take such measures?

c. Do you agree with the Minister's statement?

toolbox

Nouns

- increase (in): *augmentation*
- domestic flight: *vol intérieur*
- connecting flight: *correspondance*
- fare: *prix du billet*
- route: *itinéraire*

Adjectives & adverbs

- dramatic(ally)
- slight(ly)
- jobless
- tough /tʌf/: *difficile*
- exhausting /ɪg'zɔːstɪŋ/: *épuisant*
- wealthy = well-off
- needy: *dans le besoin*

Verbs

- take off ≠ land (plane)
- get on ≠ get off (bus / train)
- reach: *atteindre*
- link: *relier*

C Planning a gap year

MÉTHODOLOGIE
Expliquer. Argumenter → p. 155

Speak without stopping for at least one minute.
Use the following guidelines:

1. What project would you choose if you were given the opportunity of taking a gap year? The web page below will help you to make a choice but you may have other ideas.
2. What difficulties would you have to face?

plan-your-gap-year.com

MONTHLY UPDATE

SO SCHOOL RESULTS ARE OUT...

... and you feel like taking a gap year before continuing further, be it at school, university or work. For us, a gap year is less about student trips and spending a summer backpacking abroad than about voluntary work and adventure. It is not just a year out. It is a chance to take a different route and broaden your horizons.

Volunteering overseas is a great way to gain a deeper understanding of the culture of a country. It also provides skill learning and personal development through adventure, challenge, and through community, environmental projects.

YOU FEEL UP TO IT? FOLLOW US...

Win two Round the World Tickets

Enter the Round the World competition. Take the travel quiz and... **Read more >>**

Do something amazing

Help street children in Bombay
Help build and maintain centres for boys and girls, in a country where thousands of children are abandoned as their parents can no longer afford their care.

Read more >>

Camp Kenya
Live as a guest in a rural community – not as a tourist – and participate in conservation initiatives to protect wildlife and the environment.

Read more >>

Teach music or drama in New Zealand
Teach music or drama at a school in the largest city in New Zealand, Auckland. You'll work with children from all backgrounds, including Maori children.

Read more >>

Webquest — Travelling the world (TICE)

BINGO! You have won two Round the World tickets!

You can travel from east to west, or vice versa, but be careful! Your ticket has limitations: travel costs can't exceed £1,000 per person and your trip can't be more than 30,000 miles long.

1. Look at the world map on flaps II-III and plan your ideal trip.
2. Browse the web and calculate the distances, decide when the best time to go would be, compare the prices, and find out the company which best suits your plan.
3. Use a world map to present your project to the class and justify your choice.

Web resources

To plan your trip:
- www.gapyear.com
- www.statravel.com

To calculate distances:
- www.mapcrow.info/
- www.timeanddate.com/worldclock/distance.html

Taking risks

culture key Kenya → p. 139

Masha HAMILTON

Masha Hamilton is an American novelist who came to fiction-writing through journalism. She was a foreign correspondent in the Middle East and Russia. The author of four novels, she is also the founder of the *Camel Book Drive*, a world literacy programme, begun in 2007 to supply a camel-borne library in north-eastern Kenya.

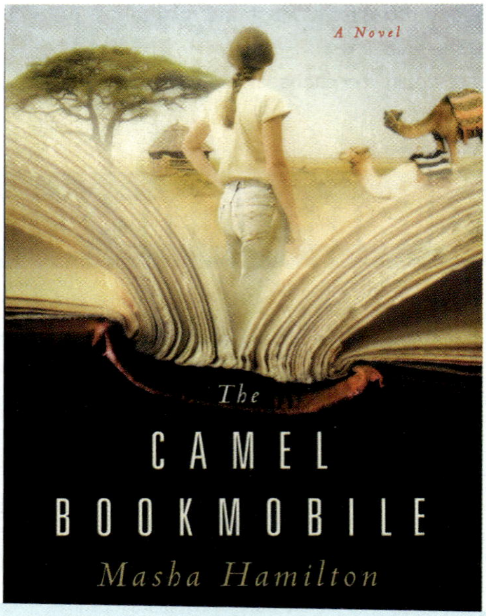

A Warming up

You are going to study an extract from a novel entitled *The Camel Bookmobile*[1]. Look at the various elements in the illustration on the book cover. What can you anticipate about the subject of the book?

Fiona turned her attention back to her bag, which still had space. What else should she take? Lifting a framed snapshot, she examined her mother as a young woman. The mother Fi had known wouldn't want to go to Africa. In fact, she wouldn't want Fi to go. Fi put the picture facedown and scanned the room, her attention drawn to a worn[2] volume of Irish poetry by her bedside. She tucked it in.

"How about the netting?" Chris called from the living room where he sat with Devi.

"Already in," Fi answered.

"And repellent?" asked Devi.

"Yes, yes." Fi waved her hand as though shooing away a gnat[3].

Early on in her research about Kenya, she'd discovered that the country's annual death toll[4] from malaria was in the tens of thousands.

She had pills; she had repellents; logically, she knew she'd be fine. Still, a figure that high jolted[5] her. *Mbu* – mosquito – had been the first Swahili word she'd learned. Sometimes the insects even dive-bombed[6] into her nightmares. Eventually, mosquitoes became a metaphor for everything she feared about this trip: all the stories she'd read about a violent and chaotic continent, plus the jitters that come with the unknown.

And what wasn't unknown? All she knew for sure, in fact, was why she was going. Fi's mom had never been a big talker, but she'd been a hero, raising four kids alone. Now it was Fi's turn to do something worthwhile.

"Fi." Chris, at the door of the bedroom, waved in the air the paper on which he'd written a list of all the items he thought she should bring and might forget. Money belt. Hat. Granola bars. "Have you been using this?" he asked half-mockingly in the tone of a teacher.

"I hate lists," Fi said.

Fi moved to the living room and plopped onto the floor across from Devi. Chris poured Fi a glass of cabernet and sat in the chair nearest her.

"You know, there's lots of illiteracy in *this* country," Devi said after a moment.

"That's why I've been volunteering after work," Fi said. "But there, it's different. They've never been exposed to libraries. Some have never held a book in their hands."

"Not to mention that it's more dangerous, which somehow makes it appealing to Fi," Chris said to Devi, shaking his head. "Nai-robbery."

Though he spoke lightly, his words echoed those of Fi's brother and two sisters – especially her brother. She was ready with a retort. "I'll mainly be in Garissa, not Nairobi," she said. "It's no more dangerous there than New York City. Anyway, I want to take some risks – different risks. Break out of my rut[7]. Do something meaningful." Then she made her tone playful. "The idealistic Irish. What can you do?"

"Sometimes idealism imposes," Chris said. "What if all they want is food and medicine?"

"You know what I think. Books are their future. A link to the modern world."

The Camel Bookmobile, Masha HAMILTON (2007)

1. /ˈbʊkməbiːl/ **2.** *(ici) vieux* **3.** /næt/ *moucheron* **4.** *nombre de victimes* **5.** *donner des frissons* **6.** *attaquer en piqué* **7.** *routine*

B Reading comprehension

WORKBOOK → p. 4-5

Turn to your *Workbook* which will help you to understand the text.

C In your own words

1. Sum up the story, with the help of the following guidelines.
   a. Who is Fiona and what has she decided to do?
   b. Explain the reasons for her decision.
   c. How do Fiona's friends and relatives react to her leaving?

D Going further

2. Analyse Fiona's feelings. Why does she think of her mother?
3. What does Fiona mean when she says she wants to *"do something meaningful"* (l. 40)?
4. Why does Fiona say that she is an *"idealistic Irish"* (l. 40)?

E Language training

5. **Savoir prononcer** YOUR CD 4-6 CD 1 7-9
6. **Pratiquer la grammaire**
   Les temps du récit

LANGUAGE WORKSHOP → p. 24

toolbox

Nouns
- role model
- disease /dɪˈziːz/: *maladie*
- aid agency: *organisation humanitaire*
- indifference

Adjectives
- apprehensive = fearful
- determined = strong-willed
- hazardous /ˈhæzədəs/ = dangerous
- illiterate /ɪˈlɪtərɪt/: *illettré*
- sceptical /ˈskeptɪkəl/
- realistic

Verbs & expressions
- pack: *faire ses bagages*
- intend = plan
- join: *rejoindre*
- bite /baɪt/: *piquer (insecte)*
- look up to = admire
- care (about): *se soucier*
- question: *remettre en question*
- make a pun: *faire un jeu de mots*
- achieve /əˈtʃiːv/ one's goal: *atteindre son but*

Your task

Write an e-mail

Six months later, Fiona sends an e-mail to her friends with this picture attached. Imagine the content of the e-mail.

MÉTHODOLOGIE
Écrire un courriel → p. 166

Another angle

A The topic

1. Use the pictures to imagine where the scene is set and imagine a story involving all these people.

B Open your ears

CD 1 10

2. You will hear three sentences spoken by two of the characters in the pictures. Can you deduce what the recording is about?

C Listen

CD 1 11-13

WORKBOOK → p. 6

3. Listen to the recording or watch the video and compare the information with your answers to questions A and B. You will find some help in your *Workbook*.

Bonus vidéo
Cross-Cultural Solutions
DVD

D In your own words

4. Explain what Jason decided to do and why he made such a decision.

5. What impact has this experience had on his life?

function box

Asking indirect questions

- I'd like to know if...
- I wonder whether...
- Could you tell me if...?
- Would you say that...?
- Is it true that...?
- How do you explain the fact that...?

Your task

Interview a student

A reporter interviews one of the students Jason had to deal with.

Student A You are the reporter. Think of the questions you would like to ask the student and get ready to react to his / her answers.

Student B You are the student. You tell the reporter how important this experience has been for you.

MÉTHODOLOGIE
Interview → p. 158

1

2

3

4

Writers' corner

Bristol, Liverpool or Edinburgh?

culture key Comenius Programme → p. 139

Your task

Write a blog entry

Your school has joined the Comenius Programme and plans to start a partnership with a British school. You have the choice between schools located in Bristol, Liverpool or Edinburgh.
Which city will your school choose? You write a blog entry on the school website to explain your preference and convince the school community. (200 words)

MÉTHODOLOGIE EXPRESSION ÉCRITE → p. 165

Education and Culture
Lifelong learning programme
COMENIUS

1. Bristol International Balloon Fiesta

2. Mathew Street Festival in Liverpool

3. Edinburgh Festival Fringe

A Get ready

1. Read about the Comenius Programme in the *Culture key* p. 139.

2. You have to choose between three British cities. Browse the web to find information about the elements below.

visitbristol.co.uk/
www.visitliverpool.com/
www.edinburgh.org/

Location
- Where are the cities located and how far are they from your own school?
- How can you get there: means of transport, fares?
- How far is it from the airport / international train station?

Places of interest
- List the places which are worth visiting in the city itself.
- Think of other places of interest in the area.
- Don't forget to mention the museums.

Historical background
- Check what happened there.

Specific events
- Check what's happening in the year to come: festivals, concerts, plays, sporting events…

3. Find out the arguments which are likely to convince your classmates but also your teachers.

function box

Suggesting and convincing
- How about / What about V-ING?
- Why don't we V...?
- Don't you think that...?
- I suggest V-ING / I suggest we (should) V...
- We should definitely V...
- I'm convinced that...
- It seems to me that...
- I'm sure you will / won't V...

B Write a blog entry about your choice

Here are a few hints:

4. The description of the city of your choice must be brief but entertaining.

5. Why not insert a few pictures?

6. Be your own critic before submitting your text. Check it to correct your usual mistakes.

Text 2

The giant trees

culture key Tasmania → p. 139

theguardian was founded in 1821 and is one of the "big four" quality British newspapers (the three others are *The Times*, *The Daily Telegraph* and *The Independent*). It is known for its left-wing political standpoint. The Sunday newspaper is *The Observer*.
Website: www.guardian.co.uk/

A Warming up

Look at the poster. What is its aim?
Who do you think issued this poster?

Clyde, 23, is a British anthropology graduate writing about his backpacking experience in Tasmania.

I was on a year out in Australia, and after a few months in the red centre I decided to go to Tasmania to escape the heat, and to see big trees. The island is home to a vast forest of Eucalyptus Regnans[1], the largest flowering plants in the world.

Within a few days of arriving I heard word of protest activity in the Upper Florentine Valley, a pristine[2] corner of virgin forest under threat from various logging projects.

I decided to hitch there, and for the last part of the journey I rode with TK, a Canadian biologist who had been living in the Florentine camp for two years. He gave me a brief history of the area as we entered the forest. These Eucalyptus Regnans, at 60m tall, may not be the biggest trees in the world – one California redwood[3] is 98m, for example – but never, TK assured me, would I feel as dwarfed by nature as when among the giants of the Florentine Valley.

The protest has been going on since 2006, when Forestry Tasmania began extending the road into the forest. Protesters live in the trees so that they won't be cut down, though there has been much confrontation and some arrests.

The local climate is incredibly wet, adding a ghostly white cover to the giant trees. Rain-soaked banners high up in the branches "Still Wild, Still Threatened" were visible from the roadside. But no amount of neck-craning can quantify the trees' size.

For an eco-friendly backpacker, the Florentine camp provided a cheap and exciting alternative to a volunteer project. Bring food donations, good conversation and a useful pair of hands and the vast Tasmanian wilderness is yours to explore. Camp life was centred on communal meals, firewood runs, clean-ups and lookout reports. Each night, wet hair and cloth steamed by a campfire under a blue tarpaulin[4]. Plates of food were passed around – curried baked beans topped with fresh parsley.

A camp veteran of six months told me how she was humbled by a spectacular light display from the aurora australis. Another veteran had a doctorate in zoology, and used the camp as a base for a statistical project on the Tasmanian devil[5] population. I spent a couple of days on the west coast's Bay of Fires – a wild, windswept clash of white-sand beaches, turquoise water, brooding[6] skies and red-stained granite rocks.

As well as being a good place to become actively involved in forest conservation, the camp was where people shared travellers' tips – a valuable resource that is often ignored in favour of a guidebook.

The Guardian – Travel section, Clyde MACFARLANE (August 21st 2010)

1. a species of eucalyptus **2.** *préservé* **3.** *séquoia* **4.** *bâche goudronnée* **5.** a carnivorous marsupial **6.** *troublant*

B Reading comprehension WORKBOOK → p. 7-8

Turn to your *Workbook* which will help you to understand the text.

C In your own words

1. Give an account of Clyde's backpacking experience. Don't forget to use link words.

D Going further

2. What can you guess about Clyde's personality?

3. Explain why ecologists protest against deforestation.

4. Would you like to embark on a similar experience? Explain why or why not.

E Language training

5. Savoir prononcer YOUR CD 7-8 CD 1 15-16

Lisez le passage de *"I was on a year…"* (l. 4) à *"… the forest."* (l. 21).

a. Dans les mots suivants la **voyelle -*a*-** en gras se prononce-t-elle : /ə/, /æ/, /ɑː/, /ɒ/, /eɪ/ ou /ɛə/?
was – Australia – Tasmania – escape – vast – largest – plants – arriving – activity – various – part – Canadian – had – camp – area

b. À quels endroits ferez-vous des **liaisons** ?

c. Vérifiez à l'écoute, puis relisez ce passage à haute voix en faisant attention aux deux points de phonologie que vous venez de travailler.

6. Pratiquer la grammaire

FOR, SINCE – Quantifieurs – Comparatifs et superlatifs

WORKBOOK → p. 9

toolbox

Nouns

- environment /ɪn'vaɪərənmənt/
- environmentalist /ɪn,vaɪərən'mentəlɪst/
- conservation: *sauvegarde, protection*
- biodiversity /,baɪəʊdaɪ'vɜːsətɪ/
- wildlife /'waɪldlaɪf/: *faune et flore*
- soil erosion
- ecosystem
- activist: *militant*

Adjectives

- adventurous /əd'ventʃərəs/
- thrilling = exciting
- hostile = inhospitable

Verbs & expressions

- give sb a lift: *prendre qqn en voiture*
- save ≠ endanger
- damage /'dæmɪdʒ/ = harm: *endommager*
- protect = preserve
- prevent from V-ING: *empêcher de*
- struggle (against)
- go off the beaten track: *aller hors des sentiers battus*

Activists protesting against forest destruction

Your task

Talk about your experience

TK tells Clyde why he decided to get involved with the Florentine camp protesters and describes his life at the camp. Put yourself in TK's shoes.

MÉTHODOLOGIE Raconter → p. 153

Grammaire | Les temps du récit

PRÉCIS GRAMMATICAL → 4, 8

A Observer et comprendre

1 Les temps du récit : formes et sens

1. *Fi's mom **had** never **been** a big talker (...).* (Text 1, p. 18, l. 21)
2. *Chris **poured** Fi a glass of cabernet and **sat** in the chair nearest her.* (Text 1, p. 19, l. 29)
3. *"What **did** your brothers and sisters **say** to you?"*
4. *Chris **didn't understand** what she **was talking** about.*

a. Classez les formes verbales des énoncés ci-dessus dans les catégories suivantes :

1. Prétérit simple **2.** Prétérit BE+ING **3.** *Pluperfect*

Traduisez ces formes verbales. Quels sont en français les temps correspondant au prétérit simple d'une part et au prétérit BE+ING d'autre part ? Quel temps avez-vous utilisé pour traduire le *pluperfect* ?

b. Associez à chaque forme verbale l'une des trois propositions ci-dessous :

1. Le prétérit simple	**a.** sert à la description d'une action en cours dans le passé.
2. Le prétérit BE+ING	**b.** sert à la narration de faits passés.
3. Le *pluperfect*	**c.** permet de faire un retour en arrière.

2 HAD : verbe ou auxiliaire ?

1. *The mother Fi **had** known wouldn't want to go to Africa.* (Text 1, p. 18, l. 3)
2. *She **had** pills (...).* (Text 1, p. 18, l. 14)

a. Dans quel énoncé HAD est-il un verbe ? Que signifie-t-il ? À quel temps est-il utilisé ?

b. Mettez cet énoncé à la forme interrogative. Quel auxiliaire devez-vous utiliser ? Dans quel énoncé HAD est-il l'auxiliaire du *pluperfect* ? Quelle est la forme du verbe dans ce cas ?

3 La contraction 'D

1. *Early on in her research about Kenya, she'**d** discovered that...* (Text 1, p. 18, l. 12)
2. *(...) logically, she knew she'**d** be fine.* (Text 1, p. 18, l. 14)

Dans quel énoncé 'D correspond-il à HAD et dans lequel à WOULD ? Justifiez votre réponse en citant les éléments du contexte qui vous permettent d'interpréter le sens de 'D. Traduisez.

Faisons le point !
Dans quel(s) cas utilise-t-on le prétérit simple, le prétérit BE+ING et le *pluperfect* ?
Quels sont les sens possibles de la contraction 'D ?

B Pratiquer

4 Mettez les énoncés suivants à la forme interrogative (?) ou négative (–).

a. She'd read that book when she was a child. (?)
b. She was still packing when he came in. (?)
c. He had the opportunity to go. (–)
d. She'd expected him to answer. (–)

5 Mettez les verbes entre parenthèses au prétérit simple, au prétérit BE+ING ou au *pluperfect*.

a. After a while, she (realize) that she (leave) one of her bags at the airport.
b. She (arrive) ten days before but she (not – have) a chance to talk to them once.
c. She (not – know) what she (do) there and suddenly she (burst) into tears.

Grammaire de l'oral | Comprendre les formes verbales au passé

6 Savoir reconnaître *HAD* et *WOULD* à l'oral CD 1 17-18

a. Écoutez ces énoncés et indiquez à la suite de chacun d'eux quels sont les mots ou les syllabes accentués. Les auxiliaires *WOULD* et *HAD* sont-ils prononcés dans leur forme pleine ?

1. *She knew that this would be the perfect place for her.*
2. *He told her that they had been there once before.*

b. Écoutez à nouveau et répétez les modèles.

7 Savoir reconnaître les temps du passé à l'oral CD 1 19

Écoutez les énoncés **a**, **b**, **c**, **d**, **e**, **f** et indiquez pour chacun d'eux si vous avez entendu la forme **1** ou **2**.

a.1. did you say	**a.2.** would you say	**d.1.** he'd ever see	**d.2.** he'd ever seen
b.1. did you say	**b.2.** would you say	**e.1.** she'd had	**e.2.** she'd have
c.1. he'd ever see	**c.2.** he'd ever seen	**f.1.** she'd had	**f.2.** she'd have

8 Écrivez la phrase que vous entendez en utilisant les formes pleines de *HAD* et *WOULD*. CD 1 20

À retenir ! À l'oral, dans un débit rapide, les auxiliaires *HAD* et *WOULD* peuvent être difficiles à distinguer. C'est le contexte (forme des verbes, compléments de temps, etc.) qui permet de comprendre le sens de la forme verbale.

Lexique | La mobilité des jeunes

Assurez-vous que vous avez bien mémorisé les mots clés de l'unité. → Keywords p. 14

9 Donnez l'équivalent anglais des mots ou expressions suivants.

a. passer d'une culture à l'autre **b.** enrichissant **c.** coutumes **d.** se sentir concerné par **e.** être sur un pied d'égalité avec **f.** avoir des préjugés contre

10 Donnez les synonymes ou les antonymes des mots suivants.

a. close = … **b.** conscious of = … **c.** open-minded ≠ …

11 Où se trouve l'accent principal dans les mots suivants ?

a. relationship **b.** solidarity **c.** tolerance **d.** multicultural **e.** different **f.** understanding

12 Complétez les phrases à l'aide des mots suivants : meaningful – overseas – volunteer – sightseeing – gapper – involved – volunteering – share – travel – broaden – gap *(deux fois).*

a. Students who plan a …1… year …2… usually want to …3… their horizons.
b. Some …4… leave as …5… . Others prefer to …6… the world.
c. I'm not interested in just going …7…, I'd rather be useful and do some …8… .
d. I want to get …9… and do something …10… .
e. She aims at bridging the …11… with people who do not …12… her values.

toolbox

Adjectives

- enthusiastic /ɪn'θuːzɪ'æstɪk/
- worried (about): *inquiet*
- astonished: *stupéfait*
- disappointed (with): *déçu*

Verbs

- plan (on doing sth): *prévoir (de faire qqch)*
- expect (to V) : *s'attendre à V*

Your task

Write an entry in your diary

You are spending your holidays in an international summer camp. On the day after your arrival, you write an entry in your diary about your first day there. **Use past tenses.**

An English-speaking world

The world is your oyster and English is your language.

A The king of languages

ENGLISH DOMINATES THE WORLD as no language ever has, and some linguists are now saying it may never be dethroned as the king of languages.

Some insist that linguistic evolution will continue to take its course over the centuries and that English could eventually die as a common language as Latin did, or Phoenician or Sanskrit or Sogdian before it.

That skepticism seems to be a minority view. Experts on the English language like David Crystal, author of *English as a Global Language*, say the world has changed so drastically[1] that history is no longer a guide. "This is the first time we actually have a language spoken genuinely globally by every country in the world," he said. "There are no precedents to help us see what will happen."

As a new millennium begins, scholars[2] say that about one-fourth of the world's population can communicate to some degree in English.

The New York Times (9th April 2007)

1. *radicalement* 2. *(ici) experts*

Read the text and find the following information.

1 Find the reason why experts believe that the English language is not likely to die as Latin did.

2 Give the proportion of the world's population who can communicate in English. Do you know how many people that makes?

B Why is English a global language?

CD 1 21

Listen to David Crystal, a linguistics professor.

What reasons does he give for the development of English as a global language?

C English language stats

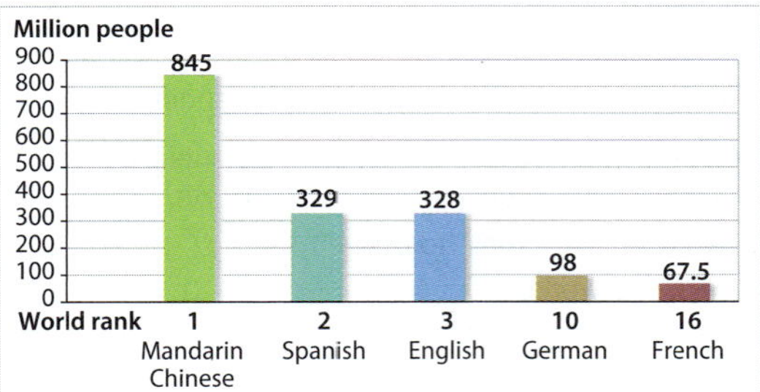

Languages by number of native speakers in 2008
(Source: Ethnologue Languages of the world, 2009)

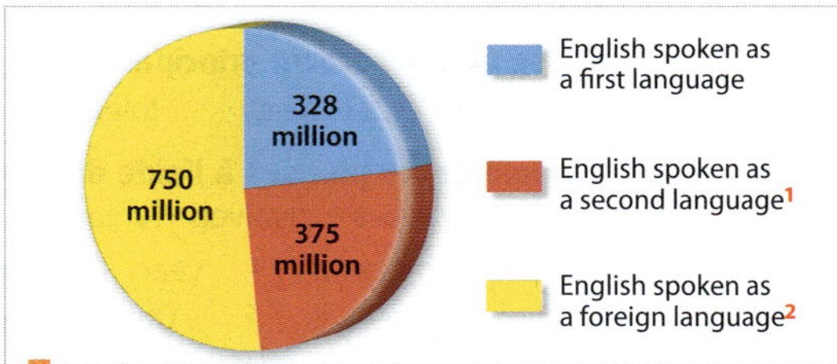

Number of English speakers in the world in 2008
(Source: British Council, 2008)

1. Second language speakers use English on a daily basis.
2. Foreign language speakers use English occasionally for business or pleasure.

Observe the two charts.

1 Which language is spoken by the greatest number of native speakers?

2 What rank does English hold by number of native speakers?

3 What is the world rank of English if you add up first, second and foreign language speakers?

4 True or false? Non-native English speakers outnumber native speakers by a ratio of 3 to 1.

5 Observe the world map on flaps II-III and say where the countries which use English as an official (or second) language are situated. Can you explain why English is used in these countries?

D Globish and Englishes

As English continues to spread, the linguists say, it is fragmenting, as Latin did, into a family of dialects – and perhaps eventually fully-fledged[1] languages – known as Englishes.

New vernaculars[2] have emerged in such places as Singapore, Nigeria and the Caribbean, although widespread literacy and mass communication may be slowing the natural process of diversification.

One enterprising scholar has translated *Don Quixote* into Spanglish, the hybrid of English and Spanish that is spoken along the borders of Mexico and the United States.

But unlike Latin and other former common languages, most scholars say English seems to be too widespread and too deeply entrenched[3] to die out. Instead, it is likely to survive in some simplified international form – sometimes called Globish or World Standard Spoken English – side by side with its offspring[4].

As a simplified form of global English emerges, the diverging forms spoken in Britain and America could become no more

than local dialects – two more Englishes alongside the Singlish spoken in Singapore or the Taglish spoken in the Philippines. A native speaker of English might need to become bilingual in his own language to converse with other speakers of global English.

The New York Times (April 9th 2007)

1. *à part entière* 2. form of a language used by ordinary people 3. *enraciné* 4. *(ici) langues dérivées*

Read the text and answer the following questions.

1 Explain the word "Globish": word formation and meaning.

2 Imagine what kind of people speak Globish.

3 What is the difference between Globish and Englishes?

4 List the various Englishes mentioned in the text.

E Is English a language killer?

CD 1 22

1 Do you think that English is likely to kill less spoken languages?

2 Listen to David Blur, a professor at Macquarie University in Sydney.

3 Does David Blur confirm or refute your first impression?

Webquest World languages

TICE

1 Browse the web so as to find out whether these statements are true or false.

Student A You visit www.vistawide.com and www.britishcouncil.org

Student B You visit www.ethnologue.com and www.learnenglishguide.com

a. There are currently 690 languages spoken around the world.

b. 94% of the world's population speak 6% of the world's languages.

c. English is an official language in Puerto Rico.

d. Mandarin Chinese is spoken by the greatest number of non-native speakers.

e. Portuguese is among the top ten languages by number of native speakers.

f. The language which has the most words is French.

g. Languages have existed since about 100,000 BC.

h. 133 languages are spoken by less than 10 people.

i. English is the official language of 268 countries.

j. Over 600,000 students a year come to study English in the UK.

2 Compare your results with your friend's and browse the web again if your answers differ.

final task

Would you like to live abroad for a while?

As a member of the International Students' Bureau (ISB), you present the advantages of international exchanges to a class and give "10 good reasons for spending a year abroad". You reply to a student's entry on the ISB's blog and write about your own experience as a volunteer in a foreign country.

1 Present "10 good reasons for spending a year abroad"

MÉTHODOLOGIE
Expliquer. Argumenter → p. 155

A List 10 reasons

The various documents you have worked on in this unit should help you to find at least ten reasons for living abroad for a while.
You can add your own good reasons of course!

B Give your reasons to the class

You must sound convincing and should not give the impression that you are reading out a list. Make complete sentences and link them.

function box

Giving arguments

- First of all...: *Avant tout*
- One of the main reasons why...
- Another good reason for V-ING...
- What's more...
- Let's not forget that...
- Last but not least: *Enfin et surtout*

Agreeing and disagreeing

- I agree / disagree with...
- It is true to say...
- So do I. / Neither do I.
- Contrary to..., I feel that...
- That's exactly how I see it.
- That's not how I see it.
- Instead of V-ING
- How can you say that...?
- I don't see things that way ...

2 Write a blog entry in reply to a student

MÉTHODOLOGIE
EXPRESSION ÉCRITE → p. 165

You have found this student's comment on the ISB's blog. You reply and give details of your own experience as a volunteer. (200-250 words)

> "... I was so disapppointed with my year abroad. It was nothing like I expected. I had imagined it would involve doing something meaningful. I wanted to help poverty-stricken people. I suppose that what I did was not utterly useless but I feel that it was nothing but a drop in the ocean... People over there need so much more..."
>
> Clive McCoy, 21 – Pennsylvania

A Decide on the content of your reply

- Do you think Clive is partly right or do you disagree with him? Prepare your arguments.
- Imagine anecdotes you can give of your experience as a volunteer.

B Organize your reply

- Your reply should start by expressing your reaction to Clive's e-mail.
- You describe your own experience.
- Conclude by saying what impact this experience has had on your life.

Check your skills

WORKBOOK → p. 10-11

A Comprendre un article de presse

Lisez cet article. Ensuite, remplissez la fiche dans votre *Workbook* et évaluez-vous en fonction des critères proposés.

Paying the price for a gap year of adventure

Welcome to "voluntourism": a booming industry that is particularly aimed at gap-year students. Around half a million of them are expected to take a break over the next 12 months, and travel companies now market scores of volunteer projects focusing mainly on animal conservation or building homes.

The average gap-year traveller, aged between 18 and 24, is spending £3,000-£4,000 on his or her trip, according to Mintel market researchers, while older escapees are blowing £6,000-£9,000 – and a fair chunk of the money is spent on charity volunteering projects.

But how productive are these projects for either the charity or the volunteer? And is it possible to sidestep the travel company projects and organise your own placement that would be better value?

Across the sector, prices can be daunting. STA Travel, one of the biggest gap-year providers, says its most popular volunteer project this year – helping to raise lions and tigers in Johannesburg for two to four weeks – costs from £1,299. And you have to pay for flights on top of that.

Patricia Barnett, a director of the independent UK charity Tourism Concern, is among those calling for firms that handle gap-year volunteers to be controlled by a new code of practice. Research by the charity revealed cases of alarming disparity between costs to volunteers and the subsequent sums of money that went directly to projects.

The Guardian (June 26th 2010)

Je me situe par rapport au CECRL **B1 → B2**

LORSQUE JE LIS CET ARTICLE :

- **B1 :** Je peux en reconnaître les points significatifs.
  Je peux deviner à l'aide du contexte le sens de certains mots inconnus.
- **B1 + :** Je peux reconnaître le schéma argumentatif suivi pour la présentation d'un problème.
  Je peux identifier, en moins de dix minutes, les principales conclusions de cet article.

B Parler d'un sujet de société

A journalist has decided to illustrate his article with this photo. He explains the reasons for his choice to his editor.

1. Aidez-vous des documents étudiés au cours de l'unité pour décrire la situation et expliquer le contenu de l'article.

2. Enchaînez vos phrases. Votre prise de parole devra durer 1 à 2 minutes.

Évaluez-vous en fonction des critères proposés dans votre *Workbook*.

Je me situe par rapport au CECRL **B1 → B2**

LORSQUE JE PARLE DE CE SUJET DE SOCIÉTÉ :

- **B1 :** Je peux décrire une situation et faire un exposé de manière simple sur un sujet étudié.
  Je peux expliquer mon opinion en donnant des arguments.
  Je peux parler de manière compréhensible même si je fais des pauses pour réfléchir.
- **B1 + :** Je peux décrire une situation et expliquer le point principal d'une idée avec assez de précision.
  Je peux développer une argumentation claire et utiliser quelques articulateurs logiques.
  Je peux m'exprimer avec une certaine aisance, malgré quelques problèmes de formulation qui entraînent de courtes pauses.

Unit 2

Mythes et héros
L'idée de progrès

Amazing people

What is a hero for you?

final task You have a summer job in a radio station and you have been asked to prepare a radio programme called "Modern day heroes". You listen to two radio reports and you decide which one to include in the programme.

Keywords

Nouns
- hero /ˈhɪərəʊ/
- heroine /ˈherəʊɪn/
- heroism /ˈherəʊɪzəm/
- courage /ˈkʌrɪdʒ/ = bravery
- coward /ˈkaʊəd/: *lâche*
- achievement: *exploit*
- deed: *action*
- rescuer: *sauveteur*
- ringleader: *chef, meneur*
- duty
- icon /ˈaɪkɒn/

Adjectives
- heroic /hɪˈrəʊɪk/
- courageous /kəˈreɪdʒəs/
- fearless = daring /ˈdɛərɪŋ/
- bold /bəʊld/ = adventurous /ədˈventʃərəs/
- risky ≠ safe
- selfless: *désintéressé*
- committed: *engagé*
- unsung (hero): *méconnu*

Verbs & expressions
- come to sb's rescue /ˈreskjuː/: *sauver, secourir qqn*
- risk one's life
- save one's life
- rebel /rɪˈbel/ (against)
- stand up for = defend
- fight (for)
- stand up to ≠ oppose
- look up to sb = admire
- sacrifice oneself
- achieve one's goal: *atteindre son but*
- take up a challenge /ˈtʃælɪndʒ/: *relever un défi*
- go beyond one's limits: *dépasser ses limites*
- overcome: *surmonter*

LANGUAGE WORKSHOP → p. 41

Robin Hood

1. What do you know about Robin Hood?

2. Describe the film still from Ridley Scott's *Robin Hood*. Do you like this kind of film? Why (not)?

3. Would you say that Robin Hood corresponds to your idea of a hero? Why (not)?

toolbox

Nouns

- bow /bəʊ/: *arc*
- arrow: *flèche*
- spear /spɪə/: *lance*
- outlaw /'aʊtlɔː/: *hors-la-loi*
- rebel /'rebl/
- the poor / the needy

Adjectives

- exposed: *à découvert*
- determined /dɪ'tɜːmɪnd/

Verbs & expressions

- shoot: *tirer*
- rob: *voler*
- break the law
- attack ≠ be under attack
- defend oneself (against)
- be at war (against)

Fighters

MÉTHODOLOGIE COMPRÉHENSION DE L'ORAL → p. 150

WORKBOOK → p. 12-13

A "I have nothing to offer…"

CD 1 23-24

MÉTHODOLOGIE
Anticiper → p. 150

Use the historical context to anticipate the words that you will certainly hear.

1. Say what you know about Winston Churchill, then read the *Culture key* to complete your answer.
2. Listen to a sentence taken from the recording. Deduce in what circumstances it was spoken.
3. Listen to the recording with the help of your *Workbook*. Don't panic! Historical documents may sometimes sound difficult because of the poor quality of the recording.
4. Give an oral account of what you've heard. Say what Winston Churchill's goal was as he spoke.

culture key Winston Churchill → p. 140

B Arrested

CD 1 25-26

MÉTHODOLOGIE
Classer, relier, hiérarchiser les informations → p. 151

Classify and link together the main elements.

1. Look at the photos, then imagine what the recording may be about.
2. You will hear four sentences. Two of them are taken from the recording. Can you guess which ones?
3. Listen to the recording. You will find some help in your *Workbook*.
4. Sum up the woman's story in your own words.

toolbox

Nouns

- criminal
- activist
- Suffragette /ˌsʌfrəˈdʒet/ Movement
- slavery: *esclavage*
- slave trade: *commerce des esclaves*
- shackles: *chaînes*
- slaver = slave ship

Adjectives

- illegal /ɪˈliːgəl/
- guilty ≠ innocent
- desegregated

Verbs & expressions

- be at war / wage war
- encourage /ɪnˈkʌrɪdʒ/
- rally to sb's support: *se rallier à qqn*
- break the law
- get / be arrested for V-ING
- convict /kənˈvɪkt/ sb (of a crime)
- abolish

culture key Emmeline Pankhurst → p. 140

C A woman's voice

CD 1 27-28

Pay attention to the different voices you will hear.

MÉTHODOLOGIE
Utiliser tous les indices → p. 150

1. Look at the photo. When do you think it was taken? Imagine what the woman is doing.
2. Now turn to the *Culture key* and compare the information given with your answer in question 1.
3. You will hear the beginning of the recording. How many voices can you hear? Whose voices could they be?

Pay attention to the heavily stressed words.

MÉTHODOLOGIE
Repérer et mémoriser la mise en relief → p. 151

4. Listen to the recording. Your *Workbook* will help you to understand it.
5. Sum up the main ideas of the recording in your own words.

Video time

Amazing Grace

DVD

culture key William Wilberforce → p. 140

A Get ready

1. Read the *Culture key* to learn about William Wilberforce.
2. Look at the picture. What detail shows that this is no ordinary ship?
3. Can you guess what the film is about?

B Watch the video

4. Watch the extract from *Amazing Grace*. Your teacher will give you a worksheet to help you.

C In your own words

5. Use the worksheet to summarize what you saw.

D Going further

6. What did you learn from this film extract?
7. Do you think William Wilberforce was a hero? Why (not)?

Amazing Grace, Michael APTED (2006)

Text 1

Real-life superheroes

The New York Times
Expect the World®

is an American daily newspaper founded in 1851 and published in New York City. It is the largest local metropolitan newspaper in the United States, behind *The Wall Street Journal* and *USA Today*. It is owned by The New York Times Company, which also publishes 18 other regional newspapers including *The International Herald Tribune* and *The Boston Globe*.
Website: www.nytimes.com/

A Warming up

Use the title and the picture to guess who these people are and what they do.

She calls herself Street Hero, says she is a former prostitute, knows martial arts and takes to the city's underbelly[1] to protect women who work the streets. Her uniform includes a black eye mask, a black bustier and black knee-high boots. Then there is Red Justice, a substitute teacher from Woodside, Queens, who wears red boxer briefs[2] over jeans, a red cape made from an old T-shirt and a sock with eyeholes to mask his identity. He trolls the subways encouraging young people to give their seats to those who need them more.

They call themselves real-life superheroes, and they were just a few of the do-gooders who gathered near Times Square yesterday for what was billed as the first meeting of a group called Superheroes Anonymous. They all declined to give their real names because they said they wanted to protect their identities.

The meeting was part news conference, part documentary film shoot and part patrol duty. There were locals and out-of-towners, most were in uniform (don't dare call them costumes) and all said they were serious about helping make their respective communities cleaner, safer and kinder places. The 13 or so who gathered yesterday are part of a growing community of activists across the country and beyond.

Chaim Lazaros, 23, a student at Columbia University and an independent filmmaker, co-founded Superheroes Anonymous along with Ben Goldman to bring to New York as many superheroes as he could for interviews and to record them for a documentary he is making about the movement.

"This is a serious job," Mr. Lazaros said. "We are out in the streets fighting crime in a legal way. But most of all we are fighting the worst crime of all, apathy."

"We're not these crazy people," said one man, Geist, who traveled to New York from Minnesota. "We just have an unorthodox approach to doing good."

The Super is a superintendent[3] of a building in Crown Heights, Brooklyn, who fixes faucets[4] and does electrical work for people in need. The Super, who also declined to give his real name, said he took on the alter ego after a friend was hurt by debris that had fallen from scaffolding[5]. "I said to myself, if we have to wait around for the city or the mayor to fix everything wrong or dangerous in this city, it'll never get done," the Super said.

He acknowledged that his self-proclaimed role – as well as what he wears – has drawn derision. He said he had been laughed at, stared at, egged and stoned.

"I don't have many friends," he said. "A lot of real-life superheroes stumble along the way. And part of it can definitely make you feel isolated, like nobody understands you."

The New York Times (October 29th 2007)

1. *(ici) quartier défavorisé* **2.** *caleçon* **3.** *gardien* **4.** *robinets* **5.** *échafaudage*

B Reading comprehension **WORKBOOK → p. 14-15**

our *Workbook* will help you to understand the text.

C In your own words

. Give an oral account of this article. Use the following uidelines.

. What do these real-life superheroes have in common?

. Sum up what Street Hero, Red Justice and The Super do.

. How do some people react when they see these real-life uperheroes?

D Going further

. What drives ordinary citizens to become real-life uperheroes?

3. Would you say that this movement is useful or not?

4. Some police departments have condemned this movement and say that America's most feared gangs, "the Crips" and "the Bloods", were also born as idealistic "community defenders". How do you explain the fact that do-gooders may turn into dangerous gang members?

E Language training

5. **Savoir prononcer** YOUR CD 9-10 CD 1 29-30

6. **Pratiquer la grammaire**

Présent simple et présent BE+ING – « faire faire »

WORKBOOK → p. 16

toolbox

Nouns

- superpower
- lawbreaker
- vigilante /ˌvɪdʒɪˈlæntɪ/: *membre d'un groupe d'autodéfense*
- good Samaritan /səˈmærɪtən/
- charity work
- the weak: *les faibles*

Adjectives

- thrilling = exciting
- unarmed
- eccentric
- law-abiding: *respectueux des lois*

Verbs & expressions

- prevent from V-ING: *empêcher de*
- act in self-defence
- break ≠ comply with the law
- take justice / the law into one's own hands
- dress up (as): *se déguiser*
- keep sb out of harm's way: *mettre qqn à l'abri*
- patrol /pəˈtrəʊl/: *patrouiller*

Your task

Discuss the real-life superhero movement

You talk with a friend about the real-life superhero movement. Decide who you want to be and note your arguments to get ready for the discussion.

Student A You think that real-life superheroes want to make the world a better place.

Student B You disagree because you think that people taking justice into their own hands can be dangerous.

MÉTHODOLOGIE
Discussion contradictoire → p. 158

Fame

A Look and listen

CD 1 31

You are going to listen to a recording about the biographies of these three celebrities. Unfortunately, during the sound mixing, various elements of these biographies were mixed up.

1. Prince William

2. Jessica Watson

1. While listening to the recording, decide which biographical elements correspond to which celebrity. Reproduce the following grid and fill it in with facts about each celeb's life.

	Prince William	Jessica Watson	John Lennon
Nationality			
Date / Place of birth			
Family members			
Activities			
Important dates			

3. John Lennon by Andy Warhol

B Speak

2. With the help of the grid, prepare an oral presentation of the celebrity you admire the most. Explain your choice to the class.

C Going further

3. Name a person who has had a great impact on you and explain why.

toolbox

Nouns

- charity: *œuvre de bienfaisance*
- pacifism /'pæsɪfɪzəm/
- idealist /aɪ'dɪəlɪst/
- private /'praɪvɪt/ life

Adjectives

- generous /'dʒenərəs/
- pacifist

Verbs & expressions

- sail (the seas): *parcourir*
- dedicate one's life to sth / V-ING
- protest /prə'test/ = speak up (against)
- denounce /dɪ'naʊns/
- make sb's life better
- raise sb's awareness (of) /ə'weənɪs/: *faire prendre conscience à qqn*
- speak one's mind: *dire ce que l'on pense*

Your task

Interview a celebrity

A reporter wants to know more about these three celebrities' achievements.

a. Decide who you want to be.

Student A You are the reporter. Write down the questions you will ask the celebrity. Get ready to react to his / her answers and to ask other unprepared questions.

Student B You are Prince William, Jessica Watson or John Lennon's widow, Yoko Ono. Imagine the questions you will be asked and jot down your answers.

b. Act out the interview.

MÉTHODOLOGIE
Interview → p. 158

Writers' corner

Rescued!

Your task

Write a newspaper article

New York City has been hit by a tidal wave. Just like many New Yorkers, the man in his office (a journalist) was saved by Spiderman. One week later, he writes an article in which he explains how Spiderman rescued him and others. (200 words)

MÉTHODOLOGIE
Rédiger un article de presse → p. 168

A Get ready

1. Look at the drawing and choose the words you will need in the *Toolbox* to describe the scene (place, people, event, consequences…).

2. Imagine the reason(s) why New York City was hit by this tidal wave.

B Write your article

3. Here are a few hints:

a. Use past tenses to describe what happened, and present tenses to express the consequences of the event and your feelings.

b. Think about a title for your article, and don't forget to write the date.

c. Remember that the journalist writing the article was also a victim. Some passages, such as the description of the scene, will be written in the first person narrative.

d. Your conclusion will insist on Spiderman's heroic action and will include personal feelings.

function box

Expressing surprise and admiration

- I couldn't believe it / my eyes!
- You can't imagine what I saw!
- It was truly amazing!
- How fantastic it was!
- It was just unbelievable!
- I really admire him for V-ING
- I was so impressed by…

toolbox

Nouns

- casualties /'kæʒjʊltɪz/: *victimes*
- damage /'dæmɪdʒ/: *dégâts*
- disaster = catastrophe /kə'tæstrəfɪ/
- the dead / the wounded /'wu:ndɪd/: *(blessés)*
- tidal wave /'taɪdl weɪv/: *raz-de-marée*
- earthquake: *tremblement de terre*

Adjectives

- flooded /'flʌdɪd: *submergé*
- trapped: *piégé*
- extraordinary /ɪk'strɔ:dnrɪ/

Verbs & expressions

- surge /sɜ:dʒ/: *déferler*
- wash away: *emporter*
- drown /draʊn/: *se noyer*
- crack: *se fissurer*
- be panic-stricken ≠ keep one's head: *garder son sang-froid*
- dive: *plonger*
- prevent from V-ING: *empêcher de*
- be grateful to sb for sth / V-ING

Text 2

What a hero is

Ernest J. GAINES

was born in 1933 on the River Lake Plantation in Oscar, Louisiana. He has written nine books of fiction and seven short stories. *A Lesson Before Dying* won the 1993 National Book Critics Circle Award. His novels are set in the plantations of the American Deep South. Four of his works have been produced into television movies.

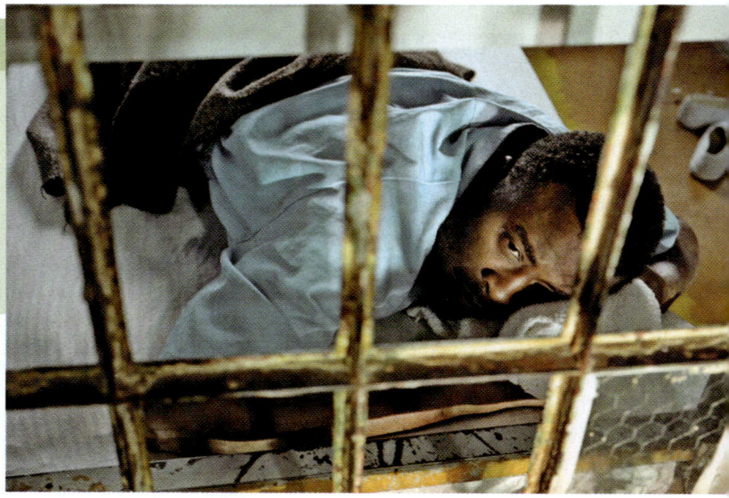

A Warming up

Read the introduction of the text, and guess what the man's thoughts and feelings are.

A Louisiana jail in the 1940s. Jefferson, 21, has been sentenced to death for a murder he did not commit. Grant Wiggins, the narrator, is the black teacher at the local plantation school.

"Jefferson," I said. "Do you know what a hero is, Jefferson? A hero is someone who does something for other people. He does something that other men don't and can't do. He is different from other men. He is above other men. No matter who those other men are, the hero, no matter who he is, is above them. I could never be a hero. I teach, but I don't like teaching. I teach because it is the only thing that an educated black man can do in the South today. I don't like it; I hate it. I don't even like living here. I want to run away. I want to live for myself and for my woman and for nobody else.

"That is not a hero. A hero does for others. He would do anything for people he loves, because he knows it would make their lives better. I am not that kind of person, but I want you to be. You could give something to her[1], to me, to those children in the quarter. You could give them something that I never could. They expect it from me, but not from you. The white people out there are saying that you don't have it – that you're a hog[2], not a man. But I know they are wrong. You have the potentials. We all have, no matter who we are.

"Those out there are no better than we are, Jefferson. They're worse. That's why they are always looking for a scapegoat, someone else to blame. I want you to show them the difference between what they think you are and what you can be. To them, you're nothing but another nigger – no dignity, no heart, no love for your people. You can prove them wrong. You can do more than I can ever do. I have always done what they wanted me to do, teach reading, writing, and arithmetic. Nothing else – nothing about dignity, nothing about identity, nothing about loving and caring. They never thought we were capable of learning these things. 'Teach those niggers how to print their names and how to figure on their fingers.' And I went along, but hating myself all the time for doing so."

"Do you know what a myth is, Jefferson?" I asked him. "A myth is an old lie that people believe in. White people believe that they're better than anyone else on earth – and that's a myth. The last thing they ever want is to see a black man stand, and think, and show that common humanity that is in us all. It would destroy their myth. They would no longer have justification for having made us slaves and keeping us in the condition we are in. As long as none of us stand, they're safe."

A Lesson Before Dying, Ernest J. GAINES (1993)

1. refers to Miss Emma, Jefferson's godmother (*marraine*) 2. *porc*

Reading comprehension

WORKBOOK → p. 17-18

urn to your *Workbook* which will help you to understand the ext.

In your own words

. Sum up the text with the help of your *Workbook*.

Going further

. What does Grant mean when he says: *"I have always one what they wanted me to do, teach reading, writing, and rithmetic."* (l. 24)?

. Do you think Grant's visit will have an impact on Jefferson? 'hy (not)?

. Explain the last sentence of the text: *"As long as none of us and, they're safe."* (l. 35)

E Language training

5. Savoir prononcer YOUR CD 11-13 CD 1 33-35

Lisez le passage de *"Those out there…"* (l. 19) à *"… for doing so."* (l. 29).

a. Dans les mots suivants la voyelle ***-o-*** se prononce-t-elle : /əʊ/, /ɜː/, /ʌ/, /uː/, /ɔː/, /aʊ/, /ə/, /ɒ/ ?
Jefferson – nothing – those – love – worse – prove – how – no – another – show – do – so – someone – more – done – on

b. Lisez à voix haute les mots suivants en vous aidant de leurs transcriptions phonétiques :

scapegoat /'skeɪpgəʊt/
dignity /'dɪgnɪtɪ/
arithmetic /ə'rɪθmətɪk/
capable /'keɪpəbl/
difference /'dɪfrəns/
heart /hɑːt/
identity /aɪ'dentɪtɪ/
figure /'fɪgə/

c. Vérifiez à l'écoute, puis relisez le passage à voix haute.

6. Pratiquer la grammaire

Les modaux (sens 1)

LANGUAGE WORKSHOP → p. 40

toolbox

Nouns
- pride: *fierté*
- failure /'feɪljə/ ≠ success
- supremacy /sʊ'preməsɪ/

Adjectives
- helpless: *désespéré*
- overwhelmed: *accablé*
- uneducated = illiterate /ɪ'lɪtərɪt/
- proud /praʊd/: *fier*
- bitter = resentful /rɪ'zentfʊl/: *amer*
- selfish / self-centred
- obedient /ə'biːdɪənt/
- superior /sʊ'pɪərɪə/ (to)
- submissive (to): *soumis (à)*

Verbs & expressions
- prove sth to oneself
- be wrongfully accused of sth / V-ING
- be worthy of sth: *être digne de qqch*
- deserve /dɪ'zɜːv/: *mériter*
- be on an equal footing with: *être sur un pied d'égalité avec*
- be an example (to sb)
- comply with = respect
- debunk /ˌdiː'bʌŋk/ a myth: *démythifier*

Your task

Write a letter after an important visit

The day after Grant's visit, Jefferson writes to Miss Emma, his godmother, to tell her about Grant's visit and the impact it has had on him.

MÉTHODOLOGIE
Écrire une lettre → p. 166

Grammaire | Les modaux (sens 1) : *CAN, COULD, MAY, SHOULD, MUST, NEED*

PRÉCIS GRAMMATICAL → 12, 13, 15, 16

A Observer et comprendre

1 Les modaux : formes et sens

1. *"He does something that other men (…)* ***can't*** *do."* (Text 2, p. 38, l. 5)
2. *"(…) it is the only thing that an educated black man* ***can*** *do (…)"* (Text 2, p. 38, l. 8)
3. *"You* ***mustn't*** *forget who you are."*
4. *"I know how you're feeling. You* ***needn't*** *tell me."*
5. *"You* ***must*** *believe me. I'm telling the truth."*
6. *"****May*** *I ask you what I am supposed to do now?"*
7. *Every prison has rules about what prisoners* ***can*** *or* ***cannot*** *do.*

a. Associez à chaque notion ci-dessous le(s) modal (modaux) qui lui correspond(ent) :

1. Obligation. **2.** Interdiction. **3.** Absence d'obligation. **4.** Permission. **5.** Capacité. **6.** Incapacité.

b. Les modaux sont-ils suivis d'un infinitif (*to* V) ou d'une base verbale (V) ?

c. Traduisez les énoncés **1** à **7**.

2 *COULD* et *COULD HAVE* / *SHOULD* et *SHOULD HAVE*

1. *"I* ***could*** *(…)* ***be*** *a hero."* (Text 2, p. 38, l. 7)
2. *"You* ***could give*** *them something that I never* ***could****."* (Text 2, p. 38, l. 15)
3. *As a child he* ***couldn't read and write*** *as well as the other children.*
4. *You* ***could have been*** *a teacher too if you had wanted to.*
5. *You* ***should*** *understand that they are no better than we are.*
6. *You* ***should*** *never* ***have told*** *them about it. It was a mistake.*

a. Associez à chaque emploi de *could* et *could have* la notion qui lui correspond le mieux :

1. Cela appartient au passé. **2.** C'est une hypothèse envisageable. **3.** Cela aurait pu se produire mais ne s'est pas produit.

Traduisez les énoncés **1**, **2**, **3** et **4**.

b. Qu'expriment *should* et *should have* : **1.** Le regret ou **2.** Le conseil ? Traduisez les énoncés **5** et **6**.

c. *Have* après *should* et *could* se construit-il avec une base verbale ou un participe passé ?

Faisons le point !
Quelles sont les traductions possibles de *could* et *could have*, *should* et *should have* ?

B Pratiquer

3 Reformulez les phrases suivantes avec *MUSTN'T, NEEDN'T, COULDN'T, SHOULD, MAY* ou *SHOULD HAVE*.

a. Why don't you leave him alone?
b. Don't worry about it!
c. You don't have to answer.
d. I don't understand why he didn't run away.
e. They were incapable of writing their names.
f. Am I allowed to stay a little longer?

4 Traduisez à l'aide des modaux *NEEDN'T, COULD, COULD HAVE, SHOULD* et *SHOULD HAVE*.

a. Je n'ai jamais pu lui parler.
b. Ce n'est pas la peine de crier !
c. Il devrait savoir ce que cela veut dire.
d. Je ne pense pas que je pourrais le refaire.
e. Il aurait pu aider d'autres gens.
f. Vous auriez dû vous taire.

Grammaire de l'oral | Comprendre les formes modales à l'oral

5 Prononcer les formes négatives et les formes en *HAVE*. CD 1 36-37

COULDN'T / COULD HAVE / SHOULDN'T / SHOULD HAVE / CAN / CAN'T

a. Écoutez ces énoncés et indiquez quelles sont les syllabes accentuées dans les formes verbales.

1. ***I couldn't be*** *a hero.* **2.** *He* ***could have been*** *a hero.*

b. Écoutez et répétez les modèles suivants.

3. *You shouldn't stay here.* **4.** *You should have stayed a little longer.*

5. *"He does something that other men don't and can't do."* (Text 2, p. 38, l. 5)

6. *"(…) it is the only thing that an educated black man can do (…)."* (Text 2, p. 38, l. 8)

À savoir ! À l'oral, dans certains cas, les formes négatives des modaux peuvent être difficiles à entendre. Il faut s'appuyer sur le contexte pour bien comprendre le sens du modal.

6 Reconnaître *COULDN'T / COULD HAVE, SHOULDN'T / SHOULD HAVE, CAN'T* et *MUSTN'T* à l'oral CD 1 38

Écoutez ces énoncés en prêtant une grande attention au contexte et indiquez si la forme entendue est la forme **1** ou **2**.

a. 1. can't tell you	**a. 2.** can tell you	**e. 1.** couldn't afford	**e. 2.** could have afforded
b. 1. can't take	**b. 2.** can take	**f. 1.** could have stayed there	**f. 2.** couldn't stay
c. 1. shouldn't let	**c. 2.** should have let	**g. 1.** mustn't find	**g. 2.** must have found
d. 1. shouldn't let	**d. 2.** should have let	**h. 1.** mustn't spend	**h. 2.** must have spent

Lexique | Courage et héroïsme

→ Keywords p. 30

Assurez-vous que vous avez bien retenu les mots clés de l'unité.

7 Donnez les synonymes ou les antonymes des mots suivants.

a. courage = … **b.** fearless = … **c.** adventurous = … **d.** risky ≠ …

8 Sélectionnez la bonne transcription phonétique de ces mots.

a. hero: /ˈhɪərəʊ/ – /ˈherəʊ/ **b.** heroine: /ˈhɪərəʊɪn/ – /ˈherəʊɪn/

9 Quelle est la syllabe accentuée dans chacun de ces mots ?

a. rescuer **b.** icon **c.** courageous **d.** achievement

10 Complétez les phrases à l'aide des mots suivants en conjugant les verbes si nécessaire :

coward – risk – fight for – stand up for – sacrifice (verb) – unsung – achieve – deeds – stand up to – duty – overcome – save – look up to – rebel – take up – rescue – beyond

a. They said that he was a …1… because he didn't …2… his boss when he was fired.

b. Emmeline Pankhurst …3… women's rights. She …4… her goal when women got the right to vote.

c. A superhero's …5… is to do good …6… and protect people.

d. She went …7… her limits, …8… all the obstacles and became president of her company.

e. He …9… his grandparents who were ready to …10… equality / equal rights and …11… against injustice.

f. A hero is someone who never hesitates to …12… a challenge and …13… himself to …14… other people.

g. There are hundreds of …15… heroes who …16… their lives to …17… people who are in danger.

toolbox

Verbs

- campaign: *faire campagne*
- get votes
- give up: *abandonner*
- have self-confidence = be confident: *avoir confiance en soi*
- doubt one's abilities
- feel low: *être déprimé*

Your task

Discuss running for leadership

There's going to be an election for the school council.

Student A You encourage your friend to run for the leadership of the school council.

Student B You express doubts about whether or not you're up to the task.

Use **modal auxiliary verbs** as often as possible.

Fictional heroes

Amazing people have always inspired film makers and comic book artists.

A The hero who never dies

1 Look at the film posters. What elements are characteristic of James Bond films?

2 Read the text, then say in what way the new James Bond is different from his predecessors.

3 Which James Bond do you prefer?

1

2

FOR ALMOST FIFTY YEARS, special agent James Bond 007 – pronounce "double O seven"– has been fighting villains with his licence to kill. The first *James Bond* film, *Dr No*, came out in 1962. *Quantum of Solace* (2008) is the 22nd Bond film. The new James Bond, British actor Daniel Craig, is the sixth actor to play 007, and he appears to be a controversial choice following five tall, dark-haired Bonds. Sean Connery, George Lazenby, Roger Moore, Timothy Dalton and Pierce Brosnan have all filled the famous tuxedo *(smoking)*, reinventing the role as the years went by just to match the age. The Bond aficionados were upset by Daniel Craig, mostly because he was blond, a little shorter than the others and very different from the Bond in Ian Fleming's books. Yet, fifty years on, everyone acknowledges that 007 does not seem to age, that he is the hero who never dies.

3

B Superheroes in comic books

1. Look at the pictures of these famous superheroes and pick out the symbolic elements.
2. Read the superheroes' biographies and say what they have in common.

1

2

3

Captain America (the alter ego of Steve Rogers) is a fictional Marvel Comics superhero who first appeared in *Captain America Comics* in 1941. He was the most popular comic book character during the wartime period. Captain America was a sort of super soldier created by the US government. He was a propaganda tool in the fight against the Nazis. His costume (an American flag motif) makes him a clear manifestation of patriotism. Even his indestructible shield bears the colours of the United States.

Wonder Woman (the alter ego of Princess Diana, an Amazon) is the first super-heroine in a male-dominated world of superheroes. She first appeared in *All Star Comics* in 1941. She was created as a feminist role model and she initially fought against the Nazis. She has extraordinary strength and she can fly. She has a Lasso of Truth, which forces anyone she catches to tell the truth, a pair of bullet-proof bracelets, a tiara that she uses as a projectile, and an invisible plane.

Captain Britain (the alter ego of Brian Braddock) is a superhero who first appeared in *Captain Britain Weekly* in 1976. He was initially intended to be a British equivalent of Captain America and was assigned to uphold[1] the laws of Britain. He has superhuman strength, speed, enhanced[2] perceptions and can fly.

1. *faire respecter* 2. *améliorées*

Webquest — Your favourite superhero

TICE

1. Browse the web to choose your favourite superhero.
2. Present your superhero to the class using the following guidelines and justify your choice:

- Real name and identity
- Aliases /ˈeɪlɪəsiz/
- Country / Planet of origin
- Occupation
- How he / she became a superhero(ine)
- Powers and abilities
- Weaknesses / Flaws
- Weapons
- Enemies

Web resources

- www.superherodb.com/characters.php
- www.marvel.com/characters/ (Click on "Browse Characters".)
- www.dccomics.com/dcu/heroes_and_villains/

final task

What is a hero for you?

You have a summer job in a radio station and you have been asked to prepare a radio programme called "Modern day heroes". You listen to two radio reports and after talking about them with a classmate you decide which one to include in the programme.

1 Listen to two radio reports

YOUR CD 14-15 CD 1 39-40

MÉTHODOLOGIE
COMPRÉHENSION DE L'ORAL → p. 150

Work with a classmate.
Student A You listen to report A.
Student B You listen to report B.
Your teacher will give you a worksheet to help you.

1

2

2 Decide which report you will choose

Which report better illustrates the programme "Modern day heroes"?

A Present your report

With the help of your worksheet, you will present your report to your friend.

B Discuss the two reports

MÉTHODOLOGIE
Discussion contradictoire → p. 158

The various documents you have worked on in this unit should help you to define what a hero is for you. Your choice of a report will be based on each student's definition of a hero.

Talk together to decide which report will be in the programme. You must react (in a positive or negative way) to your friend's arguments.

C Make your choice

After listening to and discussing each other's arguments, choose the report that you will include in the programme.

function box

Giving arguments

- First and foremost / First of all...: *Avant tout*
- One of the main reasons why...
- Another good reason for V-ING
- Besides / Moreover / What's more...
- Let's not forget that...
- Last but not least: *Enfin et surtout*

Giving one's opinion

- I feel / believe that...
- I can't help thinking that...
- To my mind / In my opinion...
- It seems to me that...

Check your skills

WORKBOOK → p. 19

A Comprendre un reportage radio

YOUR CD 16 CD 1 41

Écoutez le document sonore sur votre CD. Remplissez ensuite la fiche de votre *Workbook* et évaluez-vous en fonction des critères proposés.

Je me situe par rapport au CECRL B1 → B2

LORSQUE J'ÉCOUTE CE REPORTAGE :

- **B1 :** Je peux en comprendre les points principaux. Je comprends globalement le point de vue du locuteur.
- **B1 + :** Je peux en comprendre les informations essentielles ainsi que la plupart des détails. Je peux suivre sans difficulté le point de vue du locuteur.

B Écrire un article de presse

You are a reporter and write a press article on the event illustrated by this picture of the firefighter and the baby.

Écrivez votre article en 150-200 mots, puis évaluez-vous en fonction des critères proposés dans votre *Workbook*.

Je me situe par rapport au CECRL B1 → B2

LORSQUE J'ÉCRIS UN ARTICLE DE PRESSE :

- **B1 :** Je peux décrire des événements, réels ou imaginés, en mettant en relief la succession et la cohérence des événements et des comportements. Je peux exprimer des sentiments et des impressions dans un texte simple et articulé. Je peux supprimer en me relisant les erreurs de langue les plus importantes.
- **B1 + :** Je peux décrire des événements, sentiments et impressions de manière claire et détaillée en respectant les règles du genre en question. Les erreurs de langue sont peu nombreuses et ne gênent pas une lecture fluide de mon texte.

Art quest Iconic photos

You have certainly seen at least one of these iconic black and white photographs. They are part of American collective memory and evoke a specific period of time in US history. Some of these are photos of American heroes and others have turned ordinary people into heroes.

A photo can be iconic because of the person it represents, the event it symbolizes or its artistic qualities.

- What feelings can we read in the woman's face and in the children's attitude?
- Check the websites below to know when it was taken.
- Find information about the famous photographer who took this picture.

  - www.eyewitnesstohistory.com
  - www.berkeley.edu

1

Dorothea LANGE, *The Migrant Mother*

- What do you know about this man?
- What does he symbolize?

  - www.imdb.com/
  - www.reelclassics.com

2

Dennis STOCK, *James Dean*

3

- Which building is this woman on?
- What is she doing?
- Find out more information about her.
  - www.gallerym.com
  - www.vpphotogallery.com

Oscar GRAUBNER, *Margaret Bourke-White on top of a skyscraper*

4

Leonard FREED, *Martin Luther King back from Norway*

- Why do these women want to touch MLK's hand?
  - www.thekingcenter.org
  - www.spartacus.schoolnet.co.uk

Your task

Group work

Each group chooses one of the photographs on these pages and prepares an oral report to present to the class. Explain what historical event, if any, is referred to, or what makes the character represented famous. Don't forget to say what makes the photo iconic.
Select the most interesting information on the websites suggested. All students should speak in turn.

Unit 3

Espaces et échanges
Mythes et héros
L'idée de progrès

Born on the road

Can you imagine travelling in the USA without a car?

final task You are planning a trip to the USA with a friend. You have a discussion with him / her about the kind of trip you want to go on: a car-free trip or a mythical road trip?
You write an e-mail to a travel agency to explain your plans and ask for further information.

Keywords

Nouns

- highway /ˈhaɪweɪ/: *grande route*
- gas (Am.) = petrol (Br.): *essence*
- gas station: *station-service*
- diner /ˈdaɪnə/ (Am.): *petit restaurant*
- billboard /ˈbɪlbɔːd/: *panneau d'affichage*
- drive-in
- car plant (Am.) = car factory (Br.)
- gas guzzler: *voiture qui consomme beaucoup*
- speed limit
- consumer society
- oil crisis /ˈkraɪsɪs/
- shortage /ˈʃɔːtɪdʒ/: *pénurie*
- prosperity
- decline (noun and verb)
- a means of transport
- public transport
- car-pooling = car-sharing: *covoiturage*

Adjectives

- booming = thriving /ˈθraɪvɪŋ/: *prospère*
- increasing ≠ decreasing
- thrilling = exciting
- eco-friendly: *respectueux de l'environnement*
- economical /ˌiːkəˈnɒmɪkəl/
- individual ≠ collective
- affordable /əˈfɔːdəbl/: *abordable*

Verbs & expressions

- hit the road: *prendre la route*
- hitchhike: *faire du stop*
- give sb a lift / a ride: *prendre qqn en voiture*
- consume
- expand
- thrive: *prospérer*

LANGUAGE WORKSHOP → p. 59

The Cadillac Ranch

1. Describe the photo.

2. The Cadillac /'kædilæk/ Ranch, which lies along a Texas highway, was built in 1974. In your opinion, what was it supposed to symbolize at that time?

3. What indicates that the photo was taken much later? What could the Cadillac Ranch stand for nowadays?

4. What do you think of this work of art?

toolbox

Nouns

- sculpture /'skʌlptʃə/
- car wreck /rek/: *épave de voiture*
- graffiti /grə'fi:tɪ/
- tombstone /'tu:mstəʊn/: *pierre tombale*

Adjectives

- half-buried /'hɑ:f berɪd/: *à moitié enterré*
- planted
- nose-first
- gleaming: *brillant*
- tagged /tægd/

Verbs & expressions

- rust: *rouiller*
- praise: *faire l'éloge de*
- make fun of: *se moquer de*
- denounce

America's love affair with the road

MÉTHODOLOGIE EXPRESSION ÉCRITE → p. 165

A Henry Ford

MÉTHODOLOGIE
Rédiger des phrases correctes → p. 165

culture key The Model T → p. 141

Write Henry Ford's biography.
Use the notes below. Do not forget the appropriate link words.

1863	Born July 30 in Dearborn, Michigan. Parents: Irish immigrants, prosperous farm. Childhood: eldest of six children, disliked farm work, interest in mechanical things.
1879	Apprentice machinist.
1882	Serviced steam engines in a Detroit factory.
1888	Married Clara Bryant.
1893	Chief engineer at the Edison Company.
1896	Created the Quadricycle.
1903	Foundation of the Ford Motor company.
1908	Creation of the first "Model T".
1913	Implementation of the first moving assembly line.
By 1927	15 million Model Ts. Price down to $300. Employer with social views: paid workers more money for less work 5 day-40 hour working week.
1947	Died of a cerebral hemorrhage, buried in the Ford Cemetery, Detroit.

Ford's first self-propelled vehicle: the Quadricycle

B Car culture in the 1950s

MÉTHODOLOGIE
Enrichir sa production → p. 166

Use adjectives.

Complete using the following adjectives (several possibilities for some adjectives):
new – homely – convenient – cosy – numerous – impersonal – exhausted – dull – standardized – tasteless – friendly – hurried.

...1... roadside diners, ...2... motels, ...3... gas stations and ...4... drive-in businesses had long been part of the American landscape. Up until then they had been ...5... family-owned places with an original design meant to attract the ...6... driver's attention. But in the mid-fifties, ...7... government regulations were passed allowing large-scale industries on the interstates. So "Mom's and Pop's" places went gradually out of business. Franchising led to fast food-chains: ...8..., mass-produced, ...9... buildings adapted to accommodate motorists. The advent of ...10... drive-throughs allowed ...11... drivers to keep one hand on the wheel and the other on a ...12... burger.

C US auto industry decline

MÉTHODOLOGIE
Mots de liaison → p. 169

Compose a well-structured paragraph.

Introduce one of these link words: *on the other hand – whereas – such as – while – as a result – though.*

Ford, General Motors and Chrysler have been in decline for many reasons, ..1.. reliance[1] on discounts, mismanagement, etc. ..2.. Chrysler[2] has been taken over by a German company, ..3.. Ford has been losing market share[3] consistently for the last 10 years. ..4.. US auto decline had already set in years ago, 2005 proved fatal. ..5.. a rising demand for small cars boosted[4] the sales of Japanese automakers. Ford and GM sales fell by 24 and 20 percent, ..6.. sales for Toyota, Nissan and Hyundai rose by 10, 16 and 95 percent respectively.

Adapted from *American Chronicle* (July 4th 2006)

1. *dépendance* 2. /'kraɪslə/ 3. *part de marché* 4. *accroître*

E The ups and downs of the American car industry

MÉTHODOLOGIE
Rédiger un article de presse → p. 168

Write an article entitled "The ups and downs of the American car industry".

Use the information given in the previous exercises and the following guidelines.

1. In what way did Henry Ford revolutionize car making?
2. Explain what caused the gradual disappearance of the friendly roadside places of the 50s.
3. How can the decline of the "Big Three" car makers (Ford, General Motors, Chrysler) be explained?
4. What are the future prospects of the car industry? What will green cars be like?

D Towards green cars

MÉTHODOLOGIE
Les phrases complexes → p. 166

Combine simple sentences.

Link the two sentences with relatives or link words.

1. **a.** Electric vehicles came into existence in the 19th century.
   b. At that time, electricity was one of the preferred methods of motor vehicle propulsion.
2. **a.** Credit for building the first electric car usually goes to Robert Anderson.
   b. This Scottish inventor built an electric carriage with non-rechargeable electric cells.
3. **a.** Today's average American drives less than 40 miles per day.
   b. A typical electric vehicle is adequate for the daily driving needs of most US consumers.
4. **a.** Ford had up to now mainly relied on the making of pickup trucks and SUVs.
   b. Ford now expects to develop its production of electric vehicles.
5. **a.** Ford had announced it would make 250,000 hybrids a year.
   b. Ford admitted later it could not meet that goal due to high costs.

Video time

Easy rider

DVD

Easy Rider, Dennis HOPPER (1969)

A Get ready

1. The action is set in the late 1960s. Imagine how some Americans reacted when seeing the two men.

B Watch the video

2. Watch the extract from *Easy Rider*. Your teacher will give you a worksheet to help you.

C In your own words

3. Use the worksheet to summarize what you saw.

D Going further

4. What does the film reveal about America at that time?

Text 1

Into the West

42

culture key Mythical roads → p. 141

Jack KEROUAC
(1922-1969)
was born into a French-Canadian family in Massachusetts and studied at Columbia University in New York. A novelist and a poet he became the leader of the "Beat Generation". His most famous novel is *On The Road* (1957). Other works: *The Dharma Bums* and *The Subterraneans* (both 1958), *Doctor Sax* (1959), *Lonesome Traveler* (1960), *Big Sur* (1962).

A Warming up

Look at the photo and guess what the text is about.

And for the first time in my life, the following afternoon, I went into the West. It was a warm and beautiful day for hitchhiking. To get out of the impossible complexities of Chicago traffic I took a bus to Joliet, Illinois, went by the Joliet pen[1], stationed myself just outside town and pointed my way. All the way from New York to Joliet by bus, and I had spent more than half my money.

My first ride was a dynamite truck with a red flag, about thirty miles into great green Illinois, the truckdriver pointing out the place where Route 6, which we were on, intersects Route 66 before they both shoot west for incredible distances.

Along about three in the afternoon, after an apple pie and ice cream in a roadside stand, a woman stopped for me in a little coupe. I had a twinge of hard joy as I ran after the car. But she was a middle-aged woman, actually the mother of sons my age, and wanted somebody to help her drive to Iowa. I was all for it. Iowa! Not so far from Denver, and once I got to Denver I could relax. She drove the first few hours, at one point insisted on visiting an old church somewhere, as if we were tourists, and then I took over the wheel and, though I'm not much of a driver, drove clear through the rest of Illinois to Davenport, Iowa, via Rock Island. And here for the first time in my life I saw my beloved Mississippi River, low water, with its big rank[2] smell that smells like the raw body of America itself because it washes it up. Rock Island – railroad tracks, shacks[3], small downtown section; and over the bridge to Davenport, same kind of town, all smelling of sawdust[4] in the warm midwest sun. Here the lady had to go on to her Iowa hometown by another route, and I got out.

The sun was going down. I walked, after a few cold beers, to the edge of town, and it was a long walk. All the men were driving home from work, wearing railroad hats, baseball hats, all kinds of hats, just like after work in any town anywhere. One of them gave me a ride up the hill and left me at a lonely crossroads on the edge of the prairie[5]. It was beautiful there. The only cars that came by were farmer-cars; they gave me suspicious looks, they clanked along. Not a truck. A few cars zipped by. The sun went all the way down and I was standing in the purple darkness. Now I was scared. There weren't even any lights in the Iowa countryside; in a minute nobody would be able to see me. Luckily a man going back to Davenport gave me a lift downtown. But I was right where I started from.

On the Road, Jack KEROUAC (1957)

1. short for penitentiary /ˌpenɪˈtenʃərɪ/ **2.** *nauséabond* **3.** *cabanes* **4.** *sciure* **5.** *immense plaine au centre des États-Unis*

B Reading comprehension

WORKBOOK → p. 20-21

Read the text with the help of your *Workbook*.

C In your own words

1. Use the following guidelines to sum up the story:

a. How many drivers gave the narrator a lift that day?

b. What were the narrator's feelings about the Mississippi River?

c. When and why was the narrator scared?

D Going further

2. Analyse the narrator's feelings when the woman's coupe stopped.

3. Imagine why no farmers offered to give the narrator a lift.

4. How do you think the narrator felt at the end of the day?

5. In your opinion, why is hitchhiking forbidden in many US states nowadays?

E Language training

6. Savoir prononcer YOUR CD 17-18 CD 1 43-44

7. Pratiquer la grammaire

As if et le prétérit modal – *Any, not any* et *not a* – Place des prépositions

WORKBOOK → p. 22

toolbox

Nouns

- thumb /θʌm/: *pouce*
- backpacker: *routard*
- mixed feelings: *sentiments contradictoires*

Adjectives

- relieved: *soulagé*
- distrustful: *méfiant*
- disappointed
- safe ≠ risky
- reckless: *imprudent*
- irresponsible

Verbs & expressions

- pick up a hitchhiker: *prendre qqn en stop*
- thumb a ride / a lift = hitchhike
- be fascinated
- chat sb up (informal): *baratiner qqn*
- trust sb: *faire confiance à qqn*
- be run over: *être renversé par une voiture*
- be mugged: *se faire agresser*
- be aware /əˈweə/ of: *être conscient de*

Your task

Get information about car-sharing

A driver who does not want to travel alone has posted a note on a website offering a ride. He / She is contacted by a potential passenger who wants to know more about this car-sharing offer.
Choose your role and act out the conversation.

MÉTHODOLOGIE Conversation → p. 157

The Mother Road

culture key Mythical roads → p. 141

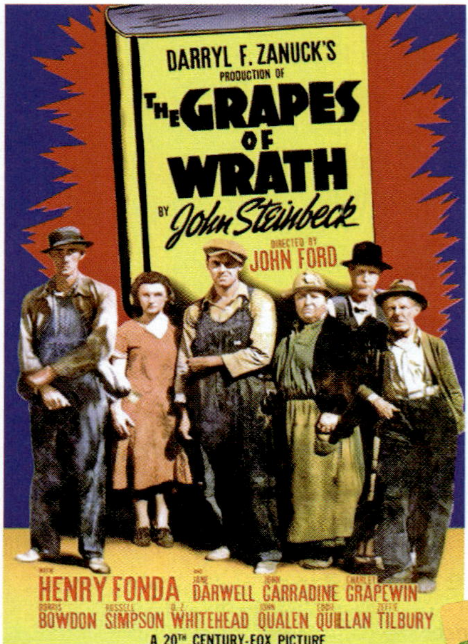

1

2

3

A The topic

1. Describe the pictures briefly (nature of the document, place, people, time…).

2. Imagine the common link between these pictures and the title.

B Open your ears (CD 1 – 45)

3. You will hear three sentences spoken by two of the interviewees. Can you guess what the recording is about?

C Listen (CD 1 – 46) WORKBOOK → p. 23

4. Listen to the recording and check whether your answers to questions A and B were right. You will find some help in your *Workbook*.

D In your own words

5. What would Jan Costner do if she went on the Mother Road?

6. Why is the Mother Road a part of American history?

function box

Asking for information

- I'd like to know…
- Have you got any idea how to…?
- Could you give me some information about…?
- Is it true that…?
- I wonder if you could tell me…
- Do you know anything about…?

Your task

Write an e-mail to ask for advice about a trip

After listening to this report you feel like travelling on Route 66. You write an e-mail to an American friend to tell him / her about the reasons why you want to go there and ask him / her for advice about this trip. (150 words)

MÉTHODOLOGIE
Écrire un courriel → p. 166

Speakers' corner

A trip to Yellowstone

PARKSCAPES CLASSIC

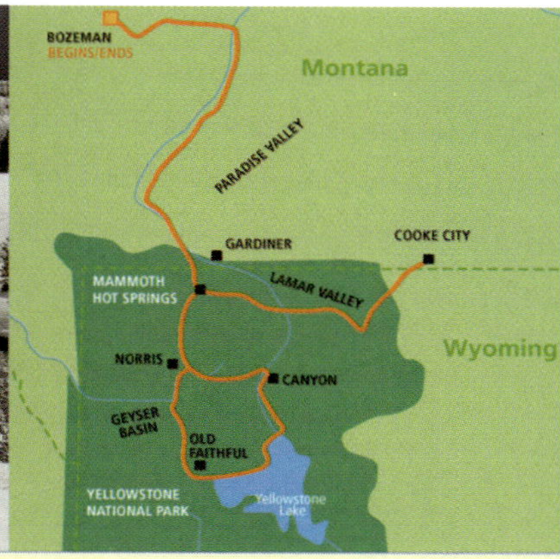

Head out to Hayden Valley in search of wolf packs that call this wintry valley home. Ride into the park's interior for more views of bison, coyotes, and trumpeter swans[1]. Walk the snow-covered boardwalk around Old Faithful and the Upper Geyser[2] Basin and return to the classic, rustic grandeur of the Old Faithful Snow Lodge. Each day of this trip offers unforgettable adventure.

WILDLIFE WATCHING – Blanketed in snow, Yellowstone comes alive with wildlife – howling wolves, huge herds[3] of bison and elk[4], playful coyotes, and soaring[5] eagles. Watch through binoculars with knowledgeable naturalists. Learn how the reintroduction of the wolves has altered the interaction of all Yellowstone wildlife.

THE QUIET SEASON – Discover the magic of winter in Yellowstone. Enjoy strolling through the heart of the park past steaming geysers and snowshoeing through pine forests.

1. *cygnes* 2. /'gi:zə/ 3. *troupeaux* 4. *élan* 5. *qui déploient leurs ailes*

A Read and speak

1. Read the leaflet. Where is Yellowstone National Park situated?

2. Find out what makes this park particularly attractive.

B Going further

3. After reading this leaflet, you try to convince a friend to go and visit the park with you next summer. Act out the conversation.

function box

Writing a formal letter

- Dear Sir / Madam,
- Could you tell me if...
- I was wondering whether...
- I would like to know if it's possible...
- Would you mind if...?
- I hope for a prompt reply.
- Hoping to hear from you shortly.
- I look forward to hearing from you...
- I would be grateful if...
- Yours sincerely / faithfully

Your task

Write a letter of enquiry

You are so enthusiastic about this park that you decide to find out if you can get a summer job there, helping the park rangers. You write a letter of enquiry to the National Park Service.

MÉTHODOLOGIE
Écrire une lettre → p. 166

Text 2

Behind the wheel

culture key The Model T, Herbert Hoover → p. 141

The Times, the oldest British national daily, was founded in 1785. This centre-right paper is regarded as one of the "big four" quality newspapers (the others being *The Guardian*, *The Independent* and *The Daily Telegraph*). In order to attract younger readers and commuters, it adopted a tabloid format in 2004. *The Times* and its sister paper *The Sunday Times* are owned by Rupert Murdoch, the world's leading publisher of English-language newspapers.
Website: www.thetimes.co.uk

A Warming up

Use the picture and the title to imagine the content of the article.

As cultural symbols go, the American car is quite young. The Model T Ford was built at the Piquette Plant in Michigan a century ago, with the first rolling off the assembly line on September 27, 1908. Only eleven cars were produced the next month. But eventually Henry Ford would build fifteen million "tin lizzies".

Modern America was born on the road, behind a wheel. The car forged some of the most enduring[1] elements of American culture: the roadside diner, the billboard, the motel, even the hamburger. For most of the last century, the automobile represented what it meant to be American – going forward at high speed to find new worlds. The road novel, the road movie, these are quintessential American ideas, born of abundant petrol, cheap cars and a never-ending interstate system, the largest public works project in history.

In 1928 Herbert Hoover imagined an America with "a chicken in every pot and a car in every garage". Ford Motion Pictures, once the largest film producer in the world, churned out[2] more than 3,000 movies extolling[3] the thrill of driving. James Dean drove a Mercury, Steve McQueen a Mustang. The names reflected a society that hurtled onward[4], never looking back, as the car transformed America from a farm-based society into an industrial giant. The love affair continues. The US now has far more cars than garages. There are 204 million registered cars, trucks and SUVs, but only 191 million drivers.

Yet the cars that drove the American Dream have helped to create a global ecological nightmare. Europe's appetite for oil has been restrained by high petrol taxes, small cars and more efficient public transport. In America, by contrast, demand for oil has grown by twenty-two per cent since 1990.

The extraordinary worldwide rise of

the middle class and the demand for an American lifestyle, of which car ownership is a key component, has fuelled a staggering[5] boom.

The horrors of excessive energy consumption, climate change and population growth have been described in detail by the American writer Thomas L. Friedman. He fears the worst, but also hopes for the best. He thinks that by using American expertise, ingenuity and cash, solutions to the energy crisis can be found.

Friedman points out that the green economy is a chance to reassert[6] American strength. "The ability to design, build and export green technologies to produce clean water, clean air and healthy and abundant food is going to be the currency of power in the New Energy Era – not the only one, but right up there with computers, microchips, information technologies and planes and tanks." The imperative here is avowedly[7] patriotic: "Green is the new red, white and blue."

The Times (September 18th 2008)

1. *persistants* 2. *produire* 3. *exalter* 4. *foncer* 5. *stupéfiant* 6. *réaffirmer* 7. *ouvertement*

B Reading comprehension

WORKBOOK → p. 24-25

Turn to your *Workbook* which will help you to understand the text.

C In your own words

1. Use your *Workbook* to sum up the article.

D Going further

2. Explain: *"Green is the new red, white and blue."* (l. 75). Do you think that Friedman's priority is to save the environment? Justify your opinion.

3. Do you think the green economy is the only way to put an end to the *"global ecological nightmare"* (l. 43)?

4. Can you name some films *"extolling the thrill of driving"* (l. 31)?

E Language training

5. Savoir prononcer YOUR CD 19-21 CD 1 48-50

a. Dans les mots suivants, les lettres ***-ea-*** se prononcent-elles : /ɪə/, /e/, /iː/, /ɪeɪ/, /iːə/ ?

meant – idea – cheap – Dean – dream – create – fear – reassert – clean – healthy

Vérifiez à l'écoute, puis prononcez ces mots.

b. Lisez une fois le passage de *"Yet the cars…"* (l. 42) à *"… since 1990."* (l. 49). Où se trouve l'accent principal dans les mots suivants : *American – ecological – nightmare – restrained – efficient – contrast – demand* ?

Vérifiez à l'écoute, puis relisez le passage à haute voix en faisant attention à l'accent de mot.

6. Pratiquer la grammaire

Le *present perfect, for, since* et *ago*

LANGUAGE WORKSHOP → p. 58

toolbox

Nouns
- pride /praɪd/: *fierté*
- fossil fuel: *combustible fossile*
- greenhouse gas
- global warming
- superpower

Adjectives
- proud: *fier*
- innovative /ˈɪnəʊˌveɪtɪv/
- paradoxical
- alternative

Verbs & expressions
- lead the market: *être en tête du marché*
- go green
- survive /səˈvaɪv/
- tackle an issue /ˈɪʃuː/: *s'attaquer à un problème*
- be ahead /əˈhed/ of
- give up: *abandonner*
- reduce (gas consumption /kənˈsʌmpʃən/): *réduire (la consommation d'essence)*

Your task

Write the summary of an article

You follow a course to become a journalist. One of the first exercises you are asked to do is to summarize the article "Behind the wheel" in 150 words.

MÉTHODOLOGIE
Résumer un article de presse → p. 168

Grammaire | Le *present perfect*, *for*, *since* et *ago*

PRÉCIS GRAMMATICAL → 5-7

A Observer et comprendre

1 ***AGO***

The Model T Ford was built (...) in Michigan a century ago (...). (Text 2, p. 56, l. 4)

Qu'exprime le complément de temps en *AGO* : **1.** « le point de départ d'une action » ou **2.** « un point de repère dans le passé » ? À quel temps est-il associé ? Traduisez ce complément.

2 ***FOR* et *SINCE***

1. ***For most of the last century***, *the automobile represented (...).* (Text 2, p. 56, l. 17)
2. *We have produced this model* ***for about twenty years now***.
3. *(...) demand for oil has grown by twenty-two per cent* ***since 1990***. (Text 2, p. 56, l. 48)

a. Qu'expriment respectivement les compléments de temps en *FOR* et *SINCE* dans les énoncés ci-dessus : **1.** « le point de départ d'une action » ou **2.** « une durée » ?

b. Quel énoncé désigne une période révolue ? Quel est le complément de temps associé à cet énoncé ? Traduisez.

c. Quel(s) énoncé(s) signifie(nt) que « l'action se poursuit au moment présent » ? Quel est le temps du verbe dans ce cas ? Quels compléments de temps sont associés à cet / ces énoncé(s) ? Traduisez.

d. Déduisez : À quels temps *FOR* peut-il être associé ? Se traduit-il toujours de la même manière ? Répondez aux mêmes questions pour *SINCE*.

3 ***Present perfect* simple et *present perfect* *BE+ING* : quelle différence ?**

1. *(...) demand for oil* ***has grown*** *by twenty-two per cent since 1990.* (Text 2, p. 56, l. 48)
2. *Demand for oil* ***has been growing*** *regularly since 1990 / for several decades.*
3. *Prices* ***have been increasing*** *continuously since 2009.*
4. *They* ***have*** *already* ***produced*** *two thousand cars.*

Qu'expriment dans les énoncés ci-dessus les compléments soulignés : **1.** « une activité continue » ou **2.** « le résultat (mesurable) d'une action » ? Indiquez pour chacun de ces compléments s'il est associé au *present perfect* simple ou au *present perfect* *BE+ING*.

Faisons le point !
Quelles sont les traductions possibles de « il y a », « depuis » et « pendant » ?
Qu'exprime le *present perfect* *BE+ING* lorsqu'il est associé à *FOR* et *SINCE* ?

B Pratiquer

4 **Mettez les verbes entre parenthèses au prétérit simple ou au *present perfect* *BE+ING*.**

a. They (produce) these cars since January.
b. They (design) this model twenty years ago.
c. I (start) this new job in July. I (work) here for two months now.
d. We (hire) these engineers two years ago. We (use) their expertise since then.

5 **Traduisez à l'aide de *FOR*, *SINCE* ou *AGO* et du prétérit ou du *present perfect* *BE+ING*.**

a. Ils vendent ce modèle depuis longtemps.
b. Pendant de nombreuses années, il a vécu aux États-Unis.
c. Les ventes *(sales)* ont augmenté *(rise)* régulièrement depuis 2000.
d. Ils ont inventé ce concept il y a un siècle.
e. Ils sont partis il y a deux mois.

Grammaire de l'oral | Reconnaître le *present perfect* à l'oral

6 Identifier les syllabes accentuées dans les formes verbales CD 1 51

Écoutez ces énoncés et indiquez quelles sont les syllabes accentuées. Les auxiliaires, les terminaisons en *-en* et en *-ing* en font-ils partie ?

1. *Ken has taken risks.* **2.** *Lou has been taking risks.*

7 Distinguer le *present perfect* du prétérit à l'oral CD 1 52

Écoutez attentivement chaque énoncé afin de bien en comprendre le sens global et indiquez si la forme entendue est la forme **1** ou **2**.

a. 1. James's run **a. 2.** James ran
b. 1. James's run **b. 2.** James ran
c. 1. She's sent **c. 2.** She sent
d. 1. My mother sent **d. 2.** My mother's sent

8 Repérer le *present perfect* BE+ING CD 1 53

Écoutez attentivement chaque énoncé afin de bien en comprendre le sens global et indiquez si la forme entendue est la forme 1 ou 2.

a. 1. He has been interviewed **a. 2.** He is being interviewed
b. 1. He has been interviewed **b. 2.** He is being interviewed
c. 1. They are staying **c. 2.** They have been staying
d. 1. They are staying **d. 2.** They have been staying

Lexique | Sur la route

Assurez-vous que vous avez bien mémorisé les mots clés de l'unité.

→ Keywords p. 48

9 Donnez les synonymes ou les antonymes des mots et expressions suivants.

a. booming = … **b.** petrol = … **c.** increasing ≠ … **d.** individual ≠ … **e.** give a ride = … **f.** factory = …

10 Donnez l'équivalent anglais des mots ou expressions suivants.

a. pénurie **b.** excitant **c.** prospérer

11 Quelle est la syllabe accentuée dans les mots suivants ?

a. economical **b.** decline **c.** prosperity **d.** expand **e.** public

12 Complétez les phrases à l'aide des mots suivants :

oil crisis – gas station – diner – gas guzzler – affordable – consume – means – highway – hit – consumer society – car-pooling – eco-friendly – billboard – hitchhike – speed limit.

a. People are turning more and more to ..1.. because it is an ..2.. ..3.. of transport.
b. He wanted to ..4.. the road. As he had little money he decided to ..5...
c. On the ..6.., he saw a ..7.. indicating a ..8.. near the ..9...
d. This car is ..10.. but it is a ..11...
e. When drivers go over the ..12.., their cars ..13.. a lot of petrol.
f. The ..14.. obliged the ..15.. to turn to green energy.

toolbox

Nouns
- mass production: *production en série*
- profitability: *rentabilité*
- supply and demand: *l'offre et la demande*

Verbs
- manufacture: *fabriquer*
- market: *commercialiser*
- compete with: *être en concurrence*

Your task

Present a revolutionary car concept
You have designed a petrol-free car. You meet the manager of a famous car company to tell him about your revolutionary concept. Act out the conversation with another student. Use the ***past simple*** and the ***present perfect*** when necessary.

Songs of the Open Road

American writers have always sung the Open Road.

A Walt Whitman (1819-1892)

CD 1 54

The poet

American poet, journalist and essayist, Walt Whitman is best known for his collection of poems *Leaves of Grass* (1855). Whitman, often called the father of free verse, disregarded rhyme and incorporated the rhythms of common speech into poetry. He believed that a poet's style should be simple. Whitman celebrated all creatures and praised natural open spaces.

Listen to an extract from "Song of the Open Road", one of the poems of *Leaves of Grass*.

1. What words show Whitman's delight in travelling the open road?
2. What sentences are good examples of Whitman's simple and natural style?

B John Steinbeck (1902-1968)

THE CARS OF THE MIGRANT PEOPLE crawled out of the side roads onto the great cross-country highway, and they took the migrant way to the West. In the daylight they scuttled[1] like bugs[2] to the westward; and as the dark caught them, they clustered[3] like bugs near to shelter and to water. And because they were lonely and perplexed, because they had all come from a place of sadness and worry and defeat, and because they were all going to a new mysterious place, they huddled[4] together; they talked together; they shared their lives, their food, and the things they hoped for in the new country. Thus it might be that one family camped near a spring, and another camped for the spring and for company, and a third because two families had pioneered the place and found it good. And when the sun went down, perhaps twenty families and twenty cars were there.

In the evening a strange thing happened: the twenty families became one family, the children were the children of all. The loss of home became one loss; and the golden time in the West was one dream.

John STEINBECK, *The Grapes of Wrath* (1939)

1. *se précipiter* 2. *insectes* 3. *se rassembler* 4. *se blottir*

The novelist

John Steinbeck was awarded the Nobel Prize in Literature for "his realistic and imaginative writing, combining as it does sympathetic humor and keen social perception." He wrote sixteen social novels, the most famous being: *Tortilla Flat* (1935), *Of Mice and Men* (1937), *East of Eden* (1952), *Travels with Charley* (1962) in which he gives an account of his three-month tour in a truck across the USA. *The Grapes of Wrath* (1939) is often considered his best work. It tells the story of Oklahoma farmers who, unable to live off their land, fled to California where they became migratory workers.

Read the passage from *The Grapes of Wrath*.

1. What happens in this passage?
2. What were the migrants' feelings along the road?
3. Make a few remarks about Steinbeck's style.
4. What effect does it produce on the reader?

C The Beat Generation

The Beat Generation writers said they were influenced by Walt Whitman. Read the text and explain in what way.

The Beat Generation writers

William Burroughs, Allen Ginsberg and Jack Kerouac were the most important writers of the American "Beat Generation" of the 1950s. They rejected what they saw as the materialism, militarism, consumerism and conformity of the 1950s. "America, where everyone is always doing what they ought," as Kerouac put it in his novel *On The Road*. So they affected nonconformist styles of dress and speech and explored the cultural underground of jazz, drug use, sexuality and Zen Buddhism.

It was Kerouac who coined the term "beat generation". It refers to *beat*en (weary people), music's *beat*, especially the beat of jazz and it referred to *beat*itudes – the belief that the entire natural world and everyone in it are blessed.

Allen Ginsberg, Jack Kerouac and Gregory Corso (1957)

D Cormac McCarthy (1933-)

The writer

Cormac McCarthy is a contemporary writer. He has written ten novels, among them *No Country for Old Men* and *The Road* which won him the Pulitzer Prize and was ranked first on *The Times* list of the best fiction and non-fiction books of the past 10 years.

The story of *The Road* follows a man and his son as they wander through a devastated landscape in search of food, shelter and warmth while keeping away from gangs of murderous outlaws. Father and son are heading for the Eastern coast with little hope of finding anything. They have nothing but the ragged clothes they're wearing. And they have themselves.

- *The Road* is a meditation on the worst and the best that we are capable of: ultimate destructiveness, desperate tenacity, and the tenderness that keeps two people alive in the face of total devastation. *Oprah's Book Club*
- *The Road* would be pure misery if not for its stunning, savage beauty. *The New York Times*
- Part of the achievement of *The Road* is its poetic description of landscapes. *The Observer*

1 Look at the film poster, read the summary of *The Road* and say why the novel is called "post-apocalyptic".

2 Read the press excerpts. What do people like about *The Road*?

Webquest — From road novels to road movies

TICE

1 The novels *The Grapes of Wrath* and *The Road* have been made into famous movies. Browse the web so as to find at least three other road novels which have been adapted for the screen.

2 Choose one of these films and give an oral account of it to the class (director, actors, synopsis...).

Web resources

- www.filmsite.org/roadfilms.html
- www.hcpl.net/read/road-novels
- www.wilmettelibrary.info/

final task

Can you imagine travelling in the USA without a car?

**You are planning a trip to the USA with a friend. You have a discussion with him / her about the kind of trip you want to go on: a car-free trip or a mythical road trip?
You write an e-mail to a travel agency to explain your plans and ask for further information.**

1 Decide on the trip you want to take

MÉTHODOLOGIE
Discussion contradictoire → p. 158

Student A You are environmentally-minded and after reading the leaflet below you try to convince your friend to go on a car-free trip in the USA.
Student B You can't imagine travelling in the USA without a car: you want to drive along the mythical Route 66!

car-free VISIT THE USA

NO NEED FOR A CAR TO ENJOY AMERICA'S LANDSCAPES... HELP US KEEP AMERICA GREEN!

Here are a few green tips for green trips:

Cycle through South Dakota!
Cycling along the 109 miles of the George S. Mickelson Trail, it's easy to see why the Black Hills of South Dakota are still sacred for the Lakota Nation.

Go hiking in the Grand Canyon!
Take a thrilling trip back in time and hike down into the Grand Canyon, back through up to six million years of erosion and four geological eras. Take extra caution hiking along the rim...

Ride a train through New England!
Train travel in the rural northeastern area of the United States is thriving again. Vintage steam engines and restored diesel locomotives take travelers through New England's countryside and along the sea coast.

Go rafting in Utah!
Moab, Utah, nestled between the red rock wonders of Arches National Park and the breathtaking forests of the La Sal Mountains is unlike any place on earth...

Don't hesitate to visit our website
www.plan-your-green-trips.com or *contact us at* "Green Trips & Co, 23 Sunset Street, San Francisco, Cal."

2 Write an e-mail to the Green Trips travel agency

MÉTHODOLOGIE
Écrire un courriel → p. 166

You have finally agreed to go on a car-free trip. You write an e-mail to Green Trips. (200-250 words)
- You explain why you have chosen an eco-friendly trip.
- You tell them about your plans and ask for more information.

Check your skills

WORKBOOK → p. 26

A Parler d'un projet de voyage

You have found this ad in a magazine and you explain why it makes you feel like travelling around California.

Expliquez en quoi cette affiche vous donne envie de faire un voyage en Californie.

1. Préparez votre prise de parole : prenez des notes mais ne rédigez pas de phrases complètes.

2. Décrivez et analysez l'affiche (origine, but) et exposez votre projet.

Votre prise de parole devra durer de 1 minute 30 à 2 minutes. Évaluez-vous en fonction des critères proposés dans votre *Workbook*.

Je me situe par rapport au CECRL B1 → B2

LORSQUE JE PARLE DE CE PROJET DE VOYAGE :

■ **B1 :** Je peux faire un exposé simple et développer les points importants avec précision.
Je peux expliquer mon opinion en donnant des arguments.
Je peux parler de manière compréhensible et sans trop hésiter, même si je fais des pauses pour réfléchir.

■ **B1 + :** Je peux m'exprimer sur ce sujet de façon claire en utilisant quelques articulateurs logiques.
J'ai un assez bon contrôle grammatical malgré quelques influences de la langue maternelle.
Je peux m'exprimer avec une certaine aisance, même si quelques problèmes de formulation entraînent de courtes pauses.

B Écrire une page de carnet de voyage

C'est votre première journée de voyage aux États-Unis. Vous êtes épuisé(e), mais vous tenez à écrire vos impressions dans votre carnet de voyage. Donnez une suite au récit de votre journée, qui commence ainsi :

"What a day! I am exhausted!..."

Écrivez 150 à 200 mots, puis évaluez-vous en fonction des critères proposés dans votre *Workbook*.

Je me situe par rapport au CECRL B1 → B2

LORSQUE J'ÉCRIS CE RÉCIT :

■ **B1 :** Je peux raconter ma journée en mettant en relief la succession et la cohérence des événements et des comportements.
Je peux exprimer des sentiments et des impressions dans un texte simple et articulé.
Je peux supprimer en me relisant les erreurs de langue les plus importantes.

■ **B1 + :** Je peux décrire des événements, sentiments et impressions de manière claire et détaillée.
Les erreurs de langue sont peu nombreuses et ne gênent pas une lecture fluide de mon texte.

Unit 4

Espaces et échanges

Mythes et héros

American dreams

Is the American dream still alive?

final task

The Drama club of your school has decided to present a modern version of the musical *West Side Story*.
You study the lyrics of a famous scene, then adapt it to the present time and act out a contradictory discussion.

Keywords

Nouns
- opportunity
- (future) prospects: *perspectives*
- achievement = accomplishment
- success ≠ failure /ˈfeɪljə/
- hardship: *épreuve*
- economic crisis /ˈkraɪsɪs/

Adjectives
- hopeful ≠ hopeless
- eager to V: *très désireux de*
- ambitious
- confident = self-assured /əˈʃʊəd/
- affordable: *que l'on peut s'offrir*
- lucrative = prosperous
- bankrupt = ruined
- unemployed = jobless

Verbs & expressions
- dream of sth / V-ING
- make it to the top
- change lives
- go from rags to riches = from extreme poverty to wealth
- overcome obstacles /ˈɒbstəklz/
- thrive = prosper
- make a dream come true: *réaliser un rêve*
- achieve /əˈtʃiːv/ = fulfil: *réaliser*
- reach a goal: *atteindre un but*
- manage *(réussir)* to V ≠ fail to V
- succeed in V-ING
- try every possible means: *mettre en œuvre tous les moyens*
- make one's way in life: *trouver sa voie*
- miss a chance: *laisser passer une occasion*
- be having a hard time
- cope with: *faire face à*

LANGUAGE WORKSHOP → p. 75

American landmarks

1. Describe the picture. What is strange about it?

2. Say all you know about the three main elements; use the Internet if necessary.

3. How do these elements symbolize the American dream?

toolbox

Nouns
- landmark : *point de repère*
- trompe-l'œil /trɒmp'lɔɪ/
- truck (Am.) = lorry (Br.): *camion*
- low-angle shot : *contre-plongée*
- beacon = torch
- flag = *drapeau*
- stars and stripes
- skyscraper: *gratte-ciel*

Adjectives
- bright (colours / lights)
- deceptive: *trompeur*

Verbs & expressions
- customize /'kʌstəmaɪz/
- flap / fly in the wind
- welcome: *accueillir*
- flee from sth: *fuir qqch*
- in search of: *à la recherche de*
- at first sight: *à première vue*

Views on the American dream

MÉTHODOLOGIE INTERACTION ORALE → p. 157

A What does "The American dream" mean to you?

MÉTHODOLOGIE
Discussion contradictoire → p. 158

Discuss your representations of the American dream.

1. Think of situations and characters illustrating the American dream in movies, TV series or real life.
Read the terms provided below. In your opinion, which of them are ingredients of the American dream?
Make a list of the most important ones.

Secure job · No taxes · Success
Social justice · Large family · Freedom
Power · Own home · Plenty of money
Fame · Self-esteem · A lot of free time
Good health · Solidarity · Opportunities

2. Compare your list with your partner's and discuss what the "American dream" means to you. Do your ideas end up in a common definition? Why (not)?

B Success stories

MÉTHODOLOGIE
Interview → p. 158

Play a game about success stories.

1. What do you know about the person in the photo?
Do you think he is representative of the American dream?

2. Browse the web to find information about other successful American people. Choose entrepreneurs (Bill Gates, Walt Disney, etc.), sportsmen, scientists, politicians... not only movie stars or singers.

3. Select one of your favourites and take notes.

4. Play the "Who am I? game" with a classmate:
Student A You ask "yes-no" or open questions to find who the famous person is.
Student B You answer Student A's questions but keep the answers imprecise so as not to reveal the character's identity too soon.
Then reverse the roles.

C "This time it's true"

MÉTHODOLOGIE
Conversation → p. 157

Have a conversation about the American dream.

1. Describe the cartoon. What period in the history of the USA does it refer to?
Explain briefly what the man is telling his children.

2. You have seen this cartoon and the quotations below in an American magazine. Discuss with your partner the vision of the American dream they convey.

"The American dream is that dream of a land in which life should be better and richer and fuller for every man, with opportunity for each according to ability or achievement."

James Truslow Adams, *Epic of America*, 1931

"There is not a black America and a white America and Latino America and Asian America – there's the United States of America. [...] a vision of America that fulfills Dr King's promise that we be judged not by the color of our skin but by the content of our character."

Barack Obama, 2004

toolbox

Nouns
- career
- discrimination
- civil liberties

Adjectives
- inspired by
- self-made
- puzzling = enigmatic

Verbs & expressions
- accomplish = achieve
- climb the social ladder
- have faith: *avoir confiance*

Webquest D Meeting *The Great Gatsby* TICE

Reading: *The Great Gatsby*, p. 136

1. Browse the web to find information about the novel entitled *The Great Gatsby*:
   - the period when the story takes place;
   - the main characters;
   - the major themes;
   - Gatsby's life and death.
2. Complete the summary of the story in the worksheet provided by your teacher.
3. After Gatsby's funeral, a journalist interviews Gatsby's neighbour, Nick, to know more about Gatsby's origins, social level, lifestyle, occupation, etc.
Student A You are the journalist. You will prepare a list of specific questions to ask Nick.
Student B You are Nick. You will use the information from the webquest and the summary to answer the questions.

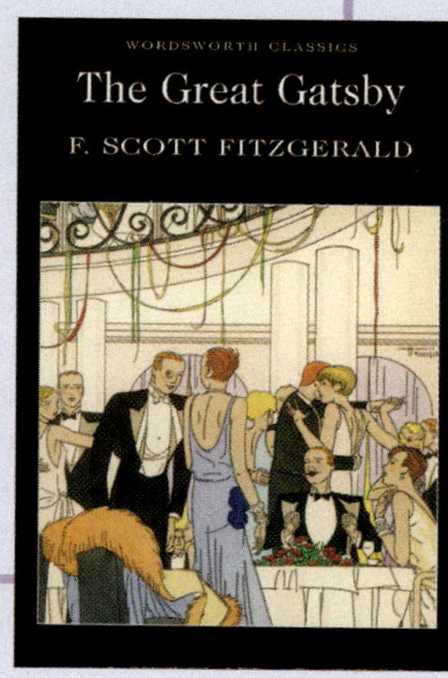

Web resources
- www.gradesaver.com/the-great-gatsby
- www.sparknotes.com/lit/gatsby

Text 1

Dreaming of America

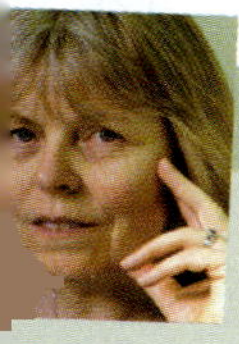

Ursula HEGI

Born in 1946 in West Germany, she moved to the United States at the age of 18. She wrote stories, reviews for *The New York Times*, and fiction about Germany. She also taught creative writing at Eastern Washington University.
She won many awards. Her latest novel is entitled *The Worst Thing I've Done* (2007).

A Warming up

Look at the picture, read the title and the first sentence of the text. What can you anticipate from them?

Stefan Blau was only thirteen when he ran away from his hometown in Germany one rainy November night in 1894. Convinced he lived in the most fascinating time possible – an age of transformation and discovery – he'd felt restless in Burgdorf. Too many traditions. Too many restrictions. America, he believed, was the country where people brought about changes instead of resisting them. But his parents didn't want to listen when he read to them about immigrants earning fortunes, about inventions, about gold in the hills; they didn't know that America had grafted itself to his mind so tenaciously that he had dreams of it every single night, dreams of an odd[1] and magnificent landscape inhabited by buffaloes and of buildings so tall they pierced the clouds.

When Stefan bought an English dictionary and memorized forty new words each day, his parents shook their heads and told him they were not about to leave Germany, and when he suggested he'd make the passage alone and send for them and his sister once he'd made his fortune, they smiled. "What a child he still is," they said to each other.

They were asleep when he left.

Although short for his age, he was sturdy and talked his way into work on a coal barge that floated north on the Rhein into Holland. When he reached Rotterdam and was unable to trade labor for passage to America, he started toward Amsterdam and walked through cold nights and days, resting in barns[2] or churches only when he was too chilled or exhausted to keep moving. But he never lost his enthusiasm because with each step – so he reminded himself – he was getting closer to America.

It was sleeting[3] the afternoon he got to Amsterdam, but he felt lucky because before nightfall he was hired as a kitchen hand on a passenger ship bound for New York.

In lower Manhattan, he found work in an elegant French restaurant, where he peeled vegetables and washed dishes with the same eagerness[4] that he would, years later, bring to his own restaurant. Only the owner was French; the rest of the staff were foreigners from other parts of Europe, who gesticulated and shouted scraps of Italian, Yiddish, Hungarian, German and fractured English. Not all had come to America as willingly as Stefan; some had fled from religion; others from family or war; but what kept each of them here was hope.

Being part of his new country would never be quite as total for Stefan as when he first arrived and wanted to be American in every way possible. How he loved the lack of convention, the instant familiarity. Here, respect had nothing to do with age but was earned with success. Class differences – that complicated ladder[5] of human worth[6] he'd grown up with – did not exist in America, he believed, and it would take him years to grasp the many subtle shadings of prejudice...

The Vision of Emma Blau, Ursula HEGI (2000)

1. strange 2. *granges* 3. sleet = snow + rain 4. /ˈiːgənɪs/ = enth**u**siasm
5. *échelle* 6. /wɜːθ/ = m**e**rit

B Reading comprehension WORKBOOK → p. 27-28

Turn to your *Workbook* which will help you to understand the text.

C In your own words

1. Sum up the story with the following guidelines:
a. Explain Stephen's dream and how his parents reacted to it.
b. How did Stephen manage to make his dream come true?
c. Was Stephen's vision of America based on reality or illusions:
1. before he left?
2. when he lived in Manhattan?

D Going further

2. Would you say that Stephen was a daydreamer?
3. Would you say that Stephen's life is a success story?
4. Imagine you are Stephen. In the same circumstances, would you have acted the same way?
5. Do you think such an adventure would be possible nowadays?

E Language training

6. **Savoir prononcer** YOUR CD 22-27 CD 2 2-7
7. **Pratiquer la grammaire**

Gérondif et infinitif LANGUAGE WORKSHOP → p. 74

toolbox

Nouns
- daredevil: *casse-cou*
- wishful thinking: *vœu pieux*
- taste for danger: *goût du risque*
- the dirty work: *les basses besognes*

Adjectives
- adv**e**nturous
- enthusi**a**stic /ɪnˌθjuːzɪˈæstɪk/
- na**i**ve
- mat**u**re
- **ch**ildish
- det**e**rmined

Verbs & expressions
- conv**i**nce = pers**ua**de /pəˈsweɪd/
- try one's luck: *tenter sa chance*
- get through to sb: *se faire comprendre*
- hold on to one's dream: *s'accrocher à son rêve*
- do one's best: *faire de son mieux*

Your task

Act out a conversation about leaving home

Imagine the conversation between Stephen and his parents when he tries to convince them to emigrate to America. Decide which part you want to play and what personality traits you want to emphasize in your character.

MÉTHODOLOGIE
Conversation → p. 157

A poll about the American dream

culture key Recession → p. 142

Bonus vidéo

Cleveland versus Wall Street

DVD

Watch an extract from this video.

A The topic

1. Describe the scene on the cover of *The Saturday Evening Post*. What does it symbolize?

2. Describe the situation of the men in the cartoon. Who or what is supposed to be responsible for it?

"I used to have the Great American Dream, but the politicians keep waking me up."

B Open your ears

CD 2 8

3. Before listening to the poll for *The New York Times*, you will hear three sentences.

Which one could be said by *The New York Times* journalist, by the photographer in the *Post* cover, by one of the tramps in the cartoon?

4. Deduce from the sentence said by the journalist:

a. what she wanted to know;

b. if the interviewers gave rather optimistic, rather pessimistic or contradictory answers.

C Listen

CD 2 9

WORKBOOK → p. 29

5. Listen to the recording and check whether your answers to questions 3 and 4 are right. You will find some help in your *Workbook*.

D In your own words

6. Using the notes in your *Workbook*, develop the various definitions people give of the American dream.

7. Does the present period of recession modify their appreciation of the American dream?

toolbox

Nouns

- tramp: *clochard*
- real estate: *bien immobilier*
- foreclosure /fɔːˈkləʊʒə/: *saisie d'un bien*
- mortgage payment: *remboursement d'un emprunt immobilier*
- social outcast: *exclu, paria*
- the haves ≠ the have-nots

Adjectives

- unfortunate: *malchanceux*
- careless: *imprudent*
- evicted: *expulsé*

Verbs & expressions

- be down and out: *être SDF*
- be had: *se faire avoir (fam.)*
- take out a loan: *faire un emprunt*
- be unaware that: *ignorer que...*
- take life as it comes
- have one bit of hard luck after another: *jouer de malchance*
- live from hand to mouth: *vivre au jour le jour*
- make ends meet: *joindre les deux bouts*

Your task

Role play: talk about a tramp's difficult life

One of the tramps you can see in the cartoon explains to *The New York Times* journalist how he tried to achieve his American dream, what problems he met and how they affected his life. He concludes by evoking the new philosophy he has developed about the American dream. Put yourself in the tramp's shoes.

MÉTHODOLOGIE
Raconter une histoire → p. 153

American dream... or nightmare?

Your task

Enter a writing contest!
To be selected you have to submit the summary of a novel entitled *American Dream... or Nightmare?* Use the notes below, decide how the story will end and write the summary of your future novel. (200-250 words)

MÉTHODOLOGIE
Écrire une histoire ou continuer un récit → p. 167

A Study the information

1. Study the information given about this married couple so as to use all of it in your summary.

2001	Wedding	
2002	• Good job in the town's finance department	• Head of a small shoe-repair business with a nice local client base
2005	• Wants more Envies his friends who can buy expensive cars and have recently purchased a big McMansion	• Happy with her life Refuses to change anything
2006	• Wants a divorce	• Decides to keep peace in the family
2007	• Starts up a company → failure	• Works full time for a large insurance company
2009	• Takes a basic job in a company → commutes 100 miles to work and back each day	• Must work over 60 hours a week just to make sure she can keep her job
2010	Buy their own McMansion way out in the country.	

culture key McMansions → p. 142

B Get ready

2. Give each character a name and make a quick portrait of each (personality traits, likes and dislikes) so as to give coherence to the story.

3. Decide if you prefer a happy ending ("American dream"...) or a sad ending ("nightmare"). Chance may play a role in the story.

4. Decide who the narrator will be (one of the characters, or an external character).

C Write your summary

5. Rephrase the indications provided in the notes.

6. Keep using the first or third person according to the type of narrative you have chosen.

toolbox

Nouns
- home owner: *propriétaire*
- odd jobs: *petits boulots*
- resentment = animosity
- financial situation
- debt

Adjectives
- jealous /'dʒeləs/ (of) = envious
- submissive: *soumis*
- doomed = unlucky, luckless
- overworked: *surmené*
- responsible for sth

Verbs & expressions
- show off: *frimer*
- can't afford: *n'a pas les moyens*
- blame sb for sth: *rejeter la responsabilité sur qqn*
- bear / have a grudge against sb: *en vouloir à qqn*
- the chances are that...: *il y a de fortes chances que...*
- for the sake of appearances: *pour sauver les apparences*
- take / catch someone unawares = surprise someone

Text 2

Gatsby is back

CD 2 10

culture key The Jazz Age, The Great Depression → p. 142

The Observer is a British Sunday quality newspaper. First published in 1791, it is the oldest national newspaper in Britain. Its political views are "left of centre". It was bought in 1993 by *The Guardian*. Website: observer.guardian.co.uk

A Warming up

What do you know about *The Great Gatsby* and its main character?

F Scott Fitzgerald's landmark[1] novel tells the story of the mysterious Jay Gatsby who sets the louche social scene of Long Island on fire[2] with his style, parties and enigmatic persona. It was hailed as emblematic of the Jazz Age of the 1920s; a portrait of decadent fun and impossible dreams complete with a poignant message of exclusion and fraud that presaged the coming Great Depression of the 1930s.

Given the spirit of the novel, it is perhaps no surprise that *The Great Gatsby* is rising again in America's cultural landscape of 2010. Across the continent, *Gatsby* is back. In New York the great Broadway hit of the summer was the epic Public Theater production *Gatz*, where the entire book is read out in an eight-hour marathon.

Literary experts believe that many of the themes associated with the book will resonate in a country coming to terms[3] with the end of a great economic boom and experiencing unemployment and hardship: they look back with longing to the Roaring Twenties and a time when the boom seemed to suggest that outrageous wealth was a possibility for everyone. It is something that many Americans facing mass unemployment and the economic wreckage left by a burst property bubble[4] can relate to.

"The 1920s were the first fetishised decade. That is part of the legacy of *The Great Gatsby*. In that sense it describes a moment of prosperity just before a crash," said Keith Gandal, a literature lecturer at City University of New York, who is teaching *Gatsby* to his students this year.

Of course, what *Gatsby* is actually about has always been hotly debated since it was published in 1925. Gandal argues that the book is in many ways dealing with the subject of a greater opening up of American society in the wake of the first world war as non-Wasp[5] Americans – as Gatsby turns out to be – are striving successfully to enter high society and take over the pillars of the American establishment.

But in most popular culture the book has been interpreted the other way round: as depicting the illusory nature of the American dream.

A poll taken by ABC News and Yahoo in September asked Americans if they thought the American dream was dead. A remarkable 43% of those surveyed replied that it was. Not surprisingly, those already rich were likely to be more receptive to the idea that it still existed than those with less money, implying the dream has become a preserve[6] of the wealthier classes. Yet that goes against its core ideal, according to which wealth and status are open to anyone provided they work hard enough.

Like Gatsby himself, a country known for its cheery optimism is coming to terms with a brutal reality check. The lessons taught by *The Great Gatsby* are living on.

The Observer (November 21st 2010)

1. *qui fait date* **2.** *révolutionner* **3.** accept something unpleasant **4.** *explosion de la bulle immobilière* **5.** White Anglo-Saxon Protestant **6.** *chasse gardée*

B Reading comprehension

WORKBOOK → p. 30-31

Your *Workbook* will help you to understand the text.

C In your own words

1. Sum up the article with the help of your *Workbook*.

D Going further

2. How do you explain the present interest for Gatsby's story?
3. Give your interpretation of the last sentence of the text: "*The lessons taught by* The Great Gatsby *are living on.*" (l. 72).
4. Imagine you are living in the Roaring Twenties. Would you be attracted by Jay Gatsby's way of life? Why (not)?

E Language training

5. Savoir prononcer

YOUR CD 28-29 — CD 2 11-12

a. La graphie ***-ou-*** des mots suivants se prononce-t-elle : /ɔː/, /ə/, /ʌ/, /uː/, /aʊ/, /aʊə/ ?

louche – hour – outrageous – course – out – round – thought – enough

b. L'accentuation des mots longs selon leur suffixe

Écoutez ces mots de 3, 4 ou 5 syllabes extraits du texte et repérez où se trouve leur accent. Pouvez-vous en déduire une règle ?

- *exclusion – depression – production*
- *enigmatic – emblematic – economic*
- *reality – prosperity – possibility – university*

6. Pratiquer la grammaire

Propositions en *that* et *what* –
Ordre des adjectifs – Place du génitif

WORKBOOK → p. 32

toolbox

Nouns

- nouveau riche /ˌnuːvəʊˈriːʃ/
- the idle /ˈaɪdl/ rich: *les riches oisifs*
- rise and fall: *grandeur et décadence*
- ruling class ≠ common people
- revival: *renaissance*

Adjectives

- extravagant /ɪkˈstrævɪgənt/ = very expensive
- illusory = false, untrue
- illicit = prohibited, illegal
- corrupted = dishonest
- decayed: *décadent*

Verbs & expressions

- lie ≠ tell the truth
- fall apart: *s'effondrer*
- bootleg: *faire de la contrebande*
- yearn /jɜːn/ (for): *désirer ardemment*
- flaunt one's wealth: *faire étalage de sa richesse*

Your task

Write an e-mail to ask about your friend's opinion

You have just read the article from *The Observer* and you'd like to know what your American friend thinks of it. You send him an e-mail telling him about the article and asking him for his opinion. (200 words)

MÉTHODOLOGIE
Écrire un courriel → p. 166

Language workshop

Grammaire | Gérondif et infinitif

PRÉCIS GRAMMATICAL → 33, 34, 35

A Observer et comprendre

1 Gérondif et infinitif : valeurs

1. *(…) they were not about* ***to leave****…* (Text 1, p. 68, l. 13)
2. *(…) when he was too chilled (…) to keep* ***moving*** (Text 1, p. 68, l. 22)
3. ***Being*** *part of his new country would never be quite as total for Stefan (…)* (Text 1, p. 69, l. 35)

Relevez, parmi les formes en gras, la forme à l'infinitif et indiquez si elle désigne pour le personnage : **1.** « un fait déjà réalisé ou en cours » ou **2.** « un fait à venir ». Qu'en est-il de la / des forme(s) au gérondif (V-*ING*) ?

2 Les prépositions

a. Observez les éléments qui suivent les prépositions en gras et déduisez : « Les prépositions peuvent être suivies de … ou bien … ». Traduisez.

1. *(…) when he read to them (…)* ***about*** *inventions (…)* (Text 1, p. 68, l. 6)
2. *(…) instead* ***of*** *resisting them (…)* (Text 1, p. 68, l. 5)
3. *He wasn't used* ***to*** *the cold.*

b. Observez les énoncés ci-dessous. Pourquoi *TO* est-il suivi du gérondif dans les énoncés **1** et **2** ? Qu'en est-il de l'énoncé **3** ? Traduisez.

1. *He wasn't used* ***to*** *sleeping out in the cold.*
2. *He didn't object* ***to*** *working with them.*
3. *he (…) wanted* ***to*** *be American (…)* (Text 1, p. 69, l. 36)

3 Propositions infinitives et propositions en -*ING*

1. *They didn't expect* ***Stefan*** */* ***him to go to America on his own.***
2. *(…) when he read (…) about* ***immigrants earning fortunes*** *(…)* (Text 1, p. 68, l. 6)
3. *It had nothing to do with* ***his*** */* ***him being an immigrant.***

a. Observez la proposition infinitive en **1** et indiquez si le sujet (souligné) est un pronom personnel sujet, un pronom personnel complément, un possessif ou un nom.

b. Analysez de la même manière le sujet des propositions en -*ING* (= au gérondif) en **2** et **3**.

> **Faisons le point !**
> **Les prépositions sont suivies soit d'un… ou bien d'un… . *TO* n'est pas toujours la marque de… . *TO* peut également être suivi… . Le sujet d'une proposition infinitive est soit un… , soit un… . Les propositions en -*ING* peuvent avoir pour sujet… .**

B Pratiquer

4 Mettez les verbes entre parenthèses à l'infinitif ou au gérondif.

a. I regret (send) that letter. It was a mistake.
b. He was busy (write) an e-mail.
c. He intends (stay) a little longer.
d. I remember (come) here before.

5 *TO* et l'infinitif / *TO* et le gérondif. Mettez les verbes à la forme qui convient.

a. Do you object to (drive) them home?
b. We're looking forward to (see) you again.
c. Next time, I'll try to (be) more reasonable.
d. He'll get used to (live) with them.

6 Écrivez un énoncé complet à partir des éléments entre parenthèses.

a. He's asked (she – join him).
b. Would you like (we – wait for you)?
c. She told (he – stay there).
d. I don't expect (they – understand me).

7 Reformulez les énoncés à l'aide d'une proposition en -*ING*.

Ex. You're too strict. I never complained about it. → *I never complained about you being too strict.*

a. He's feeling miserable. I'm worried about it. → I'm worried about…
b. He has very little money. There's nothing wrong with it. → There's nothing wrong with…
c. I didn't want to go but he insisted on it. → He insisted on…

Grammaire de l'oral | Comprendre les pronoms et les prépositions

À savoir !
Les pronoms (*he, him, they, them*, etc.), les possessifs (*his, her*, etc.) et les prépositions (*of, for*, etc.) ne sont pas accentués la plupart du temps.

8 Repérer et distinguer *her, of, have, are, a* à l'oral CD 2 13-14

a. Lisez ces énoncés tout en complétant avec la forme qui convient : *her, of, have, are, a.*

All … her friends … phoned … . They … worried about … having … hard time over there.

b. Écoutez ces énoncés. Quel son ces mots ont-ils en commun : /ɑː/ ou /ə/ ?

c. Répétez le modèle.

9 Écrivez les énoncés que vous entendez. CD 2 15

Lexique | Chance, réussite et échecs

→ Keywords p. 64

Assurez-vous que vous avez bien retenu les mots clés de l'unité.

10 Donnez les synonymes ou antonymes des mots suivants.

a. success ≠ …
b. accomplishment = …
c. too expensive ≠ …
d. prosperous = …
e. chance = …
f. self-assured = …

11 Donnez l'équivalent anglais des mots et des expressions suivants.

a. réussir, aller loin
b. surmonter des obstacles
c. réaliser un rêve
d. faire face à une situation
e. traverser une période difficile
f. prospérer

12 Recopiez les mots suivants et soulignez la syllabe accentuée.

a. affordable
b. opportunity
c. achievement
d. unemployed
e. lucrative
f. ambitious

13 Complétez les phrases à l'aide des mots et expressions suivants :

bankrupt – economic crisis – from rags to riches – hardship – jobless – miss a chance – lucrative – means – opportunity – reach – make his way – manage.

a. She was looking for a more …1… position in the firm, so she did not want to …2… and she tried every possible …3… to …4… her objective.

b. He had already survived considerable …5…, that's why he …6… to …7… in life and finally went …8….

c. Because of the …9…, he became …10… and …11…. But within six months he found a new job with a good …12… for promotion.

Your task

Have a discussion about becoming independent

Your parents never seem to agree with you. You have decided to find a job and a flat for yourself to become more independent.

Student A You tell your best friend about your problems at home and your new plans.

Student B You offer advice and try to convince your friend not to make a hasty *(précipitée)* decision. Use **infinitives** (TO V) and **gerunds** (V-ING) as often as possible.

toolbox

Verbs & expressions

- tell sb off: *réprimander*
- be ordered about: *recevoir des ordres*
- resent V-ING: *ne pas accepter de*
- stop / prevent sb from: *empêcher qqn de*
- it's no use V-ING: *cela ne vaut pas la peine de*
- it's worth V-ING: *cela vaut la peine de*

A 400-year-old dream

It all started in 1602...

A The Pilgrim Fathers

1 Read the text and explain who the Pilgrim Fathers were.

IN 1620, 102 ENGLISH PEOPLE, known as The Pilgrim Fathers, sailed from Plymouth (England) to what is now the US, on a ship called *The Mayflower*. Among them were 35 Puritans fleeing religious persecution, whose aim was to create a safe religious community in the New World. The Pilgrims established the Plymouth Colony in Massachusetts. The first winter was so hard that half of them died of hunger and illness. But the next summer gave good crops and the Native Americans helped to save food for the following winter. The Pilgrims held a big celebration, called *Thanksgiving*, to thank God and the Native Americans for their survival. The Plymouth colony joined the New England Confederation in 1643 and became part of the colony of Massachusetts in 1691.

Thanksgiving, celebrated on the fourth Thursday of November, is the most important American holiday, apart from Christmas. The traditional Thanksgiving dinner consists of typical food from North America: turkey and sweet potatoes with cranberry sauce, and pumpkin pie.

2 At the Thanksgiving dinner of 1630, one of the Pilgrim Fathers tells his grandchildren what they are celebrating.
Using elements from the picture and the text opposite, prepare his short talk and act it out.

B The beginning of a nation

1 Read the text opposite so as to memorize the main dates. Who were the Founding Fathers?

2 Browse the internet in order to:

a. complete the first famous sentence of the Declaration of Independence: *"We hold these truths…"*;

b. find the names of the Founding Fathers;

c. write a short biography of one of the Founding Fathers to be posted on a board in the classroom. (150-200 words)

THE FIRST COLONY IN NORTH AMERICA was founded in 1602 in Virginia by the British. Eighteen years later, the Pilgrim Fathers settled in Massachusetts. At the end of the 18th century, there were 13 colonies. The colonists wanted to be set free from the laws and taxes imposed by the British. The War of Revolution broke out in 1775 and the Declaration of Independence was written in 1776. The British surrendered in 1781. A Constitutional Convention was held in Philadelphia in 1787. Then the Founding Fathers wrote the Constitution which described how the new United States would be governed.

C Ellis Island

CD 2 16

1 Look at the picture, read its caption, then listen to the description and history of Ellis Island.

2 Note the information around the numbers and dates mentioned below, then sum up what you have learnt.

12,000,000 | 1892-1924 | 100,000,000 | 1954

3rd | 355 | Sept. 10th, 1990 | 35,000

August 13, 1925: a little immigrant family on the dock at Ellis Island, N.Y., just having passed the rigid examination for entry into the "land of promise", looking hopefully at New York's skyline while awaiting the government ferry to carry them on to the "land of the free".

D The growth of a nation

Immigration to the United States (Source: *Yearbook of immigration statistics 2008*, March 2009, US Department of Homeland Security)

1 Study the chart with your neighbour.

2 Give reasons to explain the peaks and troughs, with the help of the events presented below in chronological order.

- Irish potato famine
- California Gold Rush
- Pogroms in Russia against Jews
- Massive immigration from Italy
- The Great Depression
- World War 2
- Immigration Act, opening up immigration from the Third World
- Twin towers

Webquest — What countries do US immigrants come from?

TICE

Browse the web to find charts and information and say if the following statements are true or false. Correct them when necessary.

a. Between 1840 and 1860, most immigrants came from England, Germany and Ireland.

b. Immigration from Italy almost doubled during the last decade of the 19th century.

c. People from the Soviet Union immigrated massively until the 1920s.

d. In the early 20th century, Africans were specifically excluded by legislation.

e. Over 1/3 of immigrants coming from Latin America in the period 1971-1980 were Mexicans.

f. Nowadays, the majority of illegal immigrants come from Mexico and Central America.

g. In 2009, 37% of legal immigrants came from Europe.

Web resources

- www.newsbatch.com/immigration.htm
- www.dhs.gov/files/statistics

final task

Is the American dream still alive?

The Drama club of your school has decided to present a modern version of the musical *West Side Story*. You study the lyrics of a famous scene, then adapt it to the present time and act out a contradictory discussion.

1 Study the lyrics

- Read the whole song once, knowing that the part in *italics* is sung by the boys and the rest by the girls. Is this scene an agreement or a confrontation?
- Read the text again. Classify the arguments in terms of money, ethnic origin, opportunities, living conditions.
- Sum up the position of each side.

MÉTHODOLOGIE COMPRÉHENSION DE L'ÉCRIT → p. 161

AMERICA
Lyrics by S. Sondheim

I like to be in America,
Okay by me in America,
Everything free in America
For a small fee in America.

Buying on credit is so nice.
One look at us and they charge twice.
I'll have my own washing machine.
What will you have, though,
to keep clean?

Skyscrapers bloom in America.
Cadillacs zoom in America.
Industry boom in America.
Twelve in a room in America.

Lots of new housing with more space.
Lots of doors slamming in our face.
I'll get a terrace apartment.
Better get rid of your accent.

Life can be bright in America.
If you can fight in America.
Life is all right in America.
If you're all white in America.

Here you are free and you have pride.
Long as you stay on your own side.
Free to be anything you choose.
Free to wait tables and shine shoes.

Everywhere grime in America,
Organized crime in America,
Terrible time in America.
You forget I'm in America.

I think I go back to San Juan.
I know a boat you can get on.
Everyone there will give big cheer.
Everyone there will have moved here.

2 Act out a contradictory discussion

MÉTHODOLOGIE
Discussion contradictoire → p. 158

Discuss the state of the American dream nowadays.
Student A You believe in the American dream.
Student B You don't believe in it.

A Prepare your task

Using elements from the documents in this unit, prepare arguments concerning today's life in America to support your point.

B Act out the scene

- Develop your arguments with full sentences. Illustrate them with examples.
- If you interrupt your partner, remain polite.
- Don't be stiff: body language and mimics may be very eloquent.

function box

Giving one's opinion
- My feeling is that...
- What we have to realize is that...
- As a matter of fact, I am convinced that...
- I don't agree with you about that.

Contrasting
- Unlike (you), Contrary to (what you think)
- In contrast (with)
- Very different (from)

Check your skills

WORKBOOK → p. 33-34

A Comprendre un extrait de roman

Lisez le texte ci-dessous. Remplissez la fiche de votre *Workbook* et évaluez-vous en fonction des critères proposés.

The Immigrant

I handed my passport and papers to the Immigration Bureau Officer. He opened the passport and found the ten-dollar note I'd left in its centre. The note was gone before I saw it missing. Then came the questions I couldn't get wrong.

"What is your name?"

"Henry Drake."

"Where are you from?"

"London."

"Why have you come to the United States?"

"Opportunity."

So far, so easy.

But he stopped. He looked at me.

"Where are you travelling from, sir?" he asked me.

It wasn't one of the questions on the list, I knew it.

"London", I said.

He seemed to be staring at the word as I spoke it.

"You are a born Englishman, sir?"

He read my latest name.

"Mister Drake?"

"Yes."

"And how do you intend to support yourself, sir?"

That was one of the questions on the list.

"I am a salesman."

He handed me a sheet of paper.

"Could you read this for me, sir?"

"*We, the people of the United States, in order to form a more perfect union…*"

He took the paper from my fingers.

"Welcome to America", he said.

He handed me the passport and registration card, then held them back.

"But you'd want to work on your accent. *Slàn leat.*"

That shook me, but only until I climbed the last few steps and walked out into my first American sunshine.

I threw the passport into the river. I was a clean sheet.

It was the 16th of March, 1924, two years since I'd sailed out of Dublin.

Adapted from *Oh, Play That Thing*, Roddy DOYLE (2004)

Je me situe par rapport au CECRL **B1 → B2**

LORSQUE JE LIS CET EXTRAIT DE ROMAN :

- **B1 :** Je peux comprendre les informations principales qu'il contient. Je peux deviner, à l'aide du contexte, le sens de certains mots inconnus.
- **B1 + :** Je peux suivre le cours des idées et les comprendre dans certains détails. Je comprends les raisons qui poussent les personnages à agir. Je peux comprendre l'implicite.

B Prendre part à une conversation

A few weeks later, the two characters happen to meet on a train. They evoke this scene and talk freely about it.

Je me situe par rapport au CECRL **B1 → B2**

QUAND JE PRENDS PART À CETTE CONVERSATION :

- **B1 :** Je peux poser des questions spontanées. Je peux participer activement et sans préparation à une discussion sur un thème qui m'est familier, même si je dois parfois chercher mes mots. Je peux m'exprimer autrement si on ne me comprend pas.
- **B1 + :** Je peux expliquer pourquoi quelque chose pose un problème, discuter de la suite à donner. Je peux exprimer mes idées avec précision, et donner des explications, des arguments et des commentaires.

Art quest American contemporary art

Whether the American artists presented here are called neo-dadaist, hyper-realist, pop artist, neo-expressionist, graffiti artist, photo-realist or super-realist, their works reflect the great imaginative variety of the American art scene these last 50 years.

- What is represented in this painting ?
  - artchive.com/ftp_site.htm

1

Jasper JOHNS, *Map* (1963), Museum of Modern Art, New York

- What kind of artwork is this?
- Who and what is represented here?
  - www.all-art.org/
  - www.pbs.org

2

Robert RAUSCHENBERG, *Retroactive I* (1963), Wadsworth Atheneum Museum of Art, Hartford, Connecticut

- How does the artist make us feel how hard the man's work is and his frustration?
  - www.saatchi-gallery.co.uk/artists/
  - museum.oglethorpe.edu/Hanson.htm

3

Duane HANSON, *Construction Worker* (1970), Virginia Museum of Fine Arts, Richmond

4

Richard ESTES, *D Train* (1988), Smithsonian American Art Museum, Washington DC

- What kind of artwork is this?
- What does it represent?
  - http://www.artnet.com/artists
  - www.escapeintolife.com/artist-watch/richard-estes

5

Jean-Michel BASQUIAT, *Untitled* (1981), private collection

- What does Basquiat's painting *Untitled* represent for you? Observe the painting below and say which part was painted by Jean-Michel Basquiat.
- What elements are characteristic of Andy Warhol's work?
  - www.moga8.net
  - basquiat.com/
  - edu.warhol.org/

6

Jean-Michel BASQUIAT and Andy WARHOL, *6.99* (1985), Courtesy Gallery Bruno Bischofberger, Zurich

Your task

Group work

Each group chooses one of the works of art on these pages and prepares an oral report on the artist to present to the class. Say which art movement the artist is associated with. Select the most interesting information on the websites indicated. Every student in the group must speak in turn.

Unit 5

Espaces et échanges
Lieux et formes du pouvoir
L'idée de progrès

Southern voices

Can you hear the once voiceless people?

final task You are a student at a school of journalism and you are working on a project called "Southern voices". Prepare and give an audio report about South Africa today. After listening to a speech by Kevin Rudd, Australia's Prime Minister, write an article about it.

Keywords

Nouns
- tolerance ≠ intolerance
- brotherhood: *fraternité*
- diversity /daɪˈvɜːsɪtɪ/
- activist
- icon /ˈaɪkɒn/
- advocate /ˈædvəkɪt/: *défenseur*
- discrimination
- oppression
- equality ≠ inequality
- showdown = confrontation
- freedom of speech / expression
- second-class citizen: *citoyen de seconde zone*
- (white-minority) rule: *domination*

Adjectives
- cultural
- multicultural /ˌmʌltɪˈkʌltʃərəl/
- equal ≠ unequal
- disadvantaged /ˌdɪsədˈvɑːntɪdʒd/

Verbs & expressions
- voice one's opposition to
- have one's say: *dire ce que l'on pense*
- stand up for = defend (one's rights / a cause)
- stand up to = oppose
- fight for = struggle for
- demonstrate /ˈdemənstreɪt/: *manifester*
- denounce /dɪˈnaʊns/
- achieve one's goal: *atteindre son but*
- break down barriers /ˈbærɪəz/: *faire tomber les barrières*
- seek (*rechercher*) a better future /ˈfjuːtʃə/
- be on an equal footing with: *être sur un pied d'égalité avec*
- be discriminated against: *être victime de discrimination*

LANGUAGE WORKSHOP → p. 93

"Power in the voice"

1. This mural was commissioned by the British Council in South Africa for its awareness campaign "Power in the voice" in 2008. Describe it briefly.

2. How does each character express his / her voice?

3. In your opinion, why did the British Council decide to launch such a campaign?

4. Why do some artists choose to paint on walls?

toolbox

Nouns

- **ar**twork = art form
- **mi**crophone / mike
- the man in the street: *Monsieur Tout-le-monde*
- **im**pact

Adjectives

- ar**tis**tic
- cre**a**tive
- ob**jec**tive ≠ sub**jec**tive
- sym**bo**lic (of)
- **po**werful

Verbs & expressions

- put **in**to words = ex**press**
- **show**case = pre**sent**
- con**vey** (a **mes**sage): *faire passer*
- give voice to sth
- stand for = repre**sent**
- en**cou**rage /ɪnˈkʌrɪdʒ/

Focus on speaking

The Rainbow nation

MÉTHODOLOGIE EXPRESSION ORALE EN CONTINU → p. 153

culture key South Africa → p. 143

A Artists' voices

MÉTHODOLOGIE
Décrire une image → p. 155

Present and analyse a visual document.

1. Read the *Culture key* to learn more about apartheid /ə'pɑːtaɪd/, Stephen Biko and Nelson Mandela.

2. Guess the period each work of art refers to.

3. Choose one of the three artistic representations of South Africa and present it orally to the class. What message does the document convey?

toolbox

Nouns
- collage /kɒ'lɑːʒ/
- mural /'mjʊərəl/
- strip cartoon: *bande dessinée*
- hand print
- note (music)
- score: *partition musicale*
- public place

Adjectives
- illegal /ɪ'liːgəl/
- guilty ≠ innocent
- whites-only: *réservé aux Blancs*
- outrageous = shocking
- segregated ≠ desegregated
- enduring /ɪn'djʊərɪŋ/: *persistant*
- separate /'seprət/

Verbs & expressions
- take sb into custody /'kʌstədɪ/ = put sb under arrest
- heal (wounds): *guérir (blessures)*
- reconcile (to) /'rekənsaɪl/
- unite
- share: *partager*
- make up = represent

1

2

3

B Side by side

MÉTHODOLOGIE
Expliquer. Décrire une image → p. 155

alk about the evolution of South African society.

hese two photos and the following guidelines will help you.

. Describe the place, people, period, activities, feelings…

. Focus on the expression “by order” written on the notice. /hat does it imply?

. Explain what has changed in public places since the partheid laws were abolished.

1

2

C Today’s figures

MÉTHODOLOGIE
Dire les chiffres → p. 154

omment on a chart.

se the following guidelines:

. What is the largest community in South Africa?

. Analyse the evolution of the figures since 2001.

. What is particularly striking in your view? Why?

Population 2010 (50M estimate)	Unemployment rate (%)			
	2001	2006	2009	2010
Black (≈ 39.7M – 79.4%)	31.1	30.7	27.9	29.5
Coloured (≈ 4.4M – 8.8%)	21.2	18.9	19.5	22.5
Indian / Asian (≈ 1.3M – 2.6%)	16.7	11.2	11.3	10.1
White (≈ 4.6M – 9.2%)	6.9	4.7	4.6	6.4

(Source: Statistics from South African government)

Video time

Amandla! DVD

Amandla!, Lee HIRSCH (2002)

A Get ready

1. Look at the film poster and describe it briefly. What symbolic elements can you see? Can you guess what the film is about?

B Watch the video

2. Watch the extract from *Amandla!* Your teacher will give you a worksheet to help you.

C In your own words

3. Use the worksheet to summarize what you saw.

D Going further

4. To what extent can music play a role and help to bring about change in society?

Text 1

April 27th 1994

culture key South Africa → p. 143

Niq MHLONGO

is a South African writer who was born in 1973 in Soweto. His work focuses on social and economic issues such as AIDS, poverty and unemployment. *Dog Eat Dog* is his first novel. In 2006, *The New York Times* called him "one of the most high-spirited and irreverent new voices of South Africa's post-apartheid literary scene." *After Tears* (2007) is his second novel.

A Warming up

Read the *Culture key*, then describe the picture briefly (place, people, activity). What event does the title refer to?

A winding[1] fifty-metre queue stretched out from Braamfontein Civic Centre. We had been standing there for about two hours. The opportunity to vote had attracted many people; I saw a crowd of men and women the like of which I had never seen before. It was a queue of limitless hope. Many of us there thought this election would reshape our lives in the southern part of this unruly "Dark Continent".

The call to vote had drawn people from all walks of life. There were teachers and pupils, lecturers and students, sex hawkers[2] and street vendors, business people and laymen[3], employed and unemployed, unemployables and hobos[4], secretaries and housemaids, taxi drivers and sportspeople. It was the moment that most of us had been waiting for years to experience.

I was standing behind a homeless man in the queue. I often saw him sleeping on the floor in the entrance of the Braamfontein branch of the Saambou Bank. I saw him every evening when I came back to the Y[5] from the university library. As I joined the queue, I had been welcomed by the stench coming from his dirty body. I could easily tell that he hadn't touched water for days or even months.

Of course we all came there for different reasons. Our Big Brothers had promised beautiful things to those who lived a life of poverty, and I guess that the two homeless gentlemen ahead of me came to vote because of the promise of proper housing and employment. Some came to vote because of the promise of welfare grants, some because of the promise of free medical care; pensioners had come because of the promise of an increase in their grants so that it equalled that of their white counterparts.

I was standing in that queue because we had been promised access to a better education. I wanted to vote for whoever claimed to have fought tooth and nail to overthrow the apartheid government so that I now found myself admitted to a formerly whites-only institution. I felt morally obliged to return the favour to my Big Brothers. It was payback time for those who had been watching my back while I was sleeping. Now as an adult I felt that I had to recognise the Big Brothers' sacrifices.

Different political parties had mumbled their big lies to rally people to vote for them. I had not made up my mind as to which party to vote for, but I definitely wanted to see a black party in government. I didn't care that my Big Brothers were said to be still wet behind their ears[6] when it came to running a country as big as South Africa.

The marshals were doing their job effectively. Many people were coming out of the polling station, their faces covered with broad smiles after taking part in the first free and fair elections in South Africa.

Dog Eat Dog, Niq MHLONGO (2004)

1. /waɪndɪŋ/ *sinueuse* 2. *prostituées* 3. *gens sans qualification* 4. *clochards* 5. YMCA (Young Men's Christian Association) 6. inexperienced

B Reading comprehension

WORKBOOK → p. 35-36

our *Workbook* will help you to understand the text.

C In your own words

. Sum up the text with the help of the following guidelines:

. What incited so many South Africans to vote that day?

. Who did the narrator want to vote for? Why?

D Going further

. Find another title for the text and explain your choice to the ass.

. Explain *"It was a queue of limitless hope."* (l. 4).

4. Who are the *"Big Brothers"* that the narrator mentions (l. 17)? Why did he feel *"morally obliged to return the favour"* (l. 27)?

5. Explain why many people had *"their faces covered with broad smiles"* (l. 37).

E Language training

6. **Savoir prononcer** YOUR CD 30-31 CD 2 18-19

7. **Pratiquer la grammaire**

Dénombrables, indénombrables – Emploi des articles ø et *the* – *were said to be*

WORKBOOK → p. 37

toolbox

Nouns

- voting rights
- voter
- era /ˈɪərə/
- red-letter day: *jour mémorable*
- civil rights

Adjectives

- democratic /ˌdeməˈkrætɪk/
- historic = momentous /məʊˈmentəs/
- bright (future)

Verbs & expressions

- cast a vote
- elect
- queue /kjuː/ (up)
- make sth history
- go down in history: *entrer dans l'histoire*
- pin one's hopes on sb: *mettre tous ses espoirs en qqn*
- get rid of: *se débarrasser de*
- rule = govern
- be grateful to sb (for V-ING): *être reconnaissant envers qqn*

Your task

Make an audio report on Mandela's election

As a student in journalism, you have been given the following assignment:
Make an audio report on the election of Nelson Mandela in 1994 as if you had been there: describe the atmosphere, the people's reactions, and the consequences this election will certainly have on the country.

MÉTHODOLOGIE
EXPRESSION ORALE EN CONTINU → p. 153

The conscience of South Africa

A The topic

1. Look at these pictures and deduce why Desmond Tutu /ˈdɛzmənd ˈtuːtuː/ is an iconic figure in South Africa.

1

2

B Open your ears

CD 2 20

2. You will hear three sentences said by or about Desmond Tutu. Deduce what the recording is about.

C Listen

CD 2 21

WORKBOOK → p. 38

3. Listen to the recording with the help of your *Workbook*.

toolbox

Nouns
- pacifist
- opponent /əˈpəʊnənt/

Adjectives
- committed: *engagé*
- generous /ˈdʒenərəs/
- charismatic /ˌkærɪzˈmætɪk/

Verbs & expressions
- dedicate one's life to sth / V-ING
- protest /prəˈtest/ = speak up against
- make sb's life better
- raise sb's awareness (of) /əˈwɛənɪs/: *faire prendre conscience à qqn (de)*
- speak one's mind: *dire ce que l'on pense*

function box

Asking indirect questions
- I'd like to know if...
- I wonder whether...
- Could you tell me if...?
- Would you say that...?
- Is it true that...?
- How do you explain the fact that...

D In your own words

4. What has Desmond Tutu been fighting for all his life?

E Going further

5. Do you think Desmond Tutu achieved his goals? Why (not)?

Your task

Interview Desmond Tutu
A journalist interviews Desmond Tutu about his life as a human rights activist. Using elements from the recording, act out the interview.
Decide who you want to be, then reverse the roles.
Student A You are the journalist. Jot down the questions you will ask Desmond Tutu and get ready to react to his answers and to ask other unprepared questions.
Student B You are Desmond Tutu. Imagine the questions you will be asked and prepare your answers.

MÉTHODOLOGIE Interview → p. 158

Writers' corner

Resist!

Bonus vidéo

Babakiueria

DVD

Watch an extract from *Babakiueria*.

Your task

Write a newspaper article

As a student in a school of journalism you have been asked to continue an unfinished article about a demonstration by Aborigines. (200 words)

MÉTHODOLOGIE
Rédiger un article de presse → p. 168

culture key Aboriginal Australians → p. 143

SYDNEY, **26.01.11.** January 26, referred to as "Australia Day", marks the anniversary of the colonization of Australia by Great Britain. To Aborigines, however, that day is known as "Invasion Day" or "Survival Day", and it signifies the destruction of the native Aboriginal culture by English colonists and the continuing struggle for survival, justice and equality of rights by Aboriginal people.

That is why thousands of Aborigines took to the streets of Sydney today…

A Get ready

1. Read the *Culture key*, the article beginning above and the statistics below.

HOMELESSNESS (estimate 2006)
Indigenous: 9.1% of the homeless

UNEMPLOYMENT (estimate 2009)
- **Indigenous:** 18.1% (13.8% in 2007) of the total population
- **Non-indigenous:** 5.5% of the total population

EDUCATION (estimate 2006)
Indigenous students: 3.3% of the overall student population

(Source: The Australian Bureau of Statistics)

B Write your article

2. With the help of the photo above and the information from the instructions given in A, describe the general atmosphere of the demonstration, as well as its goal.

3. You may include a short interview of a protester and / or a passer-by.

4. Don't forget to use link words.

toolbox

Nouns
- banner: *banderole*
- demonstrator /ˈdemənstreɪtə/: *manifestant*
- (equal) opportunity
- the haves ≠ the have-nots: *les déshérités*
- wage gap: *écart de salaire*
- standard of living
- poverty line

Adjectives & adverbs
- determined = resolute /ˈrezəluːt/
- unfairly: *injustement*
- illiterate /ɪˈlɪtərɪt/

Verbs & expressions
- demonstrate = march
- protest /prəˈtest/ against sth
- make up = represent /ˌreprɪˈzent/
- improve = make better
- see the light at the end of the tunnel
- make ends meet: *joindre les deux bouts*
- bridge the gap: *combler le fossé*
- have had enough of sth / V-ING

Text 2

Away from home

CD 2 22

culture key The Stolen Generation → p. 143

Doris PILKINGTON
(b. 1937)
is an Aborigine. At four, she and her mother (Molly) were forcibly taken to a native settlement. Her trilogy traces the story of all the women of her own family over three generations: *Caprice: A Stockman's Daughter* (1991), *Rabbit-Proof Fence* (made into a film in 2002), *Under the Windamarra Tree* (2002).

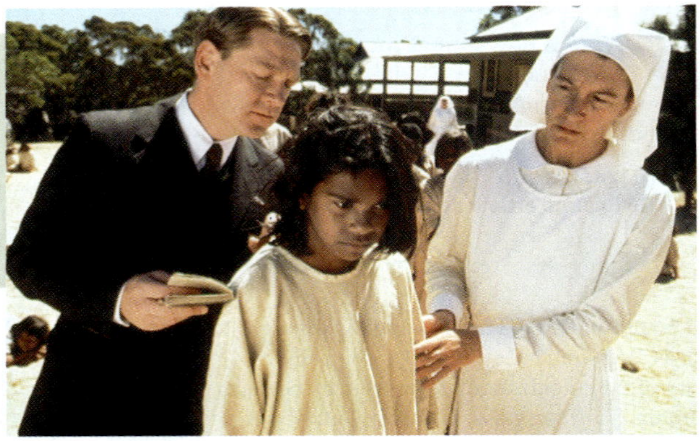

A Warming up

Read the *Culture key*, then imagine the situation in the picture.

Western Australia, 1931. Four sisters (Rosie, Molly, Daisy and Gracie) have been sent to a settlement for Aboriginal children to be educated by white people. Martha, who has lived there for a year, shows them around.

"What is that place?" asked Rosie, doing the talking for the other three.

"That's the 'boob', they lock anyone in there for punishment," Martha explained.

"What did that girl do?" asked Rosie.

"She's locked up for swearing at Miss Morgan, the teacher. She's lucky, she's only in there for two days," Martha told them about the others who had been incarcerated in the "boob".

"You should have seen the other ones who were locked up for running away," she said. "They all got seven days punishment with just bread and water. Mr Johnson shaved their heads bald and made them parade around the compound[1] so that everyone could see them. They got the strap[2] too."

The "boob" was a place of detention once described as a small, detached concrete[3] room with a sandy floor, with only a gleam of light and little ventilation. Every inmate of the settlement dreaded being incarcerated in this place. Some children were forced to spend up to fourteen days in that horrible place.

One thing on which they could all agree was that this place was certainly different from what they envisaged.

Instead of a residential school, the Aboriginal children were placed in an overcrowded dormitory. The inmates, not students, slept on beds with government-issue blankets. There were no sheets or pillow slips except on special occasions when there was an inspection by prominent officials. Then they were removed as soon as the visitors left the settlement and stored away until the next visit. On the windows there were no colourful curtains, just wire screens[4] and iron bars. It looked more like a concentration camp than a residential school for Aboriginal children.

Back at the dormitory the girls were trying to snuggle down in their cold, uninviting beds. Molly, Daisy and Gracie began to talk normally amongst themselves.

"You girls can't talk blackfulla language here, you know," came the warning from the other side of the dorm. "You gotta forget it and talk English all the time."

The girls were dumbfounded, they couldn't say anything but stare at the speaker.

"That's true," said Martha in support. "I had to do the same. They tell everybody that when they come here and go to school for the first time."

Molly couldn't believe what they had just heard. "We can't talk our old wangka," she whispered. "That's awful."

"We all know it's awful," Martha told them. "But we got over that," she added calmly.

After roll call and lights out, Molly listened to the slide of the bolt[5] and the rattle of the padlock[6], then silence. It was at that moment this free-spirited girl knew that she and her sisters must escape from this place.

Rabbit-Proof Fence, Doris PILKINGTON (1996)

1. *bâtiments* 2. *être fouetté avec une lanière de cuir* 3. *en béton* 4. *grillages* 5. *verrou* 6. *cadenas*

B Reading comprehension

WORKBOOK → p. 39-40

…rn to your *Workbook* which help you to understand the text.

C In your own words

. Sum up the text with the help of your *Workbook*.

D Going further

. What happened whenever inspectors came to visit the …ettlement? Why?

. Why did the girls have to forget their own language and …lk English all the time?

. What does the last sentence of the text reveal about …olly's personality?

toolbox

Nouns
- comfort /ˈkʌmfət/
- Aborigine /ˌæbəˈrɪdʒɪnɪ/
- identity

Adjectives
- determined /dɪˈtɜːmɪnd/ = strong-willed
- rebellious /rɪˈbeljəs/ = defiant /dɪˈfaɪənt/
- unenviable /ʌnˈenvɪəbl/
- harsh = severe /sɪˈvɪə/
- obedient /əˈbiːdɪənt/
- speechless
- deterrent /dɪˈterənt/

Verbs & expressions
- obey sb ≠ disobey /ˌdɪsəˈbeɪ/ sb
- play by the rules ≠ be against the rules
- accept ≠ resign oneself to one's fate
- rebel /rɪˈbel/
- comply with = respect
- follow orders
- be deprived of: *être dépossédé de*
- can't believe one's ears
- submit to: *se soumettre à*

E Language training

5. Savoir prononcer YOUR CD 32-34 CD 2 23-25

Lisez le passage de *"The boob was a place of detention…"* (l. 15) à *"… iron bars"* (l. 28).

a. La **marque -*ed*** des verbes suivants se prononce-t-elle : /ɪd/, /d/ ou /t/ ?
described – detached – dreaded – incarcerated – forced – envisaged

b. La **voyelle -*u*-** dans les mots suivants se prononce-t-elle : /uː/, /ə/, /ʌ/, /juː/, /ʊ/, /ɜː/ ?
up – students – issue – until – colourful – curtains – just

c. Vérifiez à l'écoute, puis relisez ce passage en tenant compte de ces points de phonologie.

6. Pratiquer la grammaire

Le style indirect LANGUAGE WORKSHOP → p. 92

Your task

Write a letter of complaint
One week later, Mr Johnson writes a letter to his superior about Molly and the other three girls, insisting on the problems that they have posed since they arrived at the settlement.

MÉTHODOLOGIE
Écrire une lettre → p. 166

Grammaire | Le style indirect

PRÉCIS GRAMMATICAL → 42

A Observer et comprendre

1 Les questions

Style direct	Style indirect
1a. *"What is that place?"* (Text 2, p. 90, l. 4)	→ **1b.** *Rosie asked them what that place was.*
2a. *"What did that girl do?"* (Text 2, p. 90, l. 7)	→ **2b.** *She asked them what that girl had done.*
3a. *"Have they been in there for long?"*	→ **3b.** *She asked them whether (if) they had been in there for long.*

a. Comparez les énoncés au style direct et au style indirect ci-dessus. L'ordre des mots (sujet / auxiliaire) est-il le même au style direct et au style indirect dans les questions ? Indiquez quels sont les changements de temps.

b. Par quel(s) mot(s) la question **3a** en *YES / NO* est-elle introduite au style indirect ?

2 Les modaux

Style direct	Style indirect
1a. *"(He) made them parade (…) so that everyone* ***could*** *see them."* (Text 2, p. 90, l. 13)	→ **1b.** *She said that he had made them parade so that everyone could see them.*
2a. *"You* ***should have*** *run away."*	→ **2b.** *She said they should have run away.*
3a. *"We* ***will*** *do the same."*	→ **3b.** *They told her they would do the same.*
4a. *"We* ***can't*** *speak our own language."*	→ **4b.** *She told the girls that they couldn't speak their own language.*

a. Parmi les modaux en gras, citez ceux qui demeurent inchangés au style indirect passé. Ces modaux sont-ils au présent ou au passé ? Déduisez : « Les modaux au … ne subissent aucun changement de temps au style indirect. »

b. Citez les modaux qui subissent un changement et indiquez lequel.

B Pratiquer

3 Réécrivez les énoncés suivants au style indirect passé à l'aide de *They asked her…*

a. "Did they find a solution?"
b. "What will happen if we run away?"
c. "How old are the girls?"
d. "Has he been talking to them?"

4 Réécrivez les énoncés suivants au style indirect passé à l'aide de *He said…*

a. "She won't regret it."
b. "I can't stand it anymore!"
c. "She could probably stay with them."
d. "We should have gone away."

5 Réécrivez les énoncés suivants au style indirect passé à l'aide de *She told them…*

a. "I had to do the same." (Text 2, p. 91, l. 38)
b. "We all know it's awful." (Text 2, p. 91, l. 42)
c. "They were locked up for swearing at him."
d. "She's had enough of this."

Grammaire de l'oral | L'intonation dans les questions et les *tags*

6 L'intonation dans les questions (CD 2 – 26)

a. Écoutez ces questions au style direct et au style indirect. Indiquez pour chaque énoncé si l'intonation est globalement montante ou descendante.

YES / NO QUESTION	**1a.** *Are you Rosie?*	→ **1b.** *She asked me whether I was Rosie.*
WH- QUESTION	**2a.** *Who's that girl?*	→ **2b.** *She asked me who that girl was.*

b. Déduisez des règles d'intonation pour les questions en *WH-* et les questions en *YES / NO* au style direct et au style indirect.

7 L'intonation dans les *tags* (CD 2 – 27-28)

a. Écoutez ces énoncés et indiquez dans chaque cas quelle est l'intonation du *tag* (en gras).

1. *She's lucky,* ***isn't she****?*
2. *He wasn't happy,* ***was he****?*
3. *He's leaving tomorrow,* ***isn't he****?*

b. Écoutez à nouveau. D'après l'intonation, indiquez si le *tag* est : **1.** une question qui exprime l'étonnement ou le doute ou bien **2.** une simple confirmation de ce qui vient d'être dit.

c. Déduisez de ce qui précède une règle d'intonation pour les *tags*.

Faisons le point ! Dans les *tags*, l'intonation montante exprime ... et l'intonation descendante... .

Lexique | Défendre ses droits

→ Keywords p. 82

Assurez-vous que vous avez bien retenu les mots clés de l'unité.

8 Donnez les synonymes ou les antonymes des mots suivants.

a. confrontation = ... **b.** oppose = ... **c.** equality ≠ ... **d.** equal ≠ ...

9 Quelle est la syllabe accentuée dans chacun de ces mots ?

a. disadvantaged **b.** multicultural **c.** discrimination **d.** diversity **e.** brotherhood

10 Complétez les phrases à l'aide des mots suivants :

rights – achieved – intolerance – demonstrated – on an equal footing – white-minority – voice – stand up – say – activist – fought for – oppression.

a. Nelson Mandela always denounced ..1.. rule. He ..2.. his goal when he was elected president of South Africa in 1994.

b. He was an anti-apartheid ..3.. who always ..4.. freedom.

c. His father always said: " ..5.. for your ..6.. and don't be afraid to have your ..7.. and ..8.. your opposition to injustice, ..9.. and ..10.. !"

d. In today's South Africa, blacks are not yet ..11.. with whites. That's why they ..12.. in the streets of Pretoria.

toolbox

Verbs and expressions

- blame for V-ING: *reprocher*
- suggest /sə'dʒest/: *suggérer*
- apologize for V-ING: *s'excuser de*
- wonder: *se demander*
- sound + adjective: *avoir l'air*
- It wasn't clear whether...: *On ne savait pas très bien si...*

Your task

Tell your friend what happened

Last night you overheard your brother arguing on the phone with his girlfriend. The following morning you tell your best friend about it. Use **indirect speech** to report the scene.

Aboriginal people and the Dreaming

Aboriginal voices can be heard all over Australia.

culture key Aboriginal Australians → p. 143

A The Aboriginal flag

Read the texts below and answer the following questions.

1 What was the Aboriginal flag designed for?

2 What do the different colours symbolize?

3 Why is the flag so important for Aboriginal people?

The Aboriginal flag was designed in 1971 by Aboriginal artist and Indigenous activist Harold Thomas. It was originally meant to symbolize the land rights movement. It became one of the two official flags of Australia in July 1995, and is now a symbol of the unity and identity of Aboriginal people.

THE ABORIGINAL FLAG is powerful, and the colours are important. And it took some time to think about it – red ochre, the red soil – the country of Australia is all red. Why I chose the sun? Because it's another colour that is used commonly in Aboriginal art – yellow ochre. But the sun is a great symbol for all people. When we look carefully at the colour black, which is an interesting one, it's more of a political inclusion, rather than a spiritual, Aboriginal concept. The black represents the pride of being black in Australia. Because, at the time, black pride came into Australian culture – during the '60s and '70s – influenced by Black American pride of their culture. If this is going to be an Aboriginal flag, it has to have black, because it represents the black people of the continent.

Harold THOMAS (March 25th 2002)

B Australia's Aboriginal heart

Read the text and answer the following questions.

1 Where is Uluru located?

2 According to the Aborigines, when was it formed?

3 Why do Aboriginal people discourage tourists from climbing Uluru?

4 Why do you think this place had its name changed?

Uluru[1], which means "great pebble[2]" in the Aboriginal language, was formerly known as Ayers Rock[3]. It is the world's largest sandstone[4] monolith and Australia's most famous natural landmark. This massive rock formation in the Red Centre is 650 million years old, 348 metres high and is a sacred place to the local Anangu Aboriginal people. It extends 2.5 km into the ground. Uluru is believed to have been formed in the Dreamtime (or Dreaming) by Dreamtime spirit people. It is believed to be inhabited by dozens of ancestral creators. Uluru is also a symbol of the Aboriginal struggle for land rights. Climbing the rock is discouraged by traditional owners for whom Uluru is a sacred site of great spiritual significance.

1. /ˌuːləˈruː/ 2. *caillou* 3. /ɛəz ˈrɒk/ 4. *grès*

C The Dreaming

CD 2 29

1 What is the Dreaming?

a. Read the text and sum up orally what the Dreaming is.
b. Describe these two works of art. What do you think they symbolize?

The Dreaming (or Dreamtime) is a term used to describe "the time before time", the time of the creation of the world in Australian Aboriginal mythology, when ancient spirit ancestors emerged from beneath the earth and from the sky to create the land forms and all living things. The dreamtime stories set down the laws for social and moral order and establish the cultural standards and customs. In these stories, landscape, animals and people are connected. To pass these stories on, Aboriginal people talk, but they have never used a written language.

The Dreaming is also illustrated in Australian Aboriginal art, one of the oldest living art traditions in the world. Aboriginal people express and identify with their spirituality in different ways. These include storytelling, community gathering, songs, dance, but also paintings and designs. The Rainbow Serpent (Ngalmudj), for example, is believed to have created riverbeds, creeks and lagoons as it moved across the country. It protected the land and its people, but it could also wreak revenge, thus symbolizing both the creative power and destructive abilities of nature.

2 Stories of the Dreaming

a. Listen to Aunty Beryl Carmichael, an Aboriginal woman, speak about storytelling.
b. How important is storytelling for her?

Webquest — Make up your own Dreaming story

TICE

1 Choose one of the two paintings of the Dreaming on this page, then browse the internet to find out more about the symbolic meaning of the elements shown.

2 Listen to the story of your choice on the websites, then sum it up to the class.

3 With the help of the websites, make up your own Dreaming story based on the painting you have chosen and tell it to the class.

Web resources

To find out more about the symbolic meaning of the elements:

- www.aboriginalartstore.com.au/
- www.didgeswedoo.com.au/

To listen to the story:

- australianmuseum.net.au/cultures

final task — Can you hear the once voiceless people?

**You are a student at a school of journalism and you work on a project called "Southern voices". Prepare and give an audio report about South Africa today.
After listening to a speech by Kevin Rudd, Australia's Prime Minister, write an article about it.**

The various documents you have worked on in this unit should help you to make your audio report and write your article.

1 Present an audio report

MÉTHODOLOGIE
EXPRESSION ORALE EN CONTINU → p. 153

A Prepare your report

- In your introduction, you will mention the apartheid era briefly.
- Focus on the positive and negative aspects of South African society over the years.
- Don't forget to mention the events that have marked South Africa's history.

B Present your report

You will have to speak between 2 and 3 minutes. Speak clearly to be understood by your classmates.

2 Write an article about a speech

YOUR CD 35 — CD 2 30

MÉTHODOLOGIE
Rédiger un article de presse → p. 168

Kevin Rudd (Canberra, February 13th 2008)

A Listen to the speech

Listen to the speech by Kevin Rudd, Australia's Prime Minister from 2007 to 2010. Your teacher will give you a worksheet to help you.

B Write an article about the speech

You report on that historic event in an article (150-200 words).

- You will insist on the main points of the speech and on its consequences for Aborigines.
- You may include a short interview of an Aborigine.

function box

Giving one's opinion
- I feel / believe that...
- I can't help thinking that...
- To my mind / In my opinion...
- It seems to me that...

Expressing surprise
- I couldn't believe my ears!
- That was unbelievable! It was incredible!
- How amazing!

Expressing consequence
- As a result of...
- Consequently...
- In the wake of...: *À la suite de...*

Check your skills

WORKBOOK → p. 41-42

A Comprendre un article de presse

Lisez cet article. Remplissez la fiche de votre *Workbook* et évaluez-vous en fonction des critères proposés.

After billions spent on stadiums now lying empty and fewer tourists than hoped for, South Africa marks six months from the kick-off of the 2010 World Cup on Saturday, asking whether it was worth it.

The tournament, Africa's first World Cup, delivered an undoubted boost to national pride, but many are ruing[1] the fact that it fell in the midst of the worst global economic recession in generations, which made the return on the country's investment fall short of its potential.

The government spent 33 billion rands (4.7 billion dollars, 3.6 billion euros) on the football extravaganza, an event officials say attracted almost 310,000 tourists and 521 million dollars in foreign spending to the economy.

But that was one-third short of the 450,000 visitors that had been forecast.

"For many businesses, the World Cup was the saviour this year," Gillian Saunders, an analyst with consulting firm Grant Thornton's Johannesburg office, told AFP.

"Without it, we would have been suffering more in this very preliminary post-recession period."

Those who see the tournament as a blessing say the money spent on roads, communications infrastructure, a new public transport system and the first high-speed train in Africa will be a lasting legacy. But critics complain that South Africa, which has 25% unemployment and staggering inequality, could have better spent the money on jobs, education and homes.

AFP (December 9th 2010)

1. *regretter amèrement*

Je me situe par rapport au CECRL B1 → B2

LORSQUE JE LIS CET ARTICLE :

■ **B1 :** Je peux en reconnaître les informations principales et distinguer l'idée essentielle des détails.
Je peux deviner, à l'aide du contexte, le sens de certains mots inconnus.

■ **B1 + :** Je peux reconnaître le schéma argumentatif suivi pour la présentation d'un problème.
Je peux identifier, en moins de dix minutes, les principales conclusions de cet article.

B Parler d'un sujet de société

You think that this cartoon is a good illustration of the situation of the indigenous and non-indigenous Australians. You explain why.

1. Aidez-vous des documents étudiés au cours de l'unité pour décrire la situation et expliquer le message du dessinateur.

2. Enchaînez vos phrases. Votre prise de parole devra durer 1 à 2 minutes.

Évaluez-vous en fonction des critères proposés dans votre *Workbook*.

Je me situe par rapport au CECRL B1 → B2

LORSQUE JE PARLE DE CE SUJET DE SOCIÉTÉ :

■ **B1 :** Je peux décrire une situation et faire un exposé de manière simple sur un sujet étudié.
Je peux justifier mon opinion en donnant des arguments.
Je peux parler de manière compréhensible, même si je fais des pauses pour réfléchir.

■ **B1 + :** Je peux décrire une situation et rendre compte d'un événement avec assez de précision.
Je peux développer une argumentation claire et utiliser quelques articulateurs logiques.
Je peux m'exprimer avec une certaine aisance malgré quelques problèmes de formulation qui entraînent de courtes pauses.

Unit 6

Espaces et échanges

Lieux et formes du pouvoir

Unwanted

What does the word "refugee" mean for you?

final task You feel concerned by the desperate situation of refugees. After listening to a radio report on a play called *Refugee*, you write a letter to the theatre company to ask them to come and perform the play in your town.

Keywords

Nouns
- migration /maɪ'greɪʃən/
- migrant /'maɪgrənt/ (noun + adj.)
- immigrant /'ɪmɪgrənt/ (noun + adj.)
- asylum /ə'saɪləm/ seeker: *demandeur d'asile*
- refugee /refju'dʒɪː/ camp
- shelter: *refuge*
- plight /plaɪt/: *situation difficile*
- smuggler: *passeur / contrebandier*
- drought /draʊt/: *sécheresse*
- flood /flʌd/: *inondation*
- starvation /stɑː'veɪʃən/ = famine
- lack (noun + verb): *manque(r)*
- citizenship: *citoyenneté*
- safety

Adjectives & adverbs
- illegal(ly)
- undocumented (Am.): *sans papiers*
- displaced
- uprooted: *déraciné*
- forced (migration)
- desperate /'despərɪt/: *prêt à tout*
- determined /dɪ'tɜːmɪnd/
- vulnerable /'vʌlnərəbl/

Verbs & expressions
- seek refuge /'refjuːdʒ/: *chercher refuge*
- claim asylum: *demander l'asile*
- flee: *fuir*
- escape /ɪs'keɪp/
- apply for: *faire une demande*
- smuggle: *faire entrer clandestinement*
- provide = supply (sb with): *fournir*
- resettle: *installer ailleurs*

LANGUAGE WORKSHOP → p. 109

Getting water

1. Describe the photo. Where could this scene take place?

2. What may explain the situation?

3. Why do some people have to move to refugee camps?

toolbox

Nouns
- developing country
- bucket /ˈbʌkɪt/: *seau*
- jerry can: *bidon d'eau*
- shortage: *pénurie*
- earthquake /ˈɜːθkweɪk/: *tremblement de terre*
- aid agency: *organisation humanitaire*

Adjectives
- drinkable: *potable*
- scarce /skɛəs/: *rare*
- polluted

Verbs & expressions
- fetch: *aller chercher*
- queue /kjuː/: *faire la queue*
- run out of: *manquer de*
- distribute

Focus on listening

Seeking refuge

WORKBOOK → p. 43-4

MÉTHODOLOGIE COMPRÉHENSION DE L'ORAL → p. 150

A What is a refugee?

CD 2 31-32

Use the photo to anticipate the content of the recording.

MÉTHODOLOGIE
Anticiper → p. 150

1. Do you know what the letters UNHCR stand for?
2. Listen to two sentences from the recording. Which do you think is the first one and which is the last?

Try to memorize the main points while listening.

MÉTHODOLOGIE
Repérer et mémoriser → p. 151

3. Listen to the recording.
4. Give a definition of a refugee from what you remember.
5. What reasons are given to explain why some people are forced to flee their country?

culture key Global refugee trends → p. 144

B Desperate to reach the UK

CD 2 33-34

MÉTHODOLOGIE
Faire des hypothèses sur le sens global d'un document → p. 151

Make hypotheses about the content of the document.

1. Imagine the link between these two pictures and the title.
2. Listen to the first sentences of the recording and make hypotheses on the nature and the topic of the document.
3. Listen to the whole document and say why London is a "paradise" for many asylum seekers.

toolbox

Nouns

- aid: *assistance*
- truck (Am.) = lorry (Br.): *camion*
- supply /sə'plaɪ/: *provision*
- civil war
- human rights
- persecution
- opportunity: *occasion*
- border patrol: *patrouille des frontières*

Adjectives

- needy: *dans le besoin*
- economic / political / religious
- ethnic /'eθnɪk/

Verbs & expressions

- assist: *aider*
- warm up
- share: *partager*
- search sb: *fouiller qqn*
- cross the border: *passer la frontière*
- play the djembe

C Illegal immigration on the decrease

CD 2 35-36

MÉTHODOLOGIE
Repérer et mémoriser les nombres → p. 151

ay attention to figures and dates.

Look at the picture.
Where do you think the scene takes place?
What's happening?

You will hear two sentences.
Which one is taken from the recording?
Do you know what this sentence refers to? If not rn to the *Culture key*.

Listen to the recording, paying particular attention figures.

Summarize the report. Your answers to the llowing questions will help you. Use link words.
What is the main idea?
How does the Border Patrol explain this situation?
What is the main reason for the present situation cording to some observers?
What is the journalist's conclusion?

culture key The US-Mexico border → p. 144

Video time

The Visitor

DVD

The Visitor, Thomas McCARTHY (2007)

A Get ready

1. Look at the film still. What is strange about the situation?
2. Imagine how the two characters are related to each other.
3. You are going to watch an extract from *The Visitor*.

Read the beginning of the film synopsis and complete your answer to question 2.

> *Walter Vale, a college professor, finds his New York apartment squatted by a young couple. Tarek is a Syrian musician, Zaineb is a Senegalese street vendor, they are both illegal immigrants. Unwilling at first, Walter finally accepts to let the couple stay in his apartment.*

B Watch the video

4. Watch the extract from the film. Your teacher will give you a worksheet to help you.

C In your own words

5. Give an oral account of the extract that you saw.

D Going further

6. Analyse Walter's reaction to the situation.
7. Do you think such an adventure is likely to change Walter's views on the plight of illegal immigrants?

Text 1

Little Bee

culture key Nigeria → p. 144

Chris CLEAVE

was born in 1973 in London. A British journalist and novelist, he drew inspiration for his novel *The Other Hand* (entitled *Little Bee* in the US and Canada) from his childhood in West Africa. The novel became increasingly popular when Nicole Kidman announced her intention to produce and star in a screen adaptation of the novel.

A Warming up

Read the introduction and imagine the two girls' feelings.

Little Bee, a Nigerian teenager, has spent two years in a British immigration detention centre. She and her Jamaican friend Yevette are about to be released.

I turned to look back at the detention officer just before we went out through the double doors. He was watching us leave. He opened his mouth, like he was going to say something, but he stopped.

"What?" I said. I realized he was going to tell us there had been a mistake. I wondered if we should run. I did not want to go back in detention. I wondered how far we would get if we ran.

The detention officer stood up. He stood there with his hands at his sides.

"Ladies?" he said.

"Yes?"

He looked down at the ground, and then up again.

"Best of luck", he said.

And we girls turned around and walked toward the light.

I pushed open the double doors, and then I froze. It was the sunlight that stopped me. I felt so fragile from the detention centre, I was afraid those bright rays of sunshine could snap me in half. I couldn't take that first step outside.

"What is de holdup, Lil Bee?"

Yevette was standing behind me. I was blocking the door for everyone.

"One moment, please."

Outside, the fresh air smelled of wet grass. It blew in my face. The smell made me panic. For two years I had smelled only bleach[1], and my nail varnish[2], and the other detainees' cigarettes. Nothing natural. Nothing like this. I felt that if I took one step forward, the earth itself would rise up and reject me. There was nothing natural about me now. I stood there in my heavy boots, a creature who had forgotten her language and learned yours, whose past had crumbled[3] to dust.

"What de hell yu waitin' fo', darlin?"

"I am scared, Yevette."

Yevette shook her head and she smiled.

"Maybe yus right to be scared, Lil Bee, cos yu a smart girl. Maybe me jus' too dumb to be 'fraid. But me spend eighteen month locked up in dat place, an if yu t'ink me dumb enough to wait one second longer on account of your tremblin' an your quakin'[4], yu better t'ink two times."

I turned round to face her and I gripped on to the door frame.

"I can't move," I said.

That is when Yevette gave me a great push in the chest and I flew backward. And that is how it was, the first time I touched the soil of England as a free woman, it was not with the soles of my boots but with the seat of my trousers[5].

"WU-ha-ha-ha!" said Yevette. "Welcome in de United Kindom, int dat glorious?"

I stood up and I smiled at Yevette.

When we came to the main gate, we stopped for a moment. Soft mist was hanging in the valleys, and the tops of the low hills were gold in the morning sun, and I smiled because the whole world was fresh and new and bright.

The Other Hand / Little Bee, Chris CLEAVE (2008)

1. *eau de Javel* 2. *vernis à ongles* 3. *s'effriter* 4. *trembler* 5. *fond de culotte*

B Reading comprehension WORKBOOK → p. 45-46

ead the text with the help of your *Workbook*.

C In your own words

. Sum up the story with the help of the following guidelines.

. What was the detention officer's attitude when the girls left e centre?

. What was Little Bee's first reaction when the door opened? How did Yevette react?

D Going further

. Analyse Little Bee's feelings in the passage.

. What strikes Little Bee as soon as she is outside?

4. What shows that the two girls have a sense of humour?

5. Imagine the reasons why the girls decided to migrate to the UK and why they spent such a long time in the detention centre.

E Language training

6. **Savoir prononcer** YOUR CD 36-37 CD 2 38-39

7. **Pratiquer la grammaire**

Subordonnées en *if* – Subordonnées en *how* – Pronoms personnels et possessifs

WORKBOOK → p. 47

toolbox

Nouns
- fear: *crainte*
- apprehension
- relief /rɪˈliːf/: *soulagement*
- delight /dɪˈlaɪt/ = joy

Adjectives
- distrustful: *méfiant*
- worried
- apprehensive = fearful
- paralyzed (with)
- realistic

Verbs & expressions
- expect: *s'attendre à*
- sympathize /ˈsɪmpəθaɪz/: *montrer de la compassion*
- wish sb luck
- care (about): *se soucier (de)*
- can't wait to V = be impatient to V
- make fun of: *se moquer de*
- be overwhelmed (with): *être submergé*
- achieve /əˈtʃiːv/ one's goal: *atteindre son but*

Your task

Call a friend to express your feelings

As soon as she is outside, Little Bee makes a phone call to a friend. Decide who you want to be and act out the conversation.

Student A You are Little Bee.

Student B You are Little Bee's friend. You were in the same situation a few years before and you're now living in London.

MÉTHODOLOGIE
Conversation au téléphone → p. 157

Speakers' corner

The same problems?

A Look and speak

1. Look at picture 1. What kind of document is it?
2. What is the woman's problem?
3. Read the caption and explain the aim of this document.

B Going further

4. Analyse the way the message is conveyed.
5. Do you think this document achieves its aim?

toolbox

Nouns
- awareness campaign: *campagne de sensibilisation*
- fate: *sort*
- bombing /ˈbɒmɪŋ/
- doorframe: *encadrement de la porte*
- toilet /ˈtɔɪlɪt/ seat
- discrepancy: *décalage*
- contrast

Adjectives
- aware of = conscious of
- devastated
- amazed = startled: *stupéfait*
- wrecked /rekt/ = in ruins
- casual /ˈkæʒjʊl/: *ordinaire*
- brave = courageous /kəˈreɪdʒəs/
- dreadful /ˈdredfʊl/: *terrible*

Verbs & expressions
- launch /lɔːntʃ/ a campaign: *lancer une campagne*
- destroy
- drop a bomb
- light up: *allumer (une cigarette)*
- hide from sb
- be caught red-handed:

1

2

6. Look at the second poster. What is its aim? Which poster is the more efficient in your view?

Your task

Have a discussion about the choice of a campaign poster

You are preparing an awareness campaign on refugees and have a discussion about how to illustrate it.
You have the choice between the documents 1 and 2.
Student A You prefer the first document.
Student B You think the second poster is better.
Act out the discussion.

MÉTHODOLOGIE
Discussion contradictoire → p. 158

Writers' corner

Iqmat's secret diary

Your task

Write an entry in Iqmat's diary
Iqmat, a young illegal Afghan immigrant, wrote how he managed to reach the United Kingdom in his diary. Imagine and write his story. (200-250 words)

MÉTHODOLOGIE EXPRESSION ÉCRITE → p. 165

A Get ready

1. Read what Iqmat told a journalist about his life.

2. The report in the Focus pages "Desperate to reach the UK" (page 100) gives you information on how Afghan immigrants try to reach London from the French coast.

An illegal immigrant

"I am 17. My parents, brother and sister were all killed in a suicide bomb attack in Afghanistan. I decided to leave my country. I knew that if I could get to the UK I would be safe. So I managed to get smuggled all the way to France. I don't want to say how I got to England because I don't want the people who helped me to get into trouble. I disappeared into an Afghan community where I met up with friends who looked after me. It was hard to get a job without papers and at first I used to panic every time I saw a policeman. But, as I had already studied some English back home, I finally managed to get a job washing minicabs."

B Write Iqmat's story

3. Here are a few hints:

a. Imagine Iqmat's feelings (hope, fear, relief) while telling his story.

b. You can also allude to his past and to his expectations.

c. Write in the first person singular and use past tenses to tell your story.

toolbox

Nouns
- jungle
- lorry: *camion*
- the Channel: *la Manche*
- Eurotunnel /ˈjʊrəʊˌtʌnl/
- stowaway /ˈstəʊəweɪ/: *passager clandestin*

Adjectives
- scared = frightened
- panic-stricken: *pris de panique*
- anxious
- open-minded
- understanding
- helpful

Verbs
- enter illegally
- arrest
- evict: *expulser*
- can't wait to = be impatient to
- sneak in: *entrer furtivement*
- sneak out

Text 2

Climate refugees

40-41

SCIENTIFIC AMERICAN was founded in 1845. It is a popular monthly magazine about science, targeting educated but not necessarily scientific readers (total circulation: 732,600).
Website: www.scientificamerican.com

Cecilia TACOLI is a senior researcher at the Institute for Environment and Development, London. Her current work focuses on rural-urban interconnections in Africa, Asia and Latin America.

A Warming up

Describe the photo and what is happening. What could be the reasons for this problem?

Millions uprooted

Experts estimate that as many as 250 million people – a population almost that of the entire United States – could be on the move by 2050. They will go because temperatures are rising and desertification has set in where rainfall is needed most. They will go because more potent monsoons[1] are making flood-prone[2] areas worse. They will go because of other water events caused by melting glaciers, rising seas and the slow and deadly seepage[3] of saline water into their wells[4] and fields. According to the Intergovernmental Panel on Climate Change, a minimum of 207 million people in Latin America, Asia and Africa will not have enough water inside a decade. In Asia, an extra 130 million people will be at risk of hunger by the middle of the century. By 2100, crop revenues in Africa will drop 90 percent.

"This will be the largest migration in history. This is not migration as we've known it before," said Edward Cameron, a former senior adviser to the government of the Maldives. "We're talking about people migrating from sensitive places into other very sensitive places."

In some ways, large-scale migration is nothing new. Humans, after all, have been on the move since early man left East Africa. But these shifts will not be the migrations of pioneers or adventurers seeking opportunities in new lands. Rather, social scientists say, they will be the movement of people who are rushed, unwanted and unprepared, into unfamiliar and perhaps hostile new environments. Most of those who will be uprooted already are living on less than $1 per day.

Scientific American (March 3rd 2009)

1. *moussons* 2. *inondables* 3. /'si:pɪdʒ/ *infiltration* 4. *puits*

Climate migration fears "misplaced"

Yes, hundreds of millions of people live in places that are highly vulnerable to climate change. But this does not mean they will all migrate.

The poorest and most vulnerable people will often find it impossible to move, as they lack the necessary funds and social support. Those who can migrate will be more likely to make short-term, short-distance movements than permanent long-term ones. Overall, long-distance international migration will be the least likely option.

Policymakers must radically alter their views of migration, and see it as a vital adaptation to climate change rather than as an unwanted consequence or a failure to adapt.

This means that poorer nations need to prepare for climate change at home by building up infrastructure and basic services in small towns located in rural areas that could become destination hubs[1] for local migrants.

Options include policies that promote access to non-farm jobs in small rural towns and a more decentralised distribution of economic opportunities.

To do so, they should first of all focus on increasing the capacity of local governments and institutions in small towns to support local economic development, provide basic services and regulate equitable access to natural resources.

Richer countries, meanwhile, need to stop panicking about a mass influx of migrants that is unlikely to happen and instead focus on helping the poorer countries to face climate change.

Cecilia TACOLI in *BBC News* (September 29th 2009)

1. *plaques tournantes / centres*

B Reading comprehension

WORKBOOK → p. 48-49

ırn to your *Workbook* which will help you to understand the ticles.

C In your own words

. Sum up each article briefly.

D Going further

. What is the aim of the journalist who wrote the article in *cientific American*?

. What figures does he give and how does he present them support his view?

. Explain in what way Cecilia Tacoli's view on climate change radically different.

. Do you feel personally concerned by climate change? hy (not)?

toolbox

Nouns

- bundle /'bʌndl/: *ballot*
- waist: *taille*
- belongings: *affaires personnelles*
- catastrophe /kə'tæstrəfɪ/ = disaster

Adjectives

- flooded: *inondé*
- filthy: *très sale*
- disastrous /dɪ'zɑ:strəs/
- starving: *affamé*
- worrying
- huge /hju:dʒ/: *énorme*
- responsible

Verbs & expressions

- swell: *grossir (rivière)*
- foretell = predict
- impress
- give a warning
- raise awareness: *rendre conscient*
- take measures /'meʒəz/
- reassure /ˌri:ə'ʃʊə/

E Language training

6. Savoir prononcer

YOUR CD 38-40 — CD 2 42-44

Dans le 2e article, lisez à haute voix le passage de *"Policymakers…"* (l. 12) à *"… local migrants"* (l. 20).

a. Faites attention à la prononciation des **diphtongues** dans les mots-ci-dessous. Les lettres soulignées se prononcent-elles : /aɪ/, /eɪ/, /əʊ/, /ɛə/, /ɪə/, /aʊ/ ?

policymakers – migration – vital – adaptation – climate – change – failure – nations – prepare – home – basic – towns – located – areas – destination – local – migrants

b. Où se trouve **l'accent principal** dans ces mots transparents ?

migration – vital – adaptation – climate – consequence – adapt – nations – prepare – infrastructure – services – rural – destination – local – migrants

c. Vérifiez à l'écoute, puis lisez à nouveau ce passage en faisant attention à ces deux points de phonologie.

7. Pratiquer la grammaire

Les modaux (sens 2)

LANGUAGE WORKSHOP → p. 108

Your task

Write an essay on the consequences of climate change

What consequences do you think climate change will have on the world's population? Draw information from the two articles studied as well as from the news reports you have certainly heard or watched about the issue. (200 words)

MÉTHODOLOGIE
Rédiger un essai → p. 168

Language workshop

Grammaire Les modaux (sens 2) : expression de la probabilité et du futur

PRÉCIS GRAMMATICAL → 10, 14-17, 39

A Observer et comprendre

1 Probabilité d'un fait présent, passé et à venir

1. *Experts estimate that as many as 250 million people (…) could* ***be*** *on the move by 2050.* (Text 2, p. 106, l. 1)
2. *They will* ***go*** *because temperatures are rising (…).* (Text 2, p. 106, l. 5)
3. *They must* ***be wondering*** *what's going on.*
4. *We may* ***have passed*** *the point of no return.*
5. *This might* ***never happen****.*

a. Classez les modaux soulignés selon le degré de probabilité qu'ils expriment : **1.** Faible probabilité (2 réponses attendues) **2.** Probabilité moyenne **3.** Forte probabilité (sens futur) **4.** Quasi-certitude.

b. Quelle forme verbale (**en gras**) trouve-t-on après le modal souligné : **a.** base verbale (infinitif sans *to*) **b.** forme *BE+ING* ou bien **c.** *HAVE* + participe passé (= *HAVE -EN*) ?

Que désigne chacune de ces formes verbales dans les énoncés ci-dessus : **1.** Un fait vu sous l'angle du déroulement **2.** Un fait vu sous l'angle du résultat ou passé **3.** Un fait à venir ? Traduisez les énoncés.

2 Les modaux et la négation : *MAY NOT* et *CAN'T*

a. Choisissez pour chaque énoncé la reformulation (**a** ou **b**) qui lui correspond le mieux.

1. *They may not know the answer.*	**a.** *It is impossible for them to know the answer.* **b.** *Perhaps they do not know the answer.*
2. *They can't have found the answer!*	**a.** *It is impossible for them to have found the answer.* **b.** *It is possible that they haven't found the answer.*

b. Traduisez les phrases **1** et **2** à l'aide de « il est impossible que » ou « il se peut que ».

3 *WILL* et les subordonnées de temps

1. *They will go when climate change* ***becomes*** *too unbearable.*
2. *When you* ***have decided*** *what you want to do, we will leave.*

Nommez le temps des verbes en gras dans les subordonnées de temps soulignées. Ces verbes désignent-ils des faits présents ou des faits à venir ? Lequel de ces verbes exprime l'idée de résultat ? Traduisez les énoncés.

Faisons le point ! Peut-on utiliser *WILL* pour exprimer le futur dans les subordonnées de temps en anglais ? Quels temps peut-on utiliser ?

B Pratiquer

4 Reformulez les énoncés à l'aide de l'amorce proposée.

a. I'm sure it has caused a great deal of damage. → It must…
b. Perhaps they are living in dreadful conditions. → They might…
c. Maybe they do not want to go. → They may…
d. I'm sure they haven't left. → They can't…

5 Traduisez à l'aide de *MUST, MAY* ou *WILL*.

a. Il se peut qu'ils ne soient pas d'accord.
b. Ils doivent être en train de chercher de nouvelles idées.
c. Quand la température augmentera *(increase)*, ils seront obligés de partir.
d. Quand cela se produira, des millions de gens s'en iront.

Grammaire de l'oral — Reconnaître l'expression de la probabilité à l'oral

6 Prononcer les formes en WILL CD 2 45

a. Écoutez ces énoncés et répétez les modèles.
1. *"This will be the largest migration in history."* (Text 2, p. 106, l. 23)
2. *"Who will be there?" he asked.* 3. *"I will," she said.* 4. *"Will they move?"*

b. Déduisez : dans quels cas peut-on prononcer WILL sous forme réduite ('LL) ?

7 Comprendre les formes modales à l'oral CD 2 46

a. Écoutez ces énoncés et indiquez quelles sont les syllabes accentuées.
1. *They could have died.* 2. *They might have been killed.* 3. *He may be sleeping.*

b. Déduisez : Les auxiliaires modaux sont-ils accentués lorsqu'ils expriment la probabilité ?

8 Écrivez les énoncés que vous entendez. CD 2 47

Lexique — Les réfugiés

→ Keywords p. 98

Assurez-vous que vous avez bien retenu les mots clés de l'unité.

9 Sélectionnez la bonne transcription phonétique des mots suivants.
a. migrant: /'maɪgrənt/ – /'mɪgrənt/ – /maɪ'grænt/
b. immigrant: /ɪ'mɪgrænt/ – /'ɪmɪgrənt/ – /ɪ'maɪgrənt/

10 Donnez les synonymes des mots suivants : a. refuge b. famine c. supply.

11 Complétez les phrases à l'aide des mots suivants :
citizenship – migration – seeker – resettle – repatriated – flee – displaced – desperate – flood – lack – smuggled – plight – applied – undocumented – drought – provide – uprooted

a. This asylum ...1... has ...2... for American ...3....
b. Pedro is an ...4... worker who decided to ...5... his country to ...6... in the USA.
c. The tsunami report focused on the terrible ...7... of the ...8... victims.
d. The refugees suffered from a severe ...9... of water because of the ...10... and had to be ...11....
e. Aid volunteers ...12... refugees with food as soon as they arrive in the camp.
f. Every week, despite strict ...13... control, hundreds of ...14... migrants are ...15... into the country.
g. He felt so ...16... in the refugee camp that he asked to be ...17....

toolbox

Nouns
- advances in: *des progrès dans*
- living standard: *le niveau de vie*

Verbs & expressions
- predict: *prédire*
- foresee: *prévoir*
- achieve one's goals: *atteindre ses buts*
- fail to: *échouer*

Your task

Talk about your future life

You don't believe that global warming will radically change the face of the world. You think that, in the future, the world will be a better place to live. You tell your friends what you think your life will be like in 2030.
Use **modal auxiliary verbs** expressing the **future** and **"probability"**.

Wanted: scientists

Not all immigrants are unwanted...

A The brain drain

1 Use the cartoon to explain what the brain drain is.
2 In your opinion, how can the brain drain be explained?
3 Read the text and check whether your answer to question 2 was right.

MANY OF THE REASONS for scientists' and engineers' migration are similar to other professionals', falling into "push factors" – reasons for leaving their home country – and "pull factors" drawing them to a host country.
"Push factors" include low wages and lack of career choices; lack of funding and / or infrastructure; political instability, poor governance, corruption and persecution.
"Pull factors" include prestige, job satisfaction, higher wages and "selective" immigration policies which favour certain types of migrant scientists and engineers.

From *Postnote* issued by the United Kingdom's Parliamentary Office of Science and Technology

B British Nobel Prize winners

CD 2 48

1 Andre Geim and Konstantin Novoselov, Nobel Prize in Physics (2010)

a. Describe the photo. What do you think is happening? Who are Geim and Novoselov?
b. Read the *Telegraph* article and explain what the expression *"immigration cap"* means.
c. Why are Geim and Novoselov mentioned in this article?

Nobel Prize winners warn against immigration cap

Britain's reputation for scientific excellence is threatened by the government's planned immigration cap, a group of Nobel prize-winning scientists have warned. It could prevent talented researchers from working in Britain, they say.

The group of eight Nobel laureates, including two Russian migrants who won the physics prize on Tuesday, claimed visa restrictions would discourage promising students and distinguished scientists from sharing their expertise with British universities and industries.

Professors Andre Geim and Konstantin Novoselov, of the University of Manchester, may have been put off coming to Britain if an immigration cap had existed when they applied to come here, they claimed. Professor Novoselov said: "If I had had a visa delay, I might have decided to go elsewhere."

The Telegraph (October 7th 2010)

The Royal Swedish Academy of Sciences announces that Russian-born scientists Geim and Novoselov share the Nobel Prize in Physics 2010 for "groundbreaking[1] experiments" with a new material expected to play a large role in electronics.

1. innovative

2 Harry Kroto, Nobel Prize in Chemistry (1996)

a. Listen to what Sir Harry Kroto told BBC Radio 4's *Today* programme.
b. Why does Harry Kroto feel particularly concerned by the new British law on immigration?

C African doctors wanted

ead the article and the statistics, then answer he following questions.

1 Why are the figures particularly striking?

2 What are the main reasons why African octors leave their countries?

3 How could the brain drain of African doctors e reduced?

Africa "being drained of doctors"

There has long been concern about the exodus of African medics, but the Human Resources for Health study suggests the problem may be greater than assumed.

The report suggested the loss of doctors often went hand-in-hand with civil strife[1], political instability and economic stagnation. Angola, Republic of Congo, Guinea-Bissau, Liberia, Mozambique, Rwanda and Sierra Leone all experienced civil war in the 1990s and all had lost 40% of their doctors by 2000.

Number of African doctors working abroad

• Mozambique: 75% • Angola: 70% • Ghana: 56% • Kenya: 51%

The UK is one of the few countries to have introduced a code preventing it from actively recruiting from sub-Saharan Africa. But despite this, Home Office figures show that 17,620 African doctors and nurses joined the NHS[2] last year.

The charity ActionAid said the brain drain was "a huge threat" to Africa.

"The UK government could do Africa a real service by upping aid levels for health systems, ensuring that desperately needed doctors and nurses stay where the need is greatest," said Nick Corby, policy officer at the charity.

1. conflict 2. National Health Service

BBC News (January 10th 2008)

D Willing to R-2-I[1]

ead the article and explain the reasons why India's brain drain to the US is in reverse.

US "reverse brain drain" to India now in full swing

According to an industry estimate, more than 60,000 Indian professionals went ack to their country last year alone, a ajority of them IT (Information technology) rofessionals.

ears ago, the Silicon Valley beckoned[2] the est IT minds from India.

ut the exchange of ideas and innovations after nearly two decades has reversed the trend. The charm of the US is wearing off. India's own Silicon Valleys are now at the forefront of innovation and they are attracting its shining lights back home from the US.

There was a time when nearly 90% of graduates passing out of the prestigious Indian Institutes of Technology (IITs) headed to the West. But not any more.

BBC News (August 19th 2010)

1. return to India 2. *attirer*

After six years working in California's Silicon Valley as IT professionals, the Niraniyas are going back to India.

Webquest — Albert Einstein TICE

1 Browse the web to find out information about Albert Einstein /ˈaɪnstaɪn/.

a. When was Albert Einstein born?

b. What were his different nationalities?

c. Why was he awarded the Nobel Prize in Physics?

d. What theory made him famous?

e. What is he doing in the photo?

f. Why did he move to the United States?

g. What did he warn President Franklin Roosevelt against?

2 Use this information to give an oral account of Einstein's life and achievements.

Web resources

- http://nobelprize.org/nobel_prizes/physics/laureates/
- http://einstein.biz/biography
- http://inventors.about.com/

final task

What does the word "refugee" mean for you?

You feel concerned by the desperate situation of refugees. After listening to a radio report on a play called *Refugee*, you write a letter to the theatre company to ask them to come and perform the play in your town.

1 Listen to a radio report

YOUR CD 41 — CD 2 49

A First read the storyline of the play *Refugee*

Refugee is a moving tale about Ludovic, a singer of protest songs, who escapes the political oppression of his native Haiti, only to find indifference, confusion, hostility and loneliness, but finally success on US shores. It's the personal story of events lived by the playwright Marc Joseph himself, and one many Americans call their own.

B Now listen to the radio report

- The worksheet your teacher will give you will help you to understand the report.

MÉTHODOLOGIE
COMPRÉHENSION DE L'ORAL → p. 150

- Explain why the interviewee is enthusiastic about the play.

2 Write a letter

Write a letter to the manager of the theatre company to ask him whether the play could be staged in your town. (200 words)

- Use the right expressions to start and end your letter.
- Prepare the content of your letter:

– You explain what the word "refugee" means for you.
– You tell the manager of the company about your reactions after hearing a report on the play *Refugee*.
– You ask him whether the company could come and stage the play in your town.
– You insist on the impact the play could have on the local community.

MÉTHODOLOGIE
Écrire une lettre → p. 166

function box

Expressing enthusiasm
- I can't wait to...!
- It must be great... / terrific...
- How interesting... / fantastic...
- I'd just love to...
- I've heard about...

Suggesting
- How / What about V-ING
- Why don't you... / Why not V...
- I suggest V-ING

Check your skills

WORKBOOK → p. 50

A Comprendre un reportage radio

YOUR CD 42 CD 2 50

Écoutez le document sonore sur votre CD. Remplissez ensuite la fiche de votre *Workbook* et évaluez-vous en fonction des critères proposés.

Je me situe par rapport au CECRL B1 → B2

LORSQUE J'ÉCOUTE CE REPORTAGE :

- **B1 :** Je peux en comprendre les points principaux.
Je comprends globalement le point de vue du locuteur.

- **B1 + :** Je peux comprendre les points principaux du reportage et la plupart des détails.
Je peux suivre sans difficulté l'argumentation et le point de vue du locuteur.

B Parler d'un sujet de société

You would like the school film club to show this documentary. You explain why to the film club members.

1. Aidez-vous des documents étudiés au cours de l'unité pour justifier votre choix.

2. Enchaînez vos phrases. Votre prise de parole devra durer 1 à 2 minutes.

Évaluez-vous en fonction des critères proposés dans votre *Workbook*.

Je me situe par rapport au CECRL B1 → B2

LORSQUE JE PARLE DE CE SUJET DE SOCIÉTÉ :

- **B1 :** Je peux décrire une situation et faire un exposé de manière simple sur un sujet étudié.
Je peux expliquer mon opinion en donnant des arguments.
Je peux parler de manière compréhensible, même si je fais des pauses pour réfléchir.

- **B1 + :** Je peux décrire une situation et expliquer le point principal d'une idée avec assez de précision.
Je peux développer une argumentation claire et utiliser quelques articulateurs logiques.
Je peux parler avec une certaine aisance, malgré quelques problèmes de formulation qui entraînent de courtes pauses.

Art quest Cinema and immigration

A film is often considered a mirror of society. Films in which immigrants or immigration play an important role are numerous. Immigration in films is either presented in a comic or a dramatic way. Whether art reflects life or life reflects art, these films present people in search of a new life far from home; they leave no one indifferent.

Look at the pictures and read the synopsis of each film. What particular immigration does each of these films focus on?

- Nazneem Ahmed, a young seventeen-year-old Bangladeshi woman, arrives with her husband Chanu Ahmed, who is twice her age in Brick Lane, London, in the early 1980s…
  - www.sonyclassics.com/bricklane/
  - www.allmovie.com/work/brick-lane-353435

Brick Lane,
Sarah GAVRON
UK (2007)

- England, 1971. George, a Pakistani immigrant, and Ella, an English woman, have seven children. They own a fish-and-chip shop in Salford, UK. George expects his family to follow his strict Pakistani ways and plans arranged marriages for his sons…
  - www.mediacircus.net/eastiseast.html
  - www.reelviews.net/movies/e/east_east.html

East is East,
Damien O'DONNELL
UK (1998)

2

3

- The film tells the story of a Mexican family separated by the US-Mexican border. It follows a young Mexican boy who, after his grandmother dies, decides to sneak across the border to find his mother...

- www.foxsearchlight.com/underthesamemoon/
- www.allmovie.com/work/under-the-same-moon-382550

Under the Same Moon,
Patricia RIGGEN
USA (2007)

- To make ends meet, two working-class single women team up to smuggle immigrants from all over the world from Canada into the United States in the trunk of a car...

- www.sonyclassics.com/frozenriver/
- www.allmovie.com/work/frozen-river-426683

Frozen River,
Courtney HUNT
USA (2008)

Your task

Group work

Each group chooses one of the films on these pages and prepares an oral report to present to the class. You will find all the information needed on the websites indicated. Every student must speak in turn. Use the following guidelines:

- **Explain the reason(s) why you chose to speak about this film.**
- **Complete the summary of the film you chose.**
- **Watch the trailer (when possible) and say if it makes you want to see the film.**
- **Say why you think the film is worth seeing or not.**

Unit 7

Lieux et formes du pouvoir
L'idée de progrès

All equal?

How far are we from equality?

final task

While doing a training course in a firm abroad, you witness a flagrant case of discrimination. You talk about it with your tutor, an executive of the company... You write an e-mail to your teacher about what has happened.

Keywords

Nouns
- equality
- second-class citizen
- glass ceiling /'si:lɪŋ/: *plafond de verre*
- career /kə'rɪə/
- affirmative action: *discrimination positive*
- opportunity: *chance, occasion*
- prejudice: *préjugés*
- job application: *demande d'emploi*

Adjectives
- equal
- (un)fair: *(in)juste*
- obvious /'ɒbvɪəs/: *évident*
- underprivileged: *défavorisé*
- open-minded = tolerant
- narrow-minded = intolerant
- responsible for
- compulsory: *obligatoire*
- bold = daring: *audacieux*
- submissive: *soumis*

Verbs & expressions
- be segregated: *être victime de ségrégation*
- be discriminated against: *être victime d'une discrimination*
- deny /dɪ'naɪ/: *nier*
- be denied: *se voir refuser (qqch)*
- be treated in the same way as: *être traité de la même façon que*
- reach: *atteindre*
- look down on: *mépriser*
- stand up for = fight for (one's rights)
- assert (one's rights): *affirmer (ses droits)*
- be on an equal footing with: *être sur un pied d'égalité avec*
- bridge the gap: *combler le fossé*
- compensate = make up for
- compete (with)
- apply for a job: *postuler (à) un emploi*

LANGUAGE WORKSHOP → p. 127

Defend equality

1. Describe the illustration briefly and say what it evokes for you.

2. Several symbols can be seen. List as many as you can and say what they represent.

3. According to the document, which groups need to stand up for their rights? Give possible reasons.

4. Can you think of other groups who may also need to fight for their rights? Why?

toolbox

Nouns

- awareness campaign: *campagne de sensibilisation*
- clenched fist: *poing serré*
- wings: *ailes*
- dove: *colombe*
- wheelchair: *fauteuil roulant*
- cross: *croix*
- arrow: *flèche*
- ethnic minority /maɪˈnɒrɪtɪ/

Adjectives & expressions

- united
- disabled = handicapped
- aware of = conscious of
- hand in hand: *main dans la main*

Verbs & expressions

- spread one's wings: *déployer ses ailes*
- struggle: *se battre*
- bring together: *rassembler*

Focus on discussing

Women's long march

MÉTHODOLOGIE INTERACTION ORALE → p. 157

A Women's quiet revolution

MÉTHODOLOGIE
Interview → p. 158

Interview the journalist who wrote the article "We did it!".

1. Look at documents **1**, **2** and **3**. What information does each of them provide?

2. Document **2** illustrates what is known as a "glass ceiling". Can you imagine what it might be and where its effects are particularly felt?

3. Use the information given in the different documents (article, pictures, graph…) and act out the interview.

Student A You deplore the fact that, for women, there is still a long way to go. You want to know more about the issue. Imagine the questions you will ask the journalist who worte the article.
Student B You are the journalist and, as your headline suggests, you are convinced that women can now say "We did it!". Get ready to answer the questions.

culture key The glass ceiling → p. 145

1

We did it!

Within the next few months women will cross the 50% mark and become the majority of the American workforce. Women already make up the majority of university graduates and the majority of professional workers in several rich countries, including the United States. Today they are running some of the organisations that once treated them as second-class citizens.

Yet even the most positive changes can be incomplete or unsatisfactory. Women are still under-represented at the top of companies. Only 2% of the bosses of America's largest companies and 5% of those in Britain are women. They are also paid significantly less than men on average. Many women feel they have to choose between their children and their careers.

The Economist (January 2nd 2010)

2

3

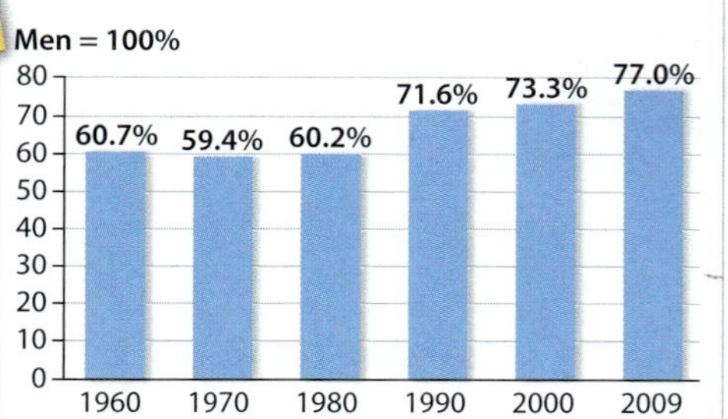

Women's Earnings as a Percentage of Men's, 1960-2009
The chart shows how much women working full-time, year-round in the United States make compared to men.
(Source: US Women's Bureau and the National Commitee on Pay Equity)

toolbox

Nouns
- wages
- income: *salaire / revenu*
- confidence: *confiance*
- self-esteem
- achievement: *réussite*
- demonstration: *manifestation*
- placard /'plækaːd/: *pancarte*

Adjectives
- intimidated
- ill-at-ease: *mal à l'aise*
- discriminatory
- condescending
- sympathetic: *compatissant*

Verbs & expressions
- climb the ladder
- make it to the top: *atteindre le sommet*
- lack: *manquer de*
- draw attention to
- concentrate / focus on: *se concentrer sur*
- speed up: *accélérer*
- depreciate
- demonstrate: *manifester*
- go on strike: *faire la grève*

B Single-sex classes

MÉTHODOLOGIE
Débat → p. 159

Debate the following statement: "Girls work better – and get better results – when they are in single-sex classes."

1. Choose your group.

Group A You agree with the statement.
Group B You disagree and are definitely in favour of co-ed (co-educational) schools.

2. Before debating: in groups, prepare several arguments to back up your views and get ready to counter the other group's arguments.

3. Debate time: each group member presents an argument.
Remember the debating rules: speak in turn, don't interrupt the others, remain polite…

C Quotas – a good idea?

MÉTHODOLOGIE
Discussion contradictoire → p. 158

Discuss a controversial proposal.

1. Look at the documents.

a. What do *The Telegraph* headline and the statistics in the chart indicate?
b. Are you surprised by these statistics?

2. Discuss the following point of view: "To compensate for past injustices, quotas should be set up in all professions".

Student A You defend the idea of quotas.
Student B You oppose the idea.

Country	%
Sweden	45
Spain	36.6
Germany	32.8
UK	22
France	18.9
USA	16.8
Brazil	8.8
Iran	2.8

Women in national parliaments
Situation as of 30 September 2010
(Source: Inter-Parliamentary Union)

Politics

Not enough women in government

There are not enough women in the coalition government, according to the new Equalities Minister who told David Cameron to do more to promote female politicians.

The Telegraph (May 15th 2010)

Video time

Made in Dagenham DVD

Made In Dagenham, Nigel COLE (2010)

A Get ready

1. Look at the photo. Describe the scene and imagine the situation.

B Watch the video

2. Watch the trailer of the film *Made in Dagenham*. Your teacher will give you a worksheet to help you.

C In your own words

3. Use the worksheet to give an oral account of this trailer.

D Going further

4. After the Dagenham strike, women's salaries were raised to 92% of what men received. Imagine the conversation which preceded this decision.

Student A You are Rita, the union leader. You explain the situation of women in your factory and why you think their salaries should be raised.
Student B You are the Minister of Employment. You try to make Rita understand that equal pay cannot be achieved at once but you show sympathy for Rita's position.

Text 1

How far we've come

culture key Slavery in the USA → p. 145

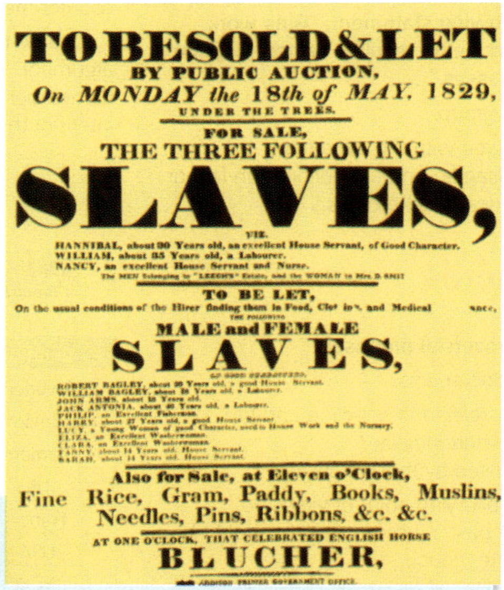

DAILY NEWS

The New York Daily News is the fifth most widely-circulated daily newspaper in the United States. The first US daily printed in tabloid form, it was founded in 1919. It has won ten Pulitzer Prizes.
Website: www.mydailynews.com

A Warming up

Study the two illustrations and link them with the title to anticipate the content of the article.

Two hundred and twenty-one years ago, the Founding Fathers wrote into the US Constitution that slaves were to be counted as three-fifths of a human being in the representative democracy that was being born.

One hundred and forty-seven years ago, the states of the South launched the Civil War to defend the white citizen's power to hold others in bondage.

One hundred and twelve years ago, the US Supreme Court ruled that laws consigning blacks to "separate but equal" facilities were constitutional.

Forty years ago, a presidential candidate declared as governor of Alabama: "Segregation now, segregation tomorrow, segregation forever." And he won the votes of ten million Americans.

And, today, this nation – so haunted by the original sin of slavery, so riven by the torments of race and yet so dedicated to the ideal that all men are created equal – has elevated a black man to the presidency.

The question asked time and time again over the past two years has been answered; Americans were ready after all – yes we were – to welcome a black man to the White House.

Fifty-two years ago, Rosa Parks refused to give up her seat on a bus to a white man.

Forty-four years ago, Lyndon Johnson pushed the Civil Rights Act of 1964 through Congress and followed with the Voting Rights Act of 1965.

Forty years ago, the Rev. Martin Luther King Jr. gave his life.

Twenty-four years ago, Oprah Winfrey got a TV talk show.

And this morning, Barack Obama is President-elect.

Fortunate are the children of all backgrounds who will grow up more trusting of America's commitment to rewarding merit regardless of skin color.

Fortunate are the members of older generations who suffered or witnessed the cruelties of racism.

Fortunate are the people of good faith – white, black and other – who have struggled to reach common ground across the racial divide.

It is a glory that so much of the American electorate of 2008 chose Obama neither because of his heritage nor despite it. They went with this son of a Kenyan father and a white mother because of the quality of his person and his approaches to the issues.

The indisputable truth is that Obama did not run for President as a black man. He ran as a Harvard Law-educated US senator who was, incidentally, a person of color.

At the same time, no one should ever forget that John McCain had the wisdom and decency never to exploit racial fears. He competed with an honor befitting the man he is.

This was an election that surely would have delighted King and of which all Americans can be proud.

We judged Barack Obama by the content of his character.

The New York Daily News (November 5th 2008)

B Reading comprehension

WORKBOOK → p. 51-52

Your *Workbook* will help you to understand the text.

C In your own words

1. Sum up the text with the help of the following guidelines.

a. List the most important stages in African-American history.

b. For what reasons can Americans be proud?

D Going further

2. Why was Obama's election such a powerful symbol? Explain the significance of the expression *"yes we were"* (l. 29).

3. Say why certain groups of people are considered to be *"fortunate"*.

4. Explain the origin of the concluding sentence: *"We judged Barack Obama by the content of his character."*

5. The journalist uses the words *"proud"*, *"fortunate"*, *"glory"*. Do you find his optimism justified? Do you think that similar elections are possible in other countries?

E Language training

6. **Savoir prononcer** YOUR CD 43-44 CD 3 2-3

7. **Pratiquer la grammaire** WORKBOOK → p. 53

Les articles et l'expression de la généralité – Emplois particuliers de l'article *a / an* – Pronoms relatifs

toolbox

Nouns

- hardship: *épreuve*
- roots: *racines*
- outcast /'aʊtkɑːst/: *exclu*
- slogan
- election campaign /ɪ'lekʃən kæm'peɪn/

Adjectives

- worthy /'wɜːðɪ/: *digne*
- pleased with: *content de*

Verbs & expressions

- overcome: *surmonter*
- ignore /ɪg'nɔː/: *ne pas tenir compte de*
- It is the first time sb has done sth: *c'est la première fois que qqn fait qqch*

function box

Expressing surprise

- Just imagine!
- Fancy that!
- How amazing!
- How surprised I was!
- How astonishing!
- Gee whiz!: *Ça alors !*

Your task

Have a phone conversation about Obama's election

It is the day after Obama's election. You have a phone conversation with your American friend.

Student A You are the French student. You express your feelings and those of people in France and ask questions about Americans' reactions.

Student B You are the American friend. You describe the exceptional events in your country and the way you and your countrymen feel.

MÉTHODOLOGIE
Conversation au téléphone → p. 157

Sport on TV

A The topic

1. Do you recognize the athlete in the photo? What is "special" about him?

2. What is his specialist discipline? Who is he competing with in the photo?

3. In your opinion, is this race perfectly "fair"? Explain.

B Open your ears CD 3 4

4. You will hear three sentences. Two of them are in the interview. Which ones? Justify.

C Listen CD 3 5

WORKBOOK → p. 54

5. Listen to the recording, and check whether your answers are right. You will find some help in your *Workbook*.

D In your own words

6. According to the people interviewed, for what positive reasons would people watch disabled sport?

7. Explain the supposed reticence of:
a. TV stations; **b.** sports fans; **c.** the "average person".

8. What is said about the man in the photo? Why is his particular case controversial?

toolbox

Nouns

- athletics /æθ'letɪks/: *athlétisme*
- track: *piste*
- limbs /lɪmz/: *membres*
- prosthetic limbs: *prothèses*
- blades: *lames*
- springs: *ressorts*

Adjectives

- disabled = handicapped
- brave: *courageux*
- sympathetic: *compatissant*

Verbs & expressions

- amputate: *amputer*
- compete (with): *concurrencer*
- get used to: *s'habituer à*
- devoted to: *consacré à*
- they can't stand / bear / put up with: *ils ne peuvent pas supporter*

function box

Expressing opinions

- Even though it's regrettable, I can't help thinking that...
- Sad though it may be, my feeling is that...
- Unfortunately, what we have to realize is that...
- I believe that...

Your task

Discuss sport on TV

Discuss the pros and cons of disabled sport on TV.

Student A You think that televising disabled sport will never be popular and give several reasons why.

Student B You disagree as you think more programmes devoted to this type of sport on TV would help people to accept handicaps more easily.

Act out the discussion.

MÉTHODOLOGIE
Discussion contradictoire → p. 158

Equality in job applications?

Your task

Write a letter to a newspaper

You've just read the following newspaper article about making anonymous job applications compulsory.

You think that the proposal sounds interesting. But you are not sure that, in practice, it will really make a difference... Write a letter to the "Readers' Opinion" column of the newspaper.

MÉTHODOLOGIE
Écrire une lettre → p. 166

A Get ready

1. Look at the photo and link it with the headline.

2. Study the definition of anonymous CVs and the information in the article. Take notes and prepare your letter.

Anonymous CVs: CVs in which information such as names, age, sex, date and place of birth, nationality and marital status will be banned.

B Write your letter

3. Structure your letter in a coherent way.

a. Begin by referring to the original article (specifying the date, the subject and the elements which caught your attention).

b. Say what you find sensible and understandable in the proposal.

c. Express your doubts about the real effectiveness of the project.

d. If you have any bright ideas, make suggestions at the end of your letter.

function box

Expressing agreement, understanding

- I perfectly understand that...
- This proposal is justified / sensible / understandable in that...
- You / They are right to suggest that...

Expressing doubts, protest

- However, I am not really sure that... / I am rather sceptical about...
- In theory, it sounds... but in practice...
- On the face of it, it seems... but in reality...
- I object to / disapprove of / protest against...
- How can they...? / What right have they to...?

Anonymous CVs

Race equality campaigners are pressing the government to make anonymous CVs compulsory in job applications. This follows research conducted by the Department of Work and Pensions, which found that job applicants whose names suggested British ancestry had a far higher chance of being invited to interview than those whose names sounded "foreign".

OK, an anonymous CV might improve the chances of someone being invited to interview but, if there is prejudice, they are likely to be rejected as soon as they walk into the interview room.

The Guardian (January 5th 2010)

Text 2

All animals are equal but...

culture key Orwell's political satires → p. 145

George ORWELL

(real name Eric Arthur Blair) was born in 1903 at Motihari, Bengal. He was educated at Eton and served with the Indian Imperial Police in Burma. He worked as a journalist for *The Tribune* and *The Observer*. His best-known works are *Nineteen Eighty-Four* and *Animal Farm*, both biting criticisms of totalitarian societies. He died in London in January 1950.

A Warming up

Study the illustration. Say what's happening and find a link between the words and their writer.

The animals have taken control of Mr. Jones's farm. The pigs, led by Napoleon and Snowball, decide to organize their new society…

The animals had their breakfast, and then Snowball and Napoleon called them together again.

"Comrades," said Snowball, "it is half-past six and we have a long day before us. Today we begin the hay harvest[1]. But there is another matter that must be attended to first."

The pigs now revealed that during the past three months they had taught themselves to read and write from an old spelling book which had belonged to Mr. Jones's children and which had been thrown on the rubbish heap. Napoleon sent for pots of black and white paint and led the way down to the five-barred gate that gave on to the main road. Then Snowball (for it was Snowball who was best at writing) took a brush between the two knuckles of his trotter[2], painted out MANOR FARM from the top bar of the gate and in its place painted ANIMAL FARM. This was to be the name of the farm from now onwards. After this they went back to the farm buildings, where Snowball and Napoleon sent for a ladder. They explained that by their studies of the past three months the pigs had succeeded in reducing the principles of Animalism to Seven Commandments. These Seven Commandments would now be inscribed on the wall; they would form an unalterable law by which all the animals on Animal Farm must live for ever after. With some difficulty, Snowball climbed up and set to work. The Commandments were written on the tarred[3] wall in great white letters that could be read thirty yards away. They ran thus:

THE SEVEN COMMANDMENTS

1. Whatever goes upon two legs is an enemy.
2. Whatever goes upon four legs, or has wings, is a friend.
3. No animal shall wear clothes.

4. No animal shall sleep in a bed.
5. No animal shall drink alcohol.
6. No animal shall kill any other animal.
7. All animals are equal.

It was very neatly written, and except that "friend" was written "freind" and one of the "S's" was the wrong way round, the spelling was correct all the way through. Snowball read it aloud for the benefit of the others. All the animals nodded in complete agreement, and the cleverer ones at once began to learn the Commandments by heart.

However, the pigs began to copy human beings and they broke the commandments one by one, even killing some rebellious animals. Curiously, whenever they broke the rules, they added some well-chosen words in order to change them – for example, "No animal shall kill any other animal WITHOUT CAUSE". Finally, the pigs had taken so much power that, one day, when the other animals looked up at the wall…

There was nothing there now except a single Commandment. It ran:
ALL ANIMALS ARE EQUAL
BUT SOME ANIMALS ARE MORE EQUAL THAN OTHERS.

Animal Farm, George ORWELL (1945)

1. *faire les foins* 2. *articulations de son pied* 3. *goudronné*

Reading comprehension

WORKBOOK → p. 55-56

urn to your *Workbook* which will help you to understand the ext.

In your own words

. Sum up the story with the help of your *Workbook*.

Going further

. What do the *"Seven Commandments"* remind you of? Give xamples to prove your point.

. Why do you think they are gradually modified?

. At the end, there is just one commandment. Say why it is ather strange.

. The pigs take power by learning to read and write. What ould Orwell's message be?

toolbox

Nouns
- knowledge /ˈnɒlɪdʒ/: *connaissances*
- skills: *compétences*
- duty: *devoir*
- struggle: *lutte*
- moral (of the story): *morale de l'histoire*

Adjectives & adverbs
- illiterate /ɪˈlɪtərɪt/: *illettré*
- evil /ˈiːvl/: *mauvais, méchant, maléfique*
- topsy-turvy: *sens dessus dessous*

Verbs & expressions
- remember: *se souvenir de*
- remind /rɪˈmaɪnd/ sb of sth: *rappeler qqch à qqn*
- make sb think of sth: *faire penser à qqch*
- sound like / seem like: *ressembler à*
- stand for: *représenter*
- symbolize: *symboliser*

E Language training

6. Savoir prononcer YOUR CD 45-46 CD 3 7-8

a. Lisez les mots suivants. Lesquels contiennent **le son** /ɔː/ comme dans les mots *more, for,* ou *saw*? Vous vérifierez ensuite à l'écoute.
aloud – cause – down – form – four – law – now – Snowball – taught – through

b. Parmi les mots suivants, lesquels sont accentués sur la **première syllabe** ? Prononcez-les, puis vérifiez à l'écoute.
begin – seven – children – again – between – written – before – matter – belonged – explained – studies – complete

7. Pratiquer la grammaire
La voix passive LANGUAGE WORKSHOP → p. 126

Your task

Write out and deliver a speech

In case the other animals do not understand the Seven Commandments, Napoleon and Snowball write a speech explaining them. Write out and deliver their speech, beginning "Dear Comrades…". (200 words)

MÉTHODOLOGIE
EXPRESSION ÉCRITE → p. 165

MÉTHODOLOGIE
EXPRESSION ORALE EN CONTINU → p. 153

Language workshop

Grammaire | La voix passive

PRÉCIS GRAMMATICAL → 43

A Observer et comprendre

1 Le passif et l'actif : formes et sens

1. *Then Snowball (...) painted* **ed** ANIMAL FARM. (Text 2, p. 124, l. 12)
2. *The words* ANIMAL FARM *were paint***ed** *on the wall.*
3. *These Seven Commandments would now be inscrib***ed** *on the wall.* (Text 2, p. 124, l. 19)

a. Quelle est la valeur de -ED dans chacun des énoncés ci-dessus ? Quel auxiliaire permet de repérer les formes passives ?

b. Quels énoncés mettent le mieux l'accent sur celui / ceux qui subissent l'action ?

2 *BEEN* ou *BEING* ?

1. *(...) an old spelling book which (...)* **had been thrown** *on the rubbish heap.* (Text 2, p. 124, l. 9)
2. *Every day, hundreds of books* **were being thrown** *away.*

Qu'indiquent respectivement la forme *had been* et la forme *were being* dans ces énoncés passifs :
1. « l'action est vue sous l'angle du déroulement » ou bien **2.** « l'action est vue sous l'angle du résultat » ? Traduisez les énoncés.

3 Les verbes prépositionnels

1. *"We must attend* **to** *this matter first."*
2. *"But there is another matter that must be attended* **to** *first."* (Text 2, p. 124, l. 6)

Quel complément la préposition *to* introduit-elle en **1** ? La place de la préposition est-elle modifiée à la voix passive en **2** ? Traduisez les énoncés **1** et **2** à l'aide du verbe « s'occuper de ». Peut-on conserver la même construction en français ?

Faisons le point !
1. Qu'indiquent respectivement la forme HAD BEEN et la forme WERE BEING dans un énoncé passif ?
2. Les verbes prépositionnels se construisent-ils de la même manière en français et en anglais à la voix passive ?

B Pratiquer

4 Réécrivez l'énoncé à la voix passive en utilisant l'élément souligné comme point de départ.

a. Somebody is watching <u>them</u> all the time.
b. They often treat <u>men and women</u> differently.
c. They had sent <u>the children</u> away.
d. They broke <u>all the rules</u> one by one.
e. They have never discussed <u>our rights</u>.
f. They are laughing at <u>you</u>.
g. They were staring at <u>us</u>.
h. We can't rely on <u>them</u>.

5 Traduisez en utilisant la voix passive.

a. Les femmes n'étaient pas représentées.
b. On ne peut plus les ignorer.
c. On nous traite très mal (présent *BE+ING*).
d. On les avait envoyés en prison.

Grammaire de l'oral | Comprendre les formes passives à l'oral

À savoir ! À l'oral, il est parfois difficile de distinguer :
– les formes en *BEEN* des formes en *BEING* ;
– les participes passés (ex. : *given*) des formes en *-ING* (ex. : *giving*).
Il faut s'appuyer sur le contexte pour interpréter correctement le sens de la forme verbale.

6 Prononcer les formes passives (CD 3 9-10)

a. Écoutez les énoncés enregistrés. Les auxiliaires *is, has, being* et *been* sont-ils accentués ?
 1. *Her mother has just been given a new job.*
 2. *He is now being interviewed by a French journalist.*

b. Répétez les modèles en veillant à bien reproduire l'accentuation.

7 Comprendre les formes passives à l'oral (CD 3 11)

Écoutez attentivement chaque énoncé afin de bien en comprendre le sens global et indiquez si la forme entendue est la forme **1** ou **2**.

a. 1. was seen	a. 2. has seen
b. 1. was seen	b. 2. is seeing
c. 1. has never been used	c. 2. is now being used
d. 1. has never been used	d. 2. is now being used
e. 1. have been accused	e. 2. are being accused
f. 1. have been nasty	f. 2. are being nasty

Lexique | Égalité et droits

Assurez-vous que vous avez bien retenu les mots clés de l'unité. → Keywords p. 116

8 Donnez les synonymes ou les antonymes des mots et expressions suivants.

a. fight for (one's rights) = … b. compensate = … c. tolerant = … d. privileged ≠ …

9 Donnez l'équivalent anglais des mots et expressions suivants.

a. discrimination positive b. obligatoire c. mépriser d. combler le fossé e. préjugés

10 Quelle est la syllabe accentuée dans les mots suivants ?

a. career b. opportunity c. obvious d. compete e. responsible f. citizen

11 Complétez les phrases à l'aide des mots et expressions suivants.

glass ceiling – unfair – equality – narrow-minded – denied – reaching – assert – apply for – compete with – treated in the same way – on an equal footing – discriminated.

a. In a society which defends …1…, it seems …2… that disabled people should be …3… access to certain public buildings.
b. When women …4… a managerial post, there is often a "…5…" which prevents them from …6… the top.
c. Forbidding African Americans to …7… other students for university places was a rather …8… policy.
d. If women were really …9… with men, they would be …10… as their male colleagues.
e. Today minorities refuse to be …11… against and fight to …12… their rights.

toolbox

Verbs
- det**ai**n: *retenir prisonnier*
- rel**ea**se: *libérer*
- s**ear**ch: *fouiller*
- prov**i**de **e**vidence: *fournir des preuves*

Your task

Make a phone call to explain what is happening to you

You are at the airport but you cannot board the plane because you have lost your passport. Two security officers have been interrogating you for an hour now. At last, they allow you to phone home. You tell your parents what's going on. Act out the phone conversation. Use **passive forms** as often as possible.

How far from equality!

Some are more equal than others...

A Poverty has a woman's face

Read the text and say whether the following statements are true or false. Justify by giving precise figures.

a. Of all the people who cannot read or write, about half of them are women.
b. Most of the world's poor are men.
c. Men work roughly half as much as women.
d. In the world's primary schools, there are just as many girls as boys.
e. Women's wages are much lower than men's.
f. Despite wage differences, men and women often share property.

Did you know?

- Of the 1.3 billion people living in poverty around the world, 70% are women.
- In the least developed countries nearly twice as many women over age 15 are illiterate compared to men.
- Two-thirds of children denied primary education are girls, and 75% of the world's 876 million illiterate adults are women.
- Women work two-thirds of the world's working hours, produce half of the world's food, and yet earn only 10% of the world's income and own less than 1% of the world's property.

Somalian women in a refugee camp

B How ethnic origin and education influence income

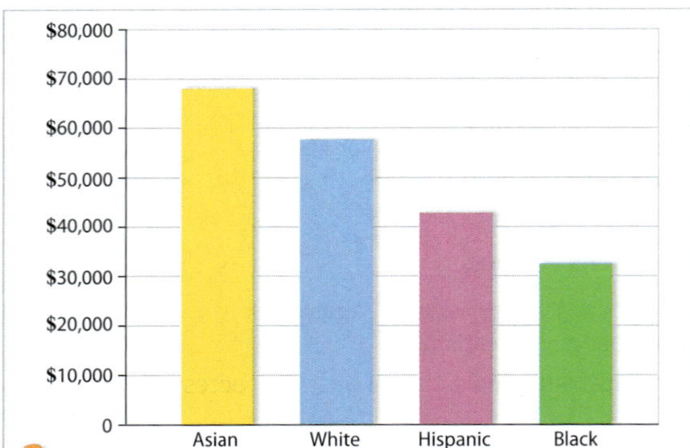

Median annual earnings by ethnic origin in the USA (2009) (Source: Data 360 Organization)

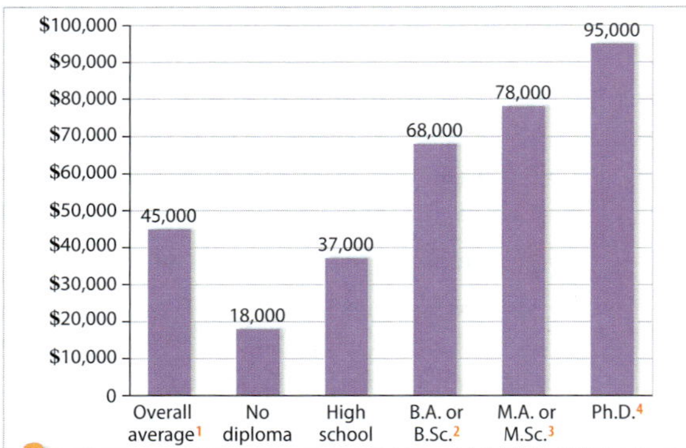

Median annual income by educational level in the USA (2006) (Source: US Census Bureau)

1. Moyenne globale 2. Licence 3. Master 4. Doctorat

Study the graphs and answer the questions.

1 What general conclusions can you draw? Does anything surprise you?
2 Which ethnic groups had a median income of over $4,000 a month? And just over $3,000 a month?
3 Who earned less than half the income of Asians? Who earned almost as much as Asians?
4 What level of education must you reach in order to earn more than the average American?
5 Which diploma seems to make your income rise most significantly?

C Giving – a way to reduce inequality?

1 Philanthropy – promoting the well-being of humanity

PHILANTHROPY HAS ALWAYS BEEN an integral part of American life – seen as a duty by the very rich or perhaps as a way of giving something back to society by fighting against inequality.

A hundred years ago, Andrew Carnegie and John D. Rockefeller spent fortunes on establishing libraries, museums and universities. Carnegie, who would say "A man who dies rich dies disgraced", spent 90% of his fortune before he died. Rockefeller's motto was "Make a lot to give a lot".

Today Bill Gates and Mark Zuckerberg, billionaires thanks to Microsoft and Facebook, have joined the ranks of America's great philanthropists by giving away colossal sums either to save the world from malaria or to fix failing schools.

2 Mark Zuckerberg, the Philanthropist

A DIFFERENT PICTURE OF FACEBOOK FOUNDER Mark Zuckerberg is emerging than the one Aaron Sorkin[1] would have you see. Instead of the fictional Zuckerberg who comes off awkward[2], insensitive and ruthless[3] in *The Social Network*, the real Mark Zuckerberg is turning out to be – well, a mensch[4].

Last week, Bill Gates and Warren Buffett announced that Zuckerberg, 27, and Facebook co-founder Dustin Moskovitz would join The Giving Pledge[5], a campaign helmed by America's wealthiest men to donate half their net worth to charity. The Facebook founders join another 57 billionaires who have already committed to the pledge, including New York City mayor Michael Bloomberg, corporate raider Carl Icahn and Star Wars creator George Lucas.

The Huffington Post (December 13th 2010)

1. director of the film *The Social Network* 2. *maladroit* 3. *impitoyable* 4. decent, responsible person with admirable characteristics 5. solemn promise

1 Read text 1. Say what very rich Americans tend to do. Why?

2 Read text 2. What two different faces of Mark Zuckerberg are evoked? What is "The Giving Pledge"?

3 Discuss the idea of "giving back".

Student A You find the philanthropists' way of fighting inequality very interesting.

Student B You disagree and think that these billionaires only act this way to give themselves a clear conscience.

Webquest From rags to riches TICE

Choose one of the following Webquests.

1. Her name is Oprah Winfrey – but who exactly is she?

Forbes Magazine included her in its 2003 list of America's billionaires, the first African-American woman to become one. In 2005, *Business Week* named her the greatest black philanthropist in American history.

a. Browse the web to find out who she is and why she is "the greatest black philanthropist in American history".

Student A You visit www.blackenterprise.com/magazine and www.blackpast.org

Student B You visit www.achievement.org and www.biography.com

b. Compare your findings and use them to write a summary of her life story.

2. Putting an end to poverty

Browse the "End Poverty 2015" website.
www.endpoverty2015.org

a. Find out what their "8 goals" are.

b. Choose one goal. Write two paragraphs explaining why you think it's important, and how this goal can be achieved.

final task

How far are we from equality?

While doing a training course in a firm abroad, you witness a flagrant case of discrimination. You talk about it with your tutor, an executive of the company – but he does not agree with your interpretation of events and defends the firm's position... You write an e-mail to your teacher about what has happened.

1 Have a discussion with your tutor

MÉTHODOLOGIE
Discussion contradictoire → p. 158

A Decide what type of discrimination you will choose

List different possible cases of discrimination in the workplace: age, gender, ethnic origin, disability. The different documents in this unit should help you to choose an example.

B Act out the conversation

With your classmate, act out the conversation between the trainee *(stagiaire)* and the tutor.

Student A You are the trainee. Explain the example of discrimination you have witnessed, giving your full support to the supposed victim.
Student B You are the tutor. React to your trainee's explanations. You explain that, even though mentalities are slowly changing, certain old-fashioned attitudes still exist.

2 Write an e-mail to your teacher

MÉTHODOLOGIE
Écrire un courriel → p. 166

- Begin by reminding your teacher who you are and what you're doing in the firm.
- Describe what you witnessed (specifying the day, the situation and what caught your attention).
- Evoke the conversation you had with your tutor. Give your tutor's position, saying whether or not you understand it.
- Make suggestions about how future cases of discrimination could be avoided.

function box

Reacting to an event
- What strikes me (the) most about this is that...
- What I find the most incredible / unpleasant / shocking is that...
- I was amazed by / stunned by / astounded by...

Expressing preference, choice
- Perhaps the firm could either do this, or do that...
- Rather than / Instead of doing this, the firm could...
- Employees would rather do this / They might prefer doing this...
- If the company chooses this solution, they will be able to...
- If the company chose this solution, they would be able to...

Check your skills

WORKBOOK → p. 57-58

A Comprendre un article de presse

Lisez cet article. Remplissez ensuite la fiche de votre *Workbook* et évaluez-vous en fonction des critères proposés.

From police chief to politician

TUESDAY'S ELECTION WAS HISTORIC for the Republican takeover of the state legislature for the first time in 38 years, but it was significant in St. Paul for another reason. The Capitol City elected its very first black lawmakers to both the House and Senate. They won the seats vacated by the state's first two Hmong[1] lawmakers.

St. Paul's black population stood at 12 percent in the 2000 Census, roughly the national average. But until now, St. Paul has never elected a black legislator to serve at the Capitol. On Tuesday, voters on the East Side elected their former police chief, John Harrington, to the state senate.

Harrington thinks his name recognition and reputation for public safety helped him win office. But he also credits his predecessor, Mee Moua, and Cy Thao, another pioneering Hmong lawmaker, for showing the city that minority representatives can do a good job representing all their constituents.

"They opened the door frankly in my mind. I can remember a time when in St. Paul, where I could show up for a call, they would ask for 'the other police,' meaning they wanted the white police to show up," he said. "Within my career of 33 years, that level of racism still existed."

During his six-year tenure as police chief, Harrington prioritized domestic violence and gang activity, and achieved notable reductions in both. He's hoping to extend that influence as a state senator.

Minnesota Public Radio (November 4th 2010)

1. ethnic group from South China

Je me situe par rapport au CECRL B1 → B2

LORSQUE JE LIS CET ARTICLE :

- **B1 :** Je peux en reconnaître les points significatifs.

  Je peux deviner, à l'aide du contexte, le sens de certains mots inconnus.

  Je peux comprendre les descriptions de sentiments ou de souhaits.

- **B1 + :** Je peux repérer le déroulement des événements évoqués, même quand le narrateur ne respecte pas leur chronologie.

  Je peux comprendre, en moins de dix minutes, les principales conclusions de cet article.

B Prendre part à une interview

A reporter is interviewing John Harrington after his election.
Decide who you want to be, get ready to react to unexpected questions and answers.
Act out the interview.

Évaluez-vous en fonction des critères proposés dans votre *Workbook*.

Je me situe par rapport au CECRL B1 → B2

QUAND JE PRENDS PART À CETTE INTERVIEW :

- **B1 :** Je peux interviewer quelqu'un sur un sujet précis si j'ai préparé le questionnaire ; je peux également poser des questions spontanées.

  Je peux participer activement et sans préparation à une discussion sur un thème qui m'est familier, même si je dois parfois chercher mes mots.

- **B1 + :** Je peux communiquer spontanément avec un bon contrôle grammatical.

  Je peux varier la formulation de ce que je souhaite dire.

  Je peux intervenir de manière adéquate dans une discussion, en utilisant des moyens d'expression appropriés.

Read the text, stopping at each box to answer the question.

The sneeze

Mary, an American teenager, and Peter, her younger brother, are in Australia, visiting their uncle. On their way back, their plane crashes and they are the only survivors – lost in the Australian Outback…

For a long time they sat in the shade of the quondong trees, the trees that had saved their lives. They were too happy to talk.

Though the edge had gone from his hunger, Peter wasn't altogether at ease. He kept looking nervously at the surrounding bush. He had a strange sort of feeling: a feeling of being watched. Several times he looked up quickly, certain there was someone there; but the bush slept on in the heat of the sun: silent, motionless, apparently deserted. Unconvinced, he sidled back to his sister.

"Mary!" he whispered. "I think there's someone here!"

"Someone here! Where?"

Disbelieving she swung round. The quondong fell to the grass. Only by snapping her teeth together did she stifle a scream of fear. For there, less than four feet away, so close that she could have stretched out an arm and touched him, was a boy. And he was ebony black and quite naked.

Describe the successive feelings of Peter and then Mary. What explains them?

The girl's first impulse was to grab Peter and run; but as her eyes swept over the stranger, her fear died slowly away. The boy was young – certainly no older than she was; he was unarmed, and his attitude was more inquisitive than threatening: more puzzled than hostile.

The three children stood looking at each other in the middle of the Australian desert. Motionless as the outcrops[1] of granite they stared, and stared, and stared. Between them the distance was less than the spread of an outstretched arm, but more than a hundred thousand years.

Brother and sister were products of the highest strata of humanity's evolution. In them the primitive had long ago been swept aside, been submerged by mechanization, been swamped[2] by scientific development, been nullified by the standardized pattern[3] of white man's way of life. They had climbed a long way up the ladder of progress; they had climbed so far, in fact, that they had forgotten how their climb had started. Coddled[4] in babyhood, psycho-analysed in childhood, nourished on predigested patent foods, provided with continuous push-button entertainment, the basic realities of life were something they'd never had to face.

How did the three children happen to be together?
Why are Mary and Peter so far away from the "basic realities of life"?

It was very different with the Aboriginal. He knew what reality was. He led a way of life that was already old when Tut-ankh-amen started to build his tomb: a way of life that had been tried and proved before the white man's continents were even lifted out of the sea. Among the secret water-holes of the Australian desert his people had lived and died, unchanged and unchanging, for twenty thousand years. Their lives were unbelievably simple. They had no homes, no crops[5], no clothes, no possessions. The few things they had, they shared: food and wives; children and laughter; tears and hunger and thirst. They walked from one water-hole to the next; they exhausted one supply of food, then moved on to another. Their lives were utterly[6] uncomplicated because they

James Vance MARSHALL

James Vance Marshall, pseudonym for the writer Donald G. Payne, was born in England in 1924. He is the author of many short stories and novels, including the highly-acclaimed *A River Ran Out of Eden* (1962) and, more recently, *Stories from the Billabong* (2008). *Walkabout*, set in Australia and describing a clash of cultures, was first published in the UK in 1959 and over the last fifty years the story has become a much-loved best-seller. In 1971, *Walkabout* was made into a film.

were devoted to one purpose, dedicated in their entirety to the waging of one battle: the battle with death. Death was their ever-present enemy. He sought them out from every dried-up salt pan[7], from the flames of every bush fire. He was never far away. Keeping him at bay was the Aboriginals' full-time job: the job they'd been doing for twenty thousand years: the job they were good at.

Why does the Aboriginal boy know more about "reality"?

The desert sun streamed down. The children stared and stared. Mary had decided not to move. To move would be a sign of weakness. She remembered being told about the man who'd come face to face with a lion, and had stared it out, had caused it to slink away[8]. That was what she'd do to the black boy; she'd stare at him until he felt the shame of his nakedness and slunk away. She thrust out her chin and glared[9]. Peter stood waiting, waiting for something to happen.

The Aboriginal was in no hurry. Time had little value to him. His next meal – the rock wallaby – was assured. Water was near. Tomorrow was also a day. For the moment he was content to examine these strange creatures at his leisure. Their clumsy[10] movements intrigued him; their lack of weapons indicated their harmlessness[11]. His eyes moved slowly, methodically, from one to another, examining them from head to foot. They were the first white people a member of his tribe had ever seen. Mary intensified her glare. But the bush boy seemed in no way perturbed.

What are the strategies adopted by Mary, Peter and the Aboriginal?

After a while, Peter started to fidget[12]. He wished someone would do something, wished something would happen. Then, quite involuntarily, he himself started a new train of events. He sneezed. It was a mighty sneeze for such a little fellow. To his sister the sneeze was a calamity. She had just intensified her stare to the point – she felt sure – of irresistibility, when the spell was shattered[13]. The bush boy's attention shifted from her to Peter. A second sneeze, even mightier than the first, shattered the silence of the bush.

Mary raised her eyes to heaven. Then a new sound made her whirl round. A gust of laughter, melodious laughter, low at first, then becoming louder, unrestrained, disproportionate, uncontrolled. She looked at the bush boy in amazement. He was doubled up with spasms of mirth[14].

Peter's sneeze had touched off one of his people's most highly-developed traits: a sense of the ridiculous. The bush boy laughed with complete abandon. He flung himself to the ground in unrestrained delight.

His mirth was infectious. It woke in Peter an instant response. The guilt that the little boy had started to feel melted away. At first apologetically, then whole-heartedly, he too started to laugh.

The barrier of twenty thousand years vanished in the twinkling of an eye.

What "event" manages to break the ice?

Walkabout, James Vance MARSHALL (1959)

1. *affleurements*
2. *englouti*
3. *modèle*
4. *couvé, dorloté*
5. *cultures*
6. *totalement*
7. *marais salant asséché*
8. *s'en aller furtivement*
9. *lancer un regard furieux*
10. *maladroits*
11. *caractère inoffensif*
12. *gigoter, remuer avec impatience*
13. *lorsque le charme fut brisé*
14. *fou rire, hilarité*

King John and the Abbot

There was once a king of England whose name was John. He was a bad king; for he was harsh and cruel to his people. He was the worst king that England ever had.

Now, there was in the town of Canterbury a rich old abbot[1] who lived in grand style in a great house called the Abbey. When King John heard of the way in which the abbot lived, he made up his mind to put a stop to it. So he sent for the old man to come and see him.

"How now, my good abbot?" he said. "I hear that you keep a far better house than I. How dare you do such a thing? Don't you know that no man in the land ought to live better than the king? And I tell you that no man shall."

"O king!" said the abbot, "I beg to say that I am spending nothing but what is my own. I hope that you will not think ill of me for making things pleasant for my friends and the brave knights[2] who are with me."

"Think ill of you?" said the king. "How can I help but think ill of you? All that there is in this broad land is mine by right; and how do you dare to put me to shame by living in grander style than I? One would think that you were trying to be king in my place."

"Oh, do not say so!" said the abbot. "For I…"

"Not another word!" cried the king. "Your fault is plain[3], and unless you can answer me three questions, your head shall be cut off, and all your riches shall be mine."

"I will try to answer them, O king!" said the abbot.

"Well, then," said King John, "as I sit here with my crown of gold on my head, you must tell me to within a day just how long I shall live. Secondly, you must tell me how soon I shall ride round the whole world; and lastly, you shall tell me what I think."

"O king!" said the abbot, "these are deep, hard questions, and I cannot answer them just now. But if you will give me two weeks to think about them, I will do the best that I can."

"Two weeks you shall have," said the king; "but if then you fail to answer me, you shall lose your head, and all your lands shall be mine."

The abbot went away very sad and in great fear. He rode to Oxford and Cambridge to see if any of the wise[4] professors could help him. But they shook their heads, and said that there was nothing about King John in any of their books.

At last, sad and sorrowful[5], he rode toward home to bid his friends and his brave knights good-bye. For now he had not a week to live.

As the abbot was riding up the lane which led to his grand house, he met his shepherd[6] going to the fields.

"Welcome home, good master!" cried the shepherd. "What news do you bring us from great King John?"

This is an old English folk-tale or ballad dating back at least to the 16th century. It is a good example of a riddle[1] song, aimed at audiences of all ages, and probably meant to suggest how important basic common sense and instinctive intelligence are.

1. *énigme*

"Sad news, sad news," said the abbot; and then he told him all that had happened.

"Cheer up, cheer up, good master," said the shepherd. "Have you never yet heard that a fool may teach a wise man wit[7]? I think I can help you out of your trouble."

"You help me!" cried the abbot. "How? how?"

"Well," answered the shepherd, "you know that everybody says that I look just like you, and that I have sometimes been mistaken for you. So, lend me your servants and your horse and your gown[8], and I will go up to London and see the king. If nothing else can be done, I can at least die in your place."

"My good shepherd," said the abbot, "you are very, very kind; and I have a mind to let you try your plan."

So the shepherd got ready to go at once. He dressed himself with great care. When all was ready, no one in the world would have thought that he was not the great man himself. Then he mounted his horse, and set out for London.

Of course the king did not know him.

"Welcome, Sir Abbot!" he said. "It is a good thing that you have come back. But, prompt as you are, if you fail to answer my three questions, you shall lose your head."

"I am ready to answer them, O king!" said the shepherd.

"Indeed, indeed!" said the king, and he laughed to himself. "Well, then, answer my first question: How long shall I live? Come, you must tell me to the very day."

"You shall live," said the shepherd, "until the day that you die, and not one day longer. And you shall die when you take your last breath, and not one moment before."

The king laughed.

"You are witty[9], I see," he said. "But we will let that pass, and say that your answer is right. And now tell me how soon I may ride round the world."

"You must rise with the sun," said the shepherd, "and you must ride with the sun until it rises again the next morning. As soon as you do that, you will find that you have ridden round the world in twenty-four hours."

The king laughed again. "Indeed," he said, "I did not think that it could be done so soon. You are not only witty, but you are wise, and we will let this answer pass. And now comes my third and last question: What do I think?"

"That is an easy question," said the shepherd. "You think that I am the abbot of Canterbury. But, to tell you the truth, I am only his poor shepherd, and I have come to beg your pardon for him and for me." And with that, he threw off his long gown.

The king laughed loud and long.

"A merry fellow you are," said he, "and you shall be the abbot of Canterbury in your master's place."

"O king! that cannot be," said the shepherd; "for I can neither read nor write."

"Very well, then," said the king, "I will give you something else to pay you for this merry joke. I will give you four pieces of silver every week as long as you live. And when you get home, you may tell the old abbot that you have brought him a free pardon from King John."

Fifty Famous Stories Retold, James BALDWIN (2005)

1. *abbé*
2. *chevaliers*
3. *évidente*
4. *sages*
5. *mélancolique*
6. *berger*
7. *intelligence*
8. *robe, toge*
9. *spirituel*

The Great Gatsby

F. Scott FITZGERALD (1896-1940)

A US writer of novels and short stories about the Jazz Age, a term he invented. The useless fun and immoral behaviour that were common in those years are described in his best-known novel, *The Great Gatsby* (1925). Fitzgerald and his wife Zelda (1900-1948) lived a wild life themselves.
In 1936, Fitzgerald moved to Hollywood to write films.

From Gatz to Gatsby

Gastby's notoriety, spread about by the hundreds who had accepted his hospitality and so become authorities upon his past, had increased all summer until he fell just short of being news.

James Gatz – that was really, or at least legally, his name. He had changed it at the age of seventeen and at the specific moment that witnessed the beginning of his career – when he saw Dan Cody's yacht drop anchor over the most insidious flat on Lake Superior. It was James Gatz who had been loafing along the beach that afternoon in a torn green jersey and a pair of canvas pants, but it was already Jay Gatsby who borrowed a rowboat, pulled out the Tuolomee, and informed Cody that a wind might catch him and break him up in half an hour.

I suppose he'd had the name ready for a long time, even then. His parents were shiftless[1] and unsuccessful farm people – his imagination had never really accepted them as his parents at all. So he invented just the sort of Jay Gatsby that a seventeen-year-old boy would be likely to invent, and to this conception he was faithful[2] to the end.

An instinct toward his future glory had led him, some months before, to the small Lutheran College of St. Olaf's in southern Minnesota. He stayed there two weeks, dismayed[3] at its ferocious indifference to the drums of his destiny, to destiny itself, and despising[4] the janitor's[5] work with which he was to pay his way through. Then he drifted back to Lake Superior, and he was still searching for something to do on the day that Dan Cody's yacht dropped anchor in the shallows[6] alongshore.

Cody was fifty years old then, a product of the Nevada silver fields, of the Yukon, of every rush for metal since seventy-five. The transactions in Montana copper[7] that made him many times a millionaire found him physically robust but on the verge of[8] soft-mindedness, and, suspecting this, an infinite number of women tried to separate him from his money.

To young Gatz, resting on his oars[9], and looking up at the railed deck, that yacht represented all the beauty and glamour in the world. I suppose he smiled at Cody – he had probably discovered that people liked him when he smiled. At any rate, Cody asked him a few questions (one of them elicited the brand-new name) and found that he was quick and extravagantly ambitious. A few days later he took him to Duluth and bought him a blue coat, six pairs of white duck trousers, and a yatching cap. And when the Tuolomee left for the West Indies and the Barbary Coast Gatsby left too. [...]

1. *paresseux*
2. *fidèle*
3. *consterné*
4. *mépriser*
5. *gardien*
6. *hauts-fonds*
7. *cuivre*
8. *au bord de*
9. *avirons*

Parties and speculations

There was music from my neighbour's house through the summer nights. In his blue gardens men and girls came and went like moths among the whisperings and the champagne and the stars.

I believe that on the first night I went to Gatsby's house I was one of the few guests who had actually been invited. People were not invited – they went there. They got into automobiles which bore them out to Long Island, and somehow they ended up at Gatsby's door. Once they were introduced by somebody who knew Gatsby, and after that they conducted themselves according to the rules of behaviour associated with an amusement park. Sometimes they came and went without having met Gatsby at all, came for the party with a simplicity of heart that was its own ticket of admission.

As soon as I arrived I made an attempt[1] to find my host, but the two or three people of whom I asked his whereabouts[2] stared at me in such an amazed way, and denied so vehemently any knowledge of his movements, that I slunk off in the direction of the cocktail table – the only place in the garden where a single man could linger without looking purposeless and alone.

I was on my way to get roaring drunk from sheer embarrassment when Jordan Baker came out of the house and stood at the head of the marble steps, leaning a little backward and looking with contemptuous interest down into the garden.

"Do you come to these parties often?" inquired Jordan of the girl beside her.

"I like to come," Lucille said. "I never care what I do, so I always have a good time. When I was here last, I tore my gown[3] on a chair, and he asked me my name and address – inside of a week I got a package from Croirier's with a new evening gown in it. Two hundred and sixty-five dollars."

"There's something funny about a fellow that'll do a thing like that," said the other girl eagerly[4]. "He doesn't want any trouble with anybody."

"Who doesn't?" I inquired.

"Gatsby. Somebody told me..."

The two girls and Jordan leaned together confidentially.

"Somebody told me they thought he killed a man once."

"I don't think it's so much that," argued Lucille sceptically; "it's more that he was a German spy[5] during the war."

"Oh, no," said the first girl, "it couldn't be that, because he was in the American army during the war." As our credulity switched back to her she leaned forward with enthusiasm. "You look at him sometimes when he thinks nobody's looking at him. I'll bet he killed a man." [...]

1. tenter
2. demander où il se trouve
3. robe du soir
4. avec empressement
5. espion

The end of a myth

After Gatsby was murdered by a man who believed he was his wife's lover, his father came to his place for the funeral.

I found Mr Gatz walking up and down excitedly in the hall. His pride in his son and his son's possessions was continually increasing and now he had something to show me.

"Jimmy sent me this picture." It was a photograph of the house, cracked in the corners and dirty with many hands. "I think it's a very pretty picture. It shows up well."

"Very well. Had you seen him lately?"

"He came out to see me two years ago and bought me the house I live in now. Of course he was broke up[1] when he run off from home, but I see now there was a reason for it. He knew he had a big future in front of him. And ever since he made a success he was very generous with me."

"Look here, this is a book he had when he was a boy. It just shows you."

He opened it at the back cover and turned it around for me to see. On the last fly-leaf[2] was printed the word SCHEDULE[3], and the date September 12, 1906. And underneath:

Rise from bed	6 A.M
Dumbbell[4] exercise and wall-scaling[5]	6.15-6.30 A.M.
Study electricity, etc.	7.15-8.15
Work	8.30-4.30 P.M.
Baseball and sports	4.30-5.00
Practise elocution, pose and how to attain it	5.00-6.00
Study needed inventions	7.00-9.00

GENERAL RESOLVES
No wasting time at Shafers or [a name, indecipherable]
No more smokeing or chewing
Bath every other day
Read one improving book or magazine per week
Save $5.00 [crossed out] $3.00 per week
Be better to parents

"I came across this book by accident," said the old man. "It just shows you, don't it? Jimmy was bound[6] to get ahead. He always had some resolves like this or something. Do you notice what he's got about improving his mind? He was always great for that."

A little before three the Lutheran minister arrived from Flushing, and I began to look involuntarily out the windows for other cars. So did Gatsby's father. And as the time passed and the servants came in and stood waiting in the hall, his eyes began to blink anxiously, and he spoke of the rain in a worried, uncertain way. The minister glanced several times at his watch, so I took him aside and asked him to wait for half an hour. But it wasn't any use. Nobody came.

The Great Gatsby, F. Scott FITZGERALD (1925)

1. *déchiré*
2. *page de garde*
3. *programme*
4. *haltères*
5. *agrès*
6. *destiné*

Culture keys

Unit 1

Gap year

→ p. 16

A gap year is a period of time – from several weeks to a year or more – when students break from formal education to do something else such as gain work experience, travel, volunteer abroad, etc.

The concept was born in the UK and, since the 1990s, taking time out has become increasingly popular with British and American students.

More and more young people from diverse backgrounds are taking a gap year and it is not the prerogative of affluent middle classes any more. An estimated 200,000 British students aged 18-25 set off on gap years in 2008.

Comenius programme

→ p. 21

The Comenius Programme, part of the European Union's Lifelong Learning Programme, is named after Jan Amos Comenius (1592-1670), a Czech educator, often considered the father of modern education.

It has two main objectives: to improve young people's understanding of the range of European cultures and languages and to help them acquire the basic skills necessary for personal development, future employment and active citizenship.

The Comenius programme focuses on:

– increasing pupil mobility across the European Union (EU);

– developing partnerships between schools in different EU Member States, with at least 3 million pupils;

– encouraging language learning, based on innovative IT[1] methods.

33 countries across Europe have joined the Comenius Programme.

1. Information Technology

Kenya

→ p. 18

- A Republic in East Africa
- Population: 39 million approx.
- Capital city: Nairobi

Human history in Kenya dates back two million years. More than forty ethnic groups live there including the Kikuyu and Maasai. The land became a German protectorate in 1885, then a British protectorate in 1890 and a British Crown colony in 1920. Kenya gained independence after a long struggle in 1963.

Kenya: Kilimanjaro (5,895 m) in the background

A series of disasters plagued Kenya in the 1990s: flooding, epidemics of malaria and cholera, ethnic clashes, economic difficulties, corruption...

Today Kenya's economy is the largest by GDP[1] in East Africa. Long based on agriculture (tea and coffee) the country has developed an important horticultural industry and is becoming more and more industrialized (telecommunications sector). It is also a renowned tourist destination; its beautiful beaches and animal reserves attract a lot of German and British tourists.

1. gross domestic product

Tasmania

→ p. 22

- A state in the Australian federation
- Population: 507,000 approx.
- Capital city: Hobart

Tasmania is an island off the south-eastern coast of the Australian continent. Originally inhabited by Australian Aborigines, it was explored by Abel J. Tasman in 1642. Taken by the British in the early 1800s and made a colony in 1825, it was used as a penal settlement until the 1850s. It became part of the Commonwealth of Australia in 1901.

Tasmania's flora and fauna is extremely diverse. The island is home to the oldest and tallest trees in the world (the Eucalyptus Regnans) and to the Tasmanian devil, a carnivorous marsupial found exclusively in Tasmania.

A Tasmanian devil

Unit 2

Winston CHURCHILL (1874-1965) → p. 32

Sir Winston Churchill was a British politician and statesman known for his leadership of the United Kingdom during World War II. He had won early fame as a war correspondent in the late 19th century. When

the Second World War broke out, he was appointed First Lord of the Admiralty. In May 1940, he became Prime Minister (PM) and Minister of Defence and remained in office until 1945. He took over the premiership again after the Conservative victory of 1951 and resigned in 1955. His refusal to consider or admit defeat during WWII, as well as his speeches and radio broadcasts helped inspire British confidence and resistance. He is the only British PM to be awarded the Nobel Prize in Literature (1953). He was also the only British PM to have been made an honorary citizen of the United States by President Kennedy in 1963. In 1965 Queen Elizabeth II granted him the honour of a state funeral. He was buried in Bladon, England. A BBC survey in January 2000 voted Sir Winston the greatest British Prime Minister of the 20th century.

Emmeline PANKHURST (1858-1928) → p. 33

She was a leading activist and a figurehead[1] for the British Suffragette Movement. In 1903 she founded the Women's Social and Political Union (WSPU), a radical organization which advocated acts of civil

disobedience. Its members carried out minor offences – chaining themselves to railings[2], setting fire to pillar boxes[3], smashing windows – to draw attention to their cause. Emmeline Pankhurst was imprisoned several times and endured force feeding after going on hunger strike. She was joined in her struggle[4] by her daughters Christabel and Sylvia. When Mrs Pankhurst died in 1928, all women in Britain had just won equal voting rights.

1. *chef de file* 2. *grilles* 3. *boîtes aux lettres* 4. *combat*

William WILBERFORCE (1759-1833) → p. 33

He was one of Britain's greatest social reformers and he served in the British Parliament from 1780 to 1825. He is best known for his active and untiring participation in getting Parliament to outlaw and abolish the slave trade throughout the British Empire. He introduced his first anti-slave trade motion in the House of Commons in 1788. The motion was defeated eleven times before the Slave Trade Act was finally passed in 1807. This act only made the slave trade illegal. Wilberforce supported the campaign for the complete abolition of slavery, and continued his involvement after 1826, when he resigned from Parliament because of his failing health. He kept campaigning against slavery, until the Slavery Abolition Act was passed through the House of Commons on July 26th 1833, just three days before he died. This Act gave freedom to all slaves in the British Empire.

Unit 3

The Model T / The Tin Lizzie

→ p. 50, 56

The **Ford Model T** (also known as the **Tin Lizzie**) is an automobile that was produced by Henry Ford's Ford Motor Company from 1908 to 1927.

The Model T was the first assembly-line car applying mass production techniques on a vast scale. This simple, affordable car brought motoring to the common middle-class American. It was produced until 1927 by which time more than 15 million models had been sold.

In 1927 the Department of Commerce census figures recorded a world total of 27,650,267 cars, of which 22,137,334, or about 80 per cent of the total, were owned by Americans.

Mythical roads

→ p. 52, 54

Route 6, also called the Grand Army of the Republic Highway, runs from Provincetown (near Boston), Massachusetts, to Long Beach (near Los Angeles), California. It is one of the longest highways in the USA (5,878 km). Route 6 goes through fourteen states, 109 counties, and 5 state capitals. In its transcontinental days, Route 6 intersected with Route 66 in two places: downtown Joliet and downtown Los Angeles.

Route 66 was the main road from Chicago to Los Angeles between 1926 and the 1960s. Many migrants going west travelled along Route 66. An estimated 210,000 people migrated to California to escape the despair of the Dust Bowl[1] in the 1930s. In John Steinbeck's novel *The Grapes of Wrath*, the highway is called "The Mother Road".

It then became a symbol of Americans' freedom of movement. A hit song, *Route 66*, was first recorded in 1946 by Nat King Cole, and has since been performed by nearly one hundred singers or groups. *Route 66* was also the name of a famous television show in the 1960s. Route 66 is 3,940 kilometres long.

1. series of severe dust storms *(tempêtes de poussière)* which affected American prairie lands, particularly in Texas and Oklahoma

Herbert HOOVER (1874-1964)

→ p. 56

Herbert Hoover was the 31st President of the United States. He served from 1929 to 1933.

When the stock market crashed in 1929, Hoover proved to be tough on the American people. He announced that he would keep a balanced budget but, to offer relief, he would cut taxes and increase public works spending. But tax relief for someone without a job was meaningless. That is why he is still thought of as an unfeeling man.

Hoover died at the age of 90 on October 20, 1964 in New York City.

Unit 4

Recession

→ p. 70

The financial crisis of 2007 to the present day was caused by a liquidity shortfall[1] in the United States banking system. It has resulted in the collapse[2] of large financial institutions, the bailout[3] of banks by national governments, and downturns in stock markets[4] around the world. In many areas, the housing market has also suffered, resulting in numerous evictions and foreclosures[5]. It is considered by many economists to be the worst financial crisis since the Great Depression of the 1930s.

1. *manque de trésorerie* 2. *chute* 3. *renflouement*
4. *baisse des marchés financiers* 5. *saisies*

McMansions

→ p. 71

A McMansion is a large new house with a mixture of styles which is judged as pretentious, tasteless or badly designed for its neighbourhood. The term McMansion compares the quality of these pseudo-luxury homes with mass-produced meals. Other terms for this type of house: Persian palace, garage Mahal.

The Jazz Age
The Roaring Twenties

→ p. 72

The name "Jazz Age" comes from the book *Tales of the Jazz Age* (1922) by F. Scott Fitzgerald. It refers to the 1920s, also called "the Roaring Twenties", a period with exciting new developments in fashion, art and music (especially jazz) and when Prohibition and flappers appeared in the USA. The Jazz Age, which started at the end of the war thanks to main stream radio and continued until the beginning of the Great Depression, has lived on in American pop culture for decades.

Prohibition, from 1919 to 1933, meant that it was illegal by national law to make or sell alcoholic drinks. Prohibition was so unpopular and so bad for business that the law was often disobeyed. It also produced criminals like Al Capone who made and sold alcohol. A few states kept prohibition laws for several years, and some counties in some states still have them.

Flappers were the typical women of the 1920s. Among the most famous were actress Louise Brooks and Zelda Sayre (F. Scott Fitzgerald's wife). They had short hair, wore short dresses, drank alcohol and enjoyed smoking and dancing, especially the Charleston. Because they developed ideas such as equality and sexual freedom, many people thought they were immoral, but they are now regarded as the first modern, independent women.

The Great Depression

→ p. 72

The Great Depression is the period of severe economic failure in most countries that lasted from 1929 until World War II. It began in the US when The New York Stock Exchange crashed on October 29th 1929, known as Black Tuesday. Many businesses and banks failed and millions of people lost their jobs. President Franklin D. Roosevelt improved the situation with his New Deal Policy, but the Great Depression only came to an end thanks to increased industrial production for the Second World War.

Unit 5

South Africa

→ p. 84, 86

- Republic of South Africa
- Capital city: Pretoria
- Largest cities: Johannesburg, Cape Town, Durban
- Population: 50.5 million (UN, 2010)
- Official languages: 11 official languages including English, Afrikaans, Sesotho, Setswana, Xhosa and Zulu

Often referred to as "the Rainbow nation", South Africa is a very racially diverse country. Black South Africans account for almost 80% of the population and the country has a very large population of Coloureds (people of mixed origins), Europeans and Indians. South Africa was ruled from 1948 to 1992 by an all-white government under the system of apartheid ("separateness" in Afrikaans), which separated people of different races and gave black people no political rights, forcing them to live in townships. Countries all over the world condemned this policy and South Africa had to leave the British Commonwealth in 1960. In the 1980s, several countries imposed trade sanctions, and in 1992, the government was forced to accept the dismantling of apartheid and to call for a general election. In 1994, the African National Congress, led by Nelson Mandela, won South Africa's first democratic election and Nelson Mandela became the first post-apartheid black President, followed by Thabo Mbeki in 1999 and 2004. Jacob Zuma, elected in 2009, is the current President.

Nelson Mandela

Nelson Mandela (b. 1918) joined the ANC in 1942 and soon got involved in the struggle against the apartheid regime. Arrested in 1964, he was convicted of sabotage, sentenced to life imprisonment and incarcerated at Robben Island Prison, off Cape Town. Released in February 1990, he negotiated the dismantling of apartheid. In 1993, he was awarded the Nobel Peace Prize "for laying the foundations for a new democratic South Africa". In 1999 he retired from politics and since then has defended numerous social and humanitarian causes.

Stephen Biko (1946-1977) was one of South Africa's best-known activists. He developed a national "Black Consciousness" movement to fight racism and apartheid. Arrested in 1977, he died in police custody, prompting international protests and a UN embargo. In 1997, five former policemen admitted killing him.

Aboriginal Australians

→ p. 89, 94

The first Australians were the Aborigines (i.e. "the original inhabitants of the country"). The Aborigines have the longest continuous cultural history of any group of people on Earth. They were sent to reservations and forced to live off government hand-outs[1]. They only got the right to vote in 1967.

1. *aumônes*

The Stolen Generation

→ p. 90

It is a term used to refer to the 35,000 Aboriginal half-caste[1] children who were forcibly removed[2] from their families by the Australian government between 1900 and 1972. These children were taken away to white settlements and schools to be assimilated and "civilized". They were raised in white foster families[3] to work as servants or farmhands. On February 13th 2008, Prime Minister Kevin Rudd gave a speech in Parliament, in which he apologized to the Stolen Generation.

1. *métis* 2. *enlever* 3. *familles d'accueil*

Unit 6

Global refugee trends

→ p. 100

Annual figures released by the United Nations refugee agency show that some 43.3 million people were forcibly displaced worldwide at the end of 2009, the highest number of people uprooted by conflict and persecution since the mid-1990s.

At the same time, according to the 2009 Global Trends report, the number of refugees voluntarily returning to their home countries has fallen to its lowest level in 20 years (source: UNHCR, June 15th 2010).

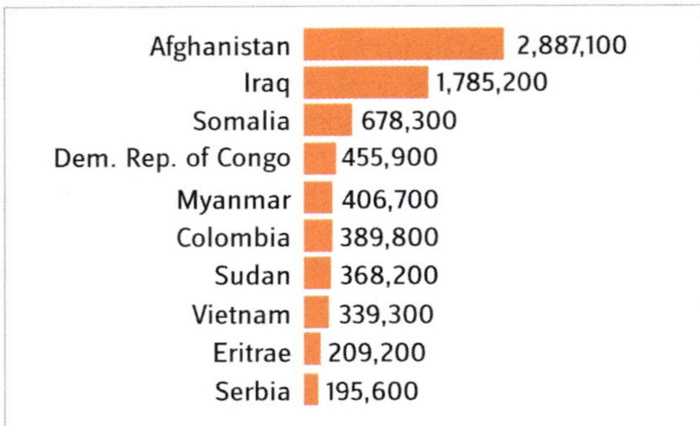

Major source countries of refugees (end 2009) (Source: UNHCR)

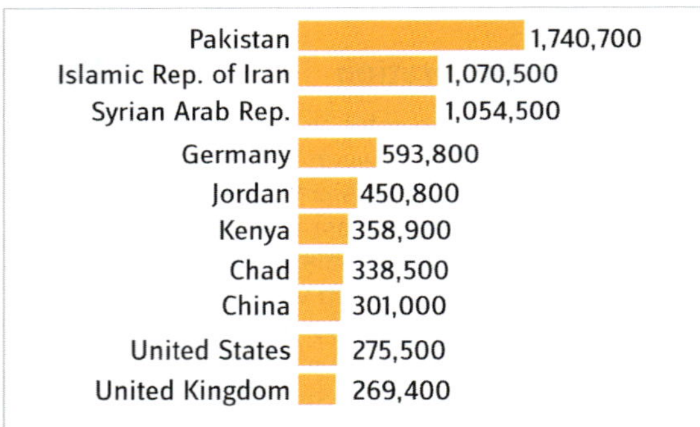

Major refugee hosting countries (end 2009) (Source: UNHCR)

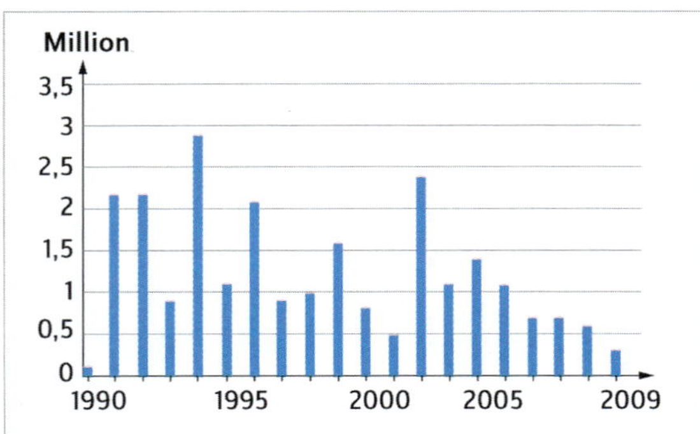

Refugee returns (1990-2009) (Source: UNHCR)

The US-Mexico border

→ p. 101

The US-Mexico border fence or border wall has been designed to prevent illegal immigration from Mexico and Latin America. Fences, walls, vehicle barriers and high-tech surveillance towers have been constructed at various places along the dusty, 1,952-mile (3,141 kilometres) boundary. In San Diego, 9 miles (14 kilometres) of a double-layered fence have been erected. In Arizona, the state most concerned by illegal crossings, 65 miles (105 kilometres) of barriers have been constructed already.

Opponents say the border fence is an ineffective deterrent[1]. They denounce the dangers of the fence for migrants who keep trying to cross the border to the US, as well as the threat for animal habitat.

1. *moyen de dissuasion*

Nigeria

→ p. 102

- A federal republic in West Africa
- Population: 154,729,000 inhabitants (8th most populous country in the world)
- Capital city: Abuja
- Largest city: Lagos

Nigerian history dates back to the 5th century BC when the Nok people, who produced beautiful terra-cotta sculptures, inhabited central Nigeria. The Portuguese and the Spaniards were the first Europeans to begin trade in Nigeria.

In the 1800s, the British started to reside in parts of the region. They annexed Lagos in 1851 and, by 1886, had seized control of the rest of the country. In 1914, it formally became the Colony and Protectorate of Nigeria, named after the big Niger river which runs through it. Nigeria obtained its independence in 1960 and became a republic in 1963. It is a member of the Commonwealth of Nations. A series of ethnic conflicts ravaged the country in the 1960s. A civil war with Biafra (1966-1970), the eastern region which had declared itself independent, caused 1 million deaths. After a series of military coups and almost 33 years of military rule, Nigeria went back to democracy in 1999 (although the international community condemned the latest elections for being flawed[1]).

Today, Nigeria is the third largest economy in Africa. It is the eighth largest oil-producer in the world, has one of the fastest growing telecommunications markets and an expanding financial services sector.

1. *frauduleuses*

Unit 7

The glass ceiling

→ p. 118

A glass ceiling is an invisible but real barrier through which the next level of advancement can be seen, but cannot be reached by a section of qualified employees. Such barriers exist due to implicit prejudice on the basis of age, ethnicity, handicap or illness, political or religious affiliation or sex. Although generally illegal, such practices exist in most countries.

The first documented use of the term appeared in an Adweek article in 1984. While the term may be casually used, the Department of Labor took it very seriously in 1991 when they issued a definition of it, stating that a glass ceiling is made up of "artificial barriers based on attitudinal or organizational bias that prevent qualified individuals from advancing upward in their organization into management-level positions."

Slavery in the USA

→ p. 120

1492: Christopher Columbus' voyage to the Americas.

1619: Virginia, first British colony, imports African slaves.

17th-18th century: Cotton and tobacco plantations established mainly in the South. Workforce provided by "chattel slavery" (ownership of a slave and his descendants).

16th to 19th century: 12 million Africans shipped as slaves to the Americas, 645,000 to the USA.

End of 18th century: Concept of "free states" and "slave states" established.

1860: Slave population in the USA had grown to 4 million.

1861-1865: Civil War. The South (Confederates) fought in order to maintain slavery – in their view the only system which would allow their economy to flourish. The North (Unionists) fought not only to preserve the unity of their country, but also to put an end to the unfair, inhuman system of slavery.

1865: 13th Amendment: Slavery abolished.

The USA in 1860.

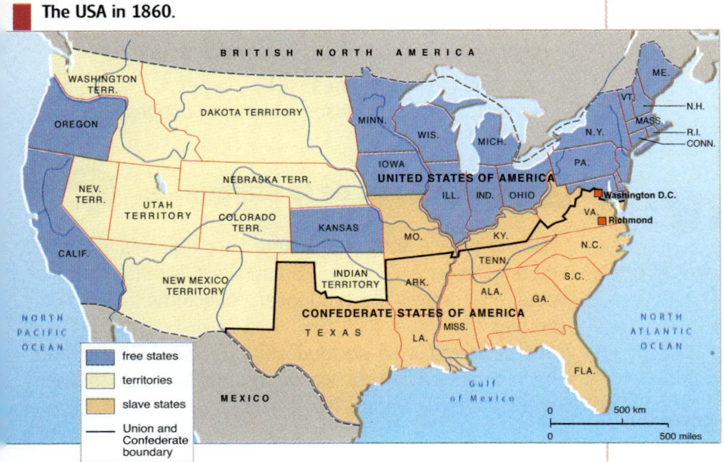

Orwell's political satires

→ p. 124

Animal Farm is a political satire of a totalitarian society ruled by a powerful dictatorship, an allegory of the Russian Revolution of 1917. The animals of "Manor Farm" revolt against their cruel human master and take control of the farm. However, despite their egalitarian principles, little by little, the pigs become dominant, gaining more power over the other animals, so much so that they become as corrupt and power-hungry as their predecessors, the humans. *Animal Farm* maintains that in every society there are leaders who, if given the opportunity, will abuse their power.

In *Nineteen Eighty-Four*, Britain is ruled by the Party, led by Big Brother whose image is ever-present. Everyone is permanently watched, and the Party's agents constantly rewrite history to suit their purposes and redesign language so that they can control people's thoughts absolutely. Winston Smith, a minor Party member, commits thought crimes by keeping a secret diary. He is interrogated by the Party with such cruelty that his spirit is broken. He surrenders his identity to the state and learns to love Big Brother. *Nineteen Eighty-Four* is considered as a bitter warning against the dangers of allowing governments to have so much power that the rights of the individual totally disappear.

Écouter et prononcer

WORKBOOK → p. 59-61

CONSEILS

Il est essentiel de connaître les symboles phonétiques afin de bien prononcer les mots. Nous utilisons partout ces symboles, en particulier dans les *Keywords* et les *Toolbox*. Vous trouverez les tableaux des symboles phonétiques sur le rabat V de votre manuel.

PRONONCER LES MOTS

A Symboles phonétiques

CD 3 12

Prononcez d'abord les six mots ci-dessous à haute voix sans regarder les transcriptions phonétiques. Puis prononcez-les en regardant les transcriptions phonétiques. Vérifiez ensuite à l'écoute.

superficial – kangaroo – catastrophe – roughly – pronunciation – psychology

superficial /ˌsuːpəˈfɪʃəl/ – *kangaroo* /ˌkæŋɡəˈruː/ – *catastrophe* /kəˈtæstrəfɪ/ – *roughly* /ˈrʌflɪ/ – *pronunciation* /prəˌnʌnsɪˈeɪʃən/ – *psychology* /saɪˈkɒlədʒɪ/

B Prononciation de la marque -*s*

CD 3 13-14

Écoutez ces deux phrases en prêtant attention à la prononciation des ***s*** en gras. Que remarquez-vous ?

Nou**s** n'avon**s** toujour**s** pa**s** vu leur**s** troi**s** cousin**s**.

*Peter'**s** friend like**s** to tell all sort**s** of storie**s** about knight**s**.*

Alors qu'en français le « s » final ne se prononce que rarement, en anglais la terminaison -***s*** des noms au pluriel, du génitif et de la 3e personne du singulier du présent se prononce systématiquement :

- /z/ après la plupart des consonnes sonores et toutes les voyelles :
  → *computers* /kəmˈpjuːtəz/ – *gardens* /ˈɡɑːdnz/ – *beds* /bedz/ – *days* /deɪz/
- /s/ après les consonnes sourdes /k/, /p/, /t/, /f/ et /θ/ :
  → *desks* /desks/ – *pipes* /paɪps/ – *lots* /lɒts/ – *photographs* /ˈfəʊtəɡræfs/ – *months* /mʌnθs/
- /ɪz/ après les consonnes /s/, /z/, /ʒ/ et /ʃ/ :
  → *misses* /ˈmɪsɪz/ – *roses* /ˈrəʊzɪz/ – *bridges* /ˈbrɪdʒɪz/ – *matches* /ˈmætʃɪz/

C Prononciation de la marque -*ed*

CD 3 15-17

Lisez la phrase suivante à haute voix, puis vérifiez votre prononciation à l'écoute. Pourquoi est-il parfois difficile pour un Français de prononcer correctement les mots en gras ?

*She **hesitated**, then **decided** it was too late. She **phoned** her friend to tell him she was **tired**, **swallowed** a sandwich and **watched** a film on TV.*

En anglais, la marque ***-ed*** se prononce de trois manières différentes :

- /d/ après toutes les voyelles et la plupart des consonnes sonores :
  → *played* /pleɪd/ – *moved* /muːvd/ – *offered* /'ɒfəd/ – *followed* /'fɒləʊd/ – *explained* /ɪk'spleɪnd/
- /t/ après les consonnes /p/, /f/, /s/, /k/ et /ʃ/ :
  → *stopped* /stɒpt/ – *bluffed* /blʌft/ – *missed* /mɪst/ – *looked* /lʊkt/ – *blushed* /blʌʃt/
- /ɪd/ uniquement après /t/ ou /d/. Il y a alors une syllabe de plus à la base verbale :
  → *participated* /pɑː'tɪsɪpeɪtɪd/ – *commanded* /kə'mɑːndɪd/

Remarque : La terminaison de certains **adjectifs** en ***-ed*** ne suit pas cette règle et se prononce /ɪd/, même si ces adjectifs sont de la même famille que le verbe.

Adjectifs	Forme verbale
– *a learned* /'lɜːnɪd/ *man*: un érudit	– *She's learned* /lɜːnd/ *her lesson.*
– *a crooked* /'krʊkɪd/ *business*: une affaire véreuse	– *I crooked* /krʊkt/ (plier) *my arm.*

Autres adjectifs dont la terminaison en ***-ed*** se prononce /ɪd/ : *beloved* /bɪ'lʌvɪd/: bien-aimé – *cursed* /'kɜːsɪd/: satané, maudit – *jagged* /'dʒægɪd/: déchiqueté – *naked* /'neɪkɪd/: nu – *sacred* /'seɪkrɪd/ – *wicked* /'wɪkɪd/: méchant, mauvais – *ragged* /'rægɪd/: en haillons

D Accent de mot

CD 3 18-19

Écoutez les paires de mots suivantes. Que remarquez-vous ?

Français	Anglais	Français	Anglais
nature	*nature*	situation	*situation*
géométrie	*geometry*	parasite	*parasite*
automobile	*automobile*	respectable	*respectable*

- Contrairement au français, les mots anglais de deux ou plusieurs syllabes comportent une syllabe accentuée, l'**accent de mot**. En phonétique, cette accentuation, appelée **accent principal**, est notée /'/ devant la syllabe accentuée :
  → *afraid* /ə'freɪd/ – *secretary* /'sekrətrɪ/ – *father* /'fɑːðə/ – *society* /sə'saɪətɪ/
- Dans les mots de plus de deux syllabes, il y a parfois un **accent secondaire** qui est noté /ˌ/ devant la syllabe accentuée :
  → *scientifically* /ˌsaɪən'tɪfɪkəlɪ/ – *disappear* /ˌdɪsə'pɪə/

E Réduction des voyelles

CD 3 20-21

Écoutez la phrase suivante. Pourquoi certains mots sont-ils parfois difficiles à comprendre pour un Français ?

The p•licem•n s•ppos•d the burgl• had prob•bly ent•r•d the l•bor•t•ry a few min•tes aft• the man•g•.

Comme l'accent de mot ne porte en général que sur une syllabe, l'autre syllabe ou les autres syllabes du mot sont **faibles**. Leurs voyelles se réduisent le plus souvent à /ə/ ou /ɪ/ :

→ *afraid* /ə'freɪd/ – *disappoint* /ˌdɪsə'pɔɪnt/ – *computer* /kəm'pjuːtə/ – *actor* /'æktə/ – *postman* /'pəʊstmən/ – *busy* /'bɪzɪ/ – *position* /pə'zɪʃən/ – *comfortable* /'kʌmfətəbl/

F Les consonnes muettes

CD 3 22-23

Lisez le passage suivant à haute voix, puis écoutez-le. Que remarquez-vous ?

Listen, I know she's not dumb: she'll write or give you an answer next Wednesday. If she could walk, no doubt she would come today.

En anglais, certaines consonnes écrites ne se prononcent pas, en particulier :

b → *dou(b)t – de(b)t – dum(b) – clim(b) – lam(b) – tom(b)* /tuːm/ – *bom(b)*

d → *We(d)nesday – gran(d)father – han(d)kerchief – han(d)some*

k → *(k)now* (et ses dérivés) – *(k)nee – (k)nife – (k)nock*

h → *(h)our – (h)onour – (h)eir – (h)onest*

l → *wa(l)k – ha(l)f – ca(l)f – fo(l)k – ta(l)k – cou(l)d – shou(l)d – wou(l)d – Linco(l)n*

p → *(p)sychology* (et ses dérivés)

s → *i(s)land – i(s)le*

t → *cas(t)le – Chris(t)mas – lis(t)en*

w → *(w)rite* (et ses dérivés) – *ans(w)er – (w)ho – (w)hose*

PRONONCER LES PHRASES

A Accent de phrase (accent syntaxique)

CD 3 24-27

Écoutez les deux phrases ci-dessous et repérez les mots accentués. À votre avis, pourquoi sont-ils accentués ?

1. *What do you know about the history of England?*
2. *She saw him when she was in London.*

Tous les mots d'une phrase ne sont pas accentués. On accentue seulement les mots **nécessaires à la compréhension du message**. En fait, l'accentuation des mots dépend de plusieurs éléments : la catégorie syntaxique, la place des mots dans la phrase et la nouveauté de l'information.

1 Catégorie syntaxique

- **Les mots porteurs de sens sont accentués.** Ces mots sont les noms, verbes, adjectifs qualificatifs, adverbes, démonstratifs, mots interrogatifs, auxiliaires avec négation, pronoms possessifs, prépositions de plus d'une syllabe et les mots *yes, no, not.*
- **Les mots-outils ne sont pas accentués.** Ces mots-outils sont les articles, conjonctions, auxiliaires sans négation, déterminants possessifs, coordinations, pronoms personnels, relatifs et prépositions d'une syllabe.

→ ***What*** *would you have* ***done*** *if he had* ***talked*** *to you in the* ***street****?*

2 Place des mots dans la phrase

Comment prononcerez-vous le mot *at* ci-dessous dans chaque cas : forme pleine ou réduite ? Vérifiez à l'écoute.

Look ***at*** *the girl he is staring* ***at****!*

Les **mots-outils** d'une seule syllabe se prononcent de deux manières, en fonction de leur place dans la phrase.

- La voyelle se prononce avec la forme **pleine** en **début ou fin de phrase**.
- La voyelle se prononce avec la forme **réduite** (en général /ə/) **pour toute autre place dans la phrase**.

Exemples de formes pleines et réduites :

Forme pleine	Forme réduite
Do it when you can /kæn/.	*I can* /kən / kn/ *do it now.*
Who were you waiting for /fɔː/?	*I was waiting for* /fə/ *you.*

B Liaisons

CD 3 28-29

Quelles liaisons ferez-vous dans la phrase ci-dessous ? Vérifiez à l'écoute.

Come over as soon as possible. I need all of you.

En général, on fait la liaison entre deux mots lorsque le premier mot se termine par une consonne ou un e muet et que le second mot commence par une voyelle (le plus souvent non accentuée). Ainsi, *Switch it off* semble se prononcer *switchitoff.*

→ *I think_I heard_a noise. – What_is she afraid_of? – I'm scared_of the dark.*

C Intonation

CD 3 30-32

Écoutez les phrases ci-dessous. L'intonation est-elle montante ou descendante ?

1. *Has your sister arrived? When will she visit us?*
2. *Don't listen to him!*
3. *You're welcome.*

1 Intonation descendante (↘)

Elle traduit une idée de certitude : la voix descend.

- Déclarations positives ou négatives
  → *She's been waiting for hours.* ↘
- Interrogations ouvertes *(wh- questions)*
  → *Why did you refuse to do it?* ↘
- Ordres
  → *Stop arguing!* ↘
- Quand le *tag* n'est pas une vraie question
  → *He can speak German, can't he?* ↘

2 Intonation montante (↗)

Elle traduit une idée d'inachèvement, de sous-entendus ou de doute : la voix monte.

- Interrogations fermées *(Yes / No questions)*
  → *Are you flying to London?* ↗
- Pour faire répéter une réponse
  → *How many people?* ↗
- Quand le *tag* est une vraie question
  → *She came yesterday, didn't she?* ↗
- Énoncé non achevé, énumération
  → *They saw Peter* ↗... *Judith* ↗...

D Mise en relief

CD 3 33-34

Selon vous, quels mots seront particulièrement mis en relief dans les phrases ci-dessous ? Vérifiez à l'écoute.

1. *He likes her but she doesn't like him.*
2. *You didn't see me, but I was there.*

Dans un contexte particulier, tout mot peut être porteur d'un accent fort accompagné d'une intonation descendante. Un mot peut être accentué afin d'obtenir un effet de contraste, d'insistance ou pour montrer la surprise.

→ ***I*** *did it.* ***You*** *didn't.*

→ *This is* ***great****!*

→ *It isn't* ***that*** *interesting!*

→ *She's not his* ***wife****. She's just a* ***friend****.*

Cette mise en relief sera d'autant plus marquée que la voix opère une chute plus grande depuis l'aigu vers le grave.

E Groupes de sens

CD 3 35-36

Écoutez les deux phrases ci-dessous. Quelle phrase avez-vous entendue en premier, **1** ou **2** ?

1. *Oliver said, "Martha is fantastic."*
2. *"Oliver," said Martha, "is fantastic."*

- Une phrase est divisée en **groupes de sens**. Ces segments de phrases sont suivis d'une pause plus ou moins marquée (schématisée ci-dessous par / [pause facultative] ou // [pause obligatoire]). En français comme en anglais, ces pauses sont essentielles pour dégager le sens de la phrase.

- La ponctuation est une aide précieuse pour délimiter un groupe de sens. Les problèmes apparaissent quand les phrases dépassent une douzaine de syllabes et qu'il n'y a pas de virgule. Il faut alors comprendre le contexte pour savoir où marquer les arrêts et donner du sens à la phrase.

- Écoutez les passages ci-dessous en prêtant attention aux pauses dues aux groupes de sens.

  → *All I have to do // is type in / the address.*

  → *Holes in the wall // where windowpanes should have been // sent a chill through the room.*

  → *"You've got to // loudly and strongly / and probably with all kinds of paper // tell the White House / what you need," // said Florida Governor Lawton Chiles / after the hurricane.*

Compréhension de l'oral

WORKBOOK → p. 62-63

CONSEILS

1. La compréhension de l'oral est une compétence difficile à maîtriser. Ne vous inquiétez pas si vous ne comprenez pas immédiatement tout. Les locuteurs répètent souvent l'idée qu'ils développent sous des formes différentes.
2. Écoutez le plus souvent possible des chansons et des émissions de radio anglophones ainsi que des *podcasts* que l'on trouve sur Internet.
3. Regardez toujours les films et les séries télévisées en version originale (sous-titrée si nécessaire mais en anglais de préférence).

A Avant l'écoute

1 Anticiper

- Tenez compte de la situation (circonstances, aide visuelle, connaissance des locuteurs) qui facilite la compréhension.
- En classe, on vous fournit quelquefois de l'aide, à partir d'une image, d'un titre, qui vous permettront d'évoquer mentalement une situation, un thème, donc de mobiliser très naturellement les connaissances que vous avez déjà (lexique, repères culturels, expérience vécue).

B Première écoute

Pourquoi est-il important d'écouter un enregistrement jusqu'au bout lors de la première écoute ?

2 Repérer l'idée principale

Vous n'avez pas le temps de prendre de notes lors de la première écoute car cela vous empêcherait de suivre l'enregistrement jusqu'au bout. Concentrez-vous afin de repérer l'idée principale qui sera sans doute formulée différemment plusieurs fois.

3 Éviter de traduire

Il ne faut surtout pas traduire ce que vous entendez. Cela vous fera perdre du temps et le fil de la conversation. Il est tout à fait possible de comprendre sans traduire.

4 Utiliser tous les indices

Utilisez tous les indices qui vous permettront de mieux comprendre ce que vous écoutez :

- la nature du document : émission de radio, flash d'information, interview, débat, discours, dialogue, etc. ;
- le nombre de voix, l'identité des locuteurs (homme, femme, adulte, enfant, etc.) ;
- les indices sonores : accent, ton de la voix, musique, applaudissements, cris, bruits de fond, etc. ;
- la gestuelle éventuelle du locuteur, en particulier lorsque vous regardez des films ou des émissions de télévision.

C Écoutes suivantes

Vous pouvez maintenant prendre des notes, mais n'écrivez que quelques mots clés car un effort est nécessaire pour stocker mentalement les informations que vous entendez.

5 Faire des hypothèses sur le sens global d'un document

Fiez-vous à votre sens logique. Comme à l'écrit, il faut s'appuyer sur les éléments connus pour compenser l'inconnu.

Au fur et à mesure de l'écoute, vous allez anticiper et émettre des hypothèses sur la suite des événements en fonction des indices perçus et des premiers éléments reconnus. La suite de l'écoute vous permettra d'ajuster vos hypothèses. Vous serez ainsi amenés à construire du sens au fil de l'écoute.

Par exemple, en cours d'écoute, la reconnaissance des mots *soundtrack, special effects* et *hero* vous permet d'émettre l'hypothèse qu'il est question d'un film.

6 Repérer et mémoriser

Les mots sont-ils tous accentués avec la même intensité en anglais ?
L'intonation dans les questions est-elle toujours montante ?

- **La mise en relief**

Soyez attentifs aux mots particulièrement mis en relief. En effet, certains mots peuvent être prononcés avec emphase afin d'obtenir un effet de contraste, d'insistance ou pour exprimer certains sentiments (surprise, enthousiasme...). Cette mise en relief n'est pas systématique, mais quand elle apparaît, elle est particulièrement significative.

- **Les mots porteurs de sens**

Dans la chaîne parlée, certains mots sont plus accentués que d'autres : ce sont les noms, les verbes, les adverbes et les adjectifs. Repérez-les car ils sont porteurs d'informations essentielles.

- **L'intonation**

Repérez et interprétez l'intonation de certains énoncés que vous trouvez essentiels : l'intonation descendante donne une idée de certitude tandis que l'intonation montante implique le doute ou un énoncé inachevé (voir « Écouter et prononcer », p. 146).

- **Les indicateurs de temps**

Soyez attentifs aux dates qui fournissent souvent des informations utiles. Mais ce ne sont pas les seules indications du moment où l'action se déroule. Les expressions de temps et les formes verbales vous mettent également sur la voie.

- **Les noms propres**

Vous ne pourrez pas toujours reconnaître les noms propres, mais vous devez reconnaître les noms de lieux les plus courants.

– britanniques :

/temz/ Thames – /'edɪnbərə/ **E**dinburgh
/'nɒtɪŋəm / **No**ttingham – /'lɛstə/ **Lei**cester
/'wʊstəʃə/ **Wo**rcestershire – /'bʌkɪŋəm/ **Bu**ckingham

– américains :

/'aɪdəˌhəʊ/ **I**daho – /'aɪəʊə/ **I**owa – /'lɪŋkən/ **Li**ncoln
/ˌɪlə'nɔɪ/ **I**llinois – /dɪ'trɔɪt/ Detr**oi**t – /ʃi'kɑːgəʊ/ Chic**a**go

- **Les nombres et les dates**

Prêtez attention aux chiffres et aux dates : il n'est pas toujours facile (même en français) de retenir du premier coup un numéro de téléphone ou un grand nombre. Il faut préalablement vous entraîner.

Soyez attentifs à l'accentuation qui peut vous aider à faire la distinction entre deux nombres dont la prononciation est proche. Par exemple : *fifty* /'fɪftɪ/ et *fifteen* /fɪf'tiːn/.

7 Classer, relier, hiérarchiser les informations

Si vous deviez, en quelques mots, transmettre à quelqu'un, qui n'en a jamais entendu parler, l'essentiel d'une histoire, d'une situation ou d'un discours, quelles informations donneriez-vous en premier lieu ?

- Posez-vous les questions suivantes : *Who? Where? When? What?*
- ***Who?*** → noms des personnages et relations qu'ils entretiennent (parents, amis, inconnus, relations professionnelles, etc.).
- ***Where?*** → dans quel pays ou dans quelle ville l'action / le dialogue se déroule-t-il ?
- ***When?*** → document contemporain ou historique, date (année, mois), saison, moment de la journée, chronologie des événements, etc.
- ***What?*** → de quoi parle-t-on ? À qui s'adresse-t-on ?

Vous n'aurez pas nécessairement de réponse à donner à toutes ces questions, mais les réponses que vous trouverez vous permettront de construire le sens du document.

- Classez les informations que vous avez mémorisées.

S'il s'agit d'un débat, essayez de classer mentalement les arguments en :
- pour / contre ;
- avantages / désavantages ;
- point de vue de X / point de vue de Y.

- S'il s'agit d'un récit, il peut être utile de classer les faits selon la chronologie :
  - passé / présent / avenir.

- Hiérarchisez les informations. Tentez de mémoriser les arguments les plus convaincants, les commentaires les plus frappants, les événements les plus marquants.

8 Revenir sur ce qui n'a pas été bien perçu

Pourquoi peut-il être difficile de comprendre certains passages ?
Doit-on chercher à comprendre les passages difficiles ?

Tentez de déduire, d'après le contexte, le sens de certains passages que vous avez mal perçus mais dont intuitivement vous sentez l'importance.

- **Les formes non accentuées**

▪ Il faut s'exercer à « deviner » la présence de formes grammaticales non accentuées, peu audibles pour quelqu'un qui n'est pas encore très bien entraîné à l'écoute et, surtout, il faut apprendre à les interpréter en s'appuyant sur le contexte. (Par exemple le son /s/ ou /z/ peut correspondre à *is, has,* le pluriel d'un nom ou le génitif.)

▪ Ces formes grammaticales fournissent des indications importantes sur les temps (auxiliaires), les intentions des personnages et leurs relations (modaux), l'identité des locuteurs (pronoms), l'orientation de l'action (voix active, voix passive), etc.

▪ Certains passages du document resteront « obscurs ». C'est normal ! Nous vous proposons tout au long du manuel et dans le fichier de l'élève des exercices de grammaire de l'oral qui vous entraîneront peu à peu à interpréter ces formes.

- **Les liaisons**

Certains mots sont « collés » à d'autres dans le flux sonore que vous entendez. Entraînez-vous à reconnaître et distinguer les mots porteurs de sens.

9 Synthétiser

- À l'issue de cette écoute active, vous aurez compris non seulement les faits présentés dans le document, mais également l'intention d'un discours ou de certaines paroles qui auront été entendues.

Vous pourrez ainsi répondre à certaines des questions suivantes :

→ Pour quelle raison l'action s'est-elle déroulée ?

→ Quelles sont les motivations des personnages ?

→ Pour quelle raison le document a-t-il été enregistré ?

→ Quelle est l'issue prévisible de la situation présentée ?

- Entraînez-vous à reconstituer le sens du document que vous venez d'entendre en en faisant un bref compte rendu oral.

Expression orale en continu

WORKBOOK → p. 64-66

CONSEILS

1. Ne rédigez pas de phrases complètes, vous seriez tentés de les lire.
2. Préparez quelques notes. Vous devez apprendre à vous exprimer à partir de phrases minimales.
3. Faites en sorte que votre auditoire ait envie de suivre votre intervention : votre regard, vos gestes, votre ton, votre dynamisme sont aussi des éléments importants pour transmettre votre message.
4. Accentuez les mots porteurs de sens et respectez les schémas intonatifs.
5. Reformulez ce que vous venez de dire si nécessaire.
6. Si vous faites une erreur, n'hésitez pas à vous auto-corriger.
7. Lorsque vous hésitez, utilisez des *gap fillers*, ne restez surtout pas muets.
8. Entraînez-vous régulièrement à parler seul pendant 1 à 2 minutes.

Gap fillers

Making yourself clear	*Giving yourself time to think*
• *I mean…*	• *Well… / So…*
• *What I mean is…*	• *Let me see… / Let me think…*
• *… if you see what I mean…*	• *You see / know…*
• *Does that make sense?*	• *… just a **mo**ment*
• *In **o**ther words…*	• *Now, what's the word…?*
• *What I'm tr**y**ing to say is…*	• *How shall I put it?*

A Raconter

Quelle est l'erreur à éviter lorsque vous vous préparez à rendre compte d'un article ?

1. Reprendre des phrases complètes de l'article.
2. Écrire des mots clés.
3. Faire un plan de son intervention.

1 Rendre compte d'un article, d'un film

Soyez concis, ne vous perdez pas dans les détails mais pensez à donner les informations relatives aux cinq questions : *Where? When? Who? What? Why?*

2 Raconter une histoire, parler de son expérience

- Mettez en relief les mots importants, parlez avec emphase, le ton de votre voix rendra votre histoire plus crédible.
- N'hésitez pas à donner des détails : décrire les lieux, l'atmosphère, les personnages, les sentiments, etc.

3 Utiliser des mots de liaison

Que ce soit pour rendre compte d'un article ou d'un film ou pour raconter une histoire ou votre expérience, vous avez besoin de mots de liaison vous permettant d'enchaîner vos énoncés et de situer les événements dans le temps.

- *first*
- *then*
- ***af**terwards:* ensuite
- ***fi**nally*
- *as:* au moment où, comme
- *as soon as:* dès que
- *while:* pendant que
- ***mean**while:* pendant ce temps
- *at the same time*

B Dire les chiffres et les dates

Figures

- 0 → *zero* /ˈzɪərəʊ/
- 200 → *two hundred* /ˈhʌndrəd/
- 7,000 → *seven thousand* /ˈθaʊzənd/

La virgule permet de séparer les groupes de trois chiffres.

- 644 → *six hundred and forty-four*
- 1814 → *one thousand eight hundred and fourteen*
- 6.1 → six *point* /pɔɪnt/ one

Le point correspond à une décimale : six virgule un.

- 20,763 → *twenty thousand seven hundred and sixty-three*
- 2,345,678 → *two million three hundred forty-five thousand six hundred and seventy-eight*
- *dozens of* / *scores of* (des vingtaines) / *hundreds of* / *thousands of* / *millions of*...

hundred, thousand, million **prennent la marque du pluriel quand ils renvoient à une quantité indéfinie.**

Calculations

- 2 + 5 = 7 → *two plus* /plʌs/ *five equals* /ˈiːkwəlz/ *seven*
- 18 −12 → *eighteen minus* /ˈmaɪnəs/ *twelve*
- 16 x 3 → *sixteen multiplied* /ˈmʌltɪplaɪd/ *by three*
- 40 : 4 → *forty divided* /dɪˈvaɪdɪd/ *by four*

Ordinals

- 1st → *the first*
- 2nd → *the second*
- 3rd → *the third*
- 4th → *the fourth*
- 5th → *the fifth*...
- 10th → *the tenth*
- 11th → *the eleventh*
- 12th → *the twelfth*
- 13th → *the thirteenth*...
- 21st → *the twenty-first*...

Dates

- *April 28* → *April the twenty-eighth* / *the twenty-eighth of April*
- *1603* → *sixteen-o-three*
- *1953* → *nineteen fifty-three*
- *2012* → *two thousand (and) twelve* / *twenty-twelve*

Lengths

- *1 inch* (pouce) → 2.54 cm
- *1 foot* → 30.4 cm
- *1 yard* → 91.4 cm
- *1 mile* → 1,609 m

C Commenter un graphique

Connaissez-vous la différence entre *a pie chart, a bar chart, a line chart*?

1 Nommer les graphiques

Il faut d'abord savoir nommer les graphiques les plus courants et dire ce qu'ils indiquent :

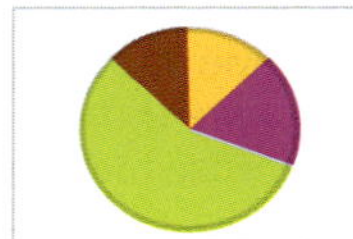

Pie chart

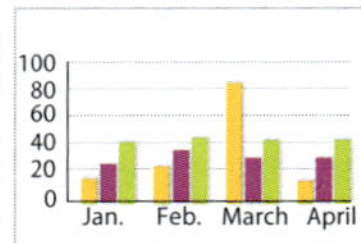

Bar chart

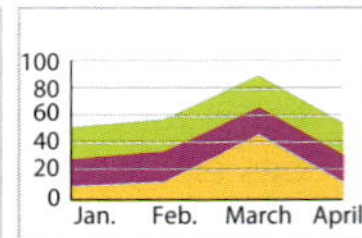

Line chart

This graph shows / illustrates /depicts...
This pie chart underlines / outlines...
This bar chart highlights / emphasizes...
This line chart brings out...

2 Analyser les tendances

Il vous faut ensuite analyser les tendances *(trends)* indiquées par le graphique. Attention aux prépositions qui suivent les noms ou les verbes.

Verbs	*Nouns*
Movement: *Upward* ↗	
• *increase (by 2%)* • *rise (to $36)* • *go up (to)* • *reach a peak* (atteindre un sommet) • *skyrocket* (monter en flèche)	• *increase (in* + GN): augmentation • *rise (in)*: hausse • *recovery (in* + GN): redressement • *peak*
Movement: *Downward* ↘	
• *decrease (by 0.5%)* • *drop (from 3.5% to 1.2%)* • *go down / fall (to)* • *decline (in the number of...)* • *collapse (in prices)*	• *decrease (in)*: diminution • *drop (in)* • *fall / trough* /trɒf/: creux • *decline (in)* • *collapse (in)*: effondrement

Les adjectifs et adverbes suivants vous permettront de décrire ces tendances :

- *dramatic(ally)*: (de manière) spectaculaire
- *sharp(ly)*: fort(ement)
- *significant(ly)*: sensible(ment)
- *slight(ly)*: léger (légèrement)
- *a little*
- *rapid(ly)*
- *gradual(ly)*
- *steady(ily)*: régulier (régulièrement)
- *slowly*

Temperatures

La conversion entre degrés (*degrees* /dɪˈgriːz/) Celsius et degrés Fahrenheit est difficile à mémoriser : (1.8 x °C) + 32 = °F. Il est préférable de ne retenir que quelques températures clés.

Celsius /ˈselsɪəs/	− 5°	0°	5°	10°	15°	20°	25°	30°	35°	100°
Fahrenheit /ˈfærənhaɪt/	23°	32°	41°	50°	59°	68°	77°	86°	95°	212°

D Expliquer

Vous serez sans doute amenés à prendre la parole pour :
- expliquer le comportement ou les sentiments des personnages ;
- rendre compte d'un problème d'actualité ;
- expliquer le fonctionnement d'un objet ;
- présenter les résultats d'une enquête ;
- exprimer ce qu'il y a d'implicite dans un document.

Les mots de liaison vous permettant d'exprimer le but, la cause ou la conséquence vous seront utiles ici.

But
- *in **or**der (not) to:* afin de (ne pas)
- *so that:* pour que

Cause
- *as:* comme
- *be**cause** of:* à cause de
- *since:* puisque

Conséquence
- ***there**fore / as a re**sult** / that's why*
- *as a re**sult** of…*
- ***con**sequently…*
- *in the wake of:* à la suite de

E Argumenter

Si vous voulez défendre votre point de vue, remettre en cause les arguments présentés, il faut être convaincant :
- n'oubliez pas que la gestuelle est importante (regard, gestes, sourire) ;
- baissez la voix en fin de phrase ;
- donnez des exemples si nécessaire ;
- introduisez vos arguments et concluez en utilisant les expressions ci-dessous.

- *I feel / be**lie**ve that…*
- *I can't help **thin**king that…*
- *to my **mind**…*
- *in my o**pin**ion…*
- *in **fact** / as a **ma**tter of fact:* en fait
- *a**bo**ve all:* par-dessus tout
- *on the **one** hand:* d'une part
- *on the **o**ther hand:* d'autre part
- *ho**w**ever / **yet** / **though**:* cependant
- *as **far** as… is con**cer**ned*
- *ac**cor**ding to:* selon (impossible avec *me* ou *us*)
- *for **in**stance / for ex**am**ple*
- *that is to say*
- *in con**clu**sion / to con**clu**de*

F Décrire

1 Décrire une image

- Lors de l'étude d'une image, vous devez d'abord la présenter brièvement :
  - nature, origine probable, période, pays, auteur (si vous le connaissez) ;
  - sujet général (en quelques mots) ;
  - objectif du document (en quelques mots).

Parlez, si nécessaire, de la composition de l'image, décrivez l'image en insistant sur les éléments les plus importants.

Parmi les expressions ci-dessous, choisissez celles dont vous aurez besoin pour décrire cette photo.

- *in the **fo**reground:* au premier plan
- *in the **ba**ckground:* à l'arrière-plan
- *at the top / **bo**ttom:* en haut / bas
- *in the **dis**tance:* au loin
- *a**bo**ve* /ə'bʌv/: au-dessus (de)
- *a**round**:* autour (de)
- *be**low*** /bɪ'ləʊ/: au-dessous (de)
- *in **front** of:* devant
- *in**side**:* à l'intérieur (de)
- *on the **o**ther side (of):* de l'autre côté (de)
- ***o**pposite* /'ɒpəzɪt/: en face (de)

- Analysez ensuite l'image en vous efforçant :
  - de comparer les personnages ou les éléments ;
  - d'imaginer les sentiments des personnages ;
  - d'imaginer ce qui s'est passé avant et va se passer après ;
  - d'expliquer les intentions de l'artiste ou du photographe.
- Faites part de vos réactions devant cette image.

2 Décrire une publicité

Quels éléments retrouve-t-on la plupart du temps dans les publicités ?
Qui est la cible, selon vous, de cette publicité ?

- **Éléments d'une publicité**

Une publicité contient en général tout ou partie des éléments suivants :

- *c**a**tchphrase* (accroche) : elle a pour but, avec l'image, d'attirer l'attention ;
- *text* / *caption* (légende) : ils informent sur les caractéristiques du produit ;
- *sl**o**gan* /'sləʊgən/ : il est le signe distinctif d'une marque ;
- *brand name* (nom de la marque) ;
- *l**o**go* /'ləʊgəʊ/ : il permet de reconnaître immédiatement une marque ;
- *pr**o**duct name* (nom du produit).

- **Cible**

Vous devez définir la **cible** *(target)*, c'est-à-dire les acheteurs potentiels. Une cible est visée selon plusieurs critères : *sex, age, occup**a**tion, social cl**a**ss, tastes, **i**nterests, needs, sp**e**nding / p**u**rchasing* /'pɜːtʃəsɪŋ/ *power*, etc.

- **Réactions**

Une publicité a un but précis : *attr**a**ct, win sb **o**ver* (séduire), *app**ea**l to, inf**o**rm, conv**i**nce, persu**a**de* /pə'sweɪd/, *warn sb ab**ou**t* (prévenir), etc. Vous devez donc toujours parler de vos réactions.

Interaction orale

WORKBOOK → p. 67-68

CONSEILS

L'interaction orale est une activité langagière complexe puisqu'il s'agit non seulement de comprendre votre interlocuteur et de vous exprimer à votre tour, mais également de réagir et de vous adapter à ses propos.

Il ne faut cependant pas hésiter à entrer dans la discussion, même si vous n'êtes pas sûrs de vous. C'est ainsi que vous progresserez…

1. Regardez votre interlocuteur.
2. Parlez suffisamment fort.
3. Accompagnez vos paroles de gestes pour convaincre.
4. Répétez les instructions éventuelles, posez des questions si vous n'êtes pas sûrs d'avoir compris.
5. Lancez-vous…

A Conversation

Comment s'assurer que votre interlocuteur suit bien la conversation ?

- Observez votre interlocuteur, l'expression de son visage et ses gestes sont aussi porteurs de sens.

- Celui qui parle ne doit pas se perdre dans les détails mais aller à l'essentiel pour intéresser son interlocuteur. Certaines expressions permettent de s'assurer que l'interlocuteur suit la conversation.

- *Do you know what I mean?*
- *… if you see what I mean…*
- *Do you under**stand**?*
- *Do I make my**self** clear?*

- Celui à qui on s'adresse doit réagir en montrant qu'il écoute et doit indiquer s'il comprend, s'il souhaite faire répéter ou s'il veut des explications complémentaires. L'intonation est importante et est elle-même porteuse de sens.

- ***Re**ally?*
- *I see…*
- *Oh yes…*
- *Hem…*
- *How **in**teresting!*
- *I know / I see what you mean.*
- *I'm **so**rry, I didn't hear / catch what you said.*
- *Could you say that a**gai**n, please?*

B Conversation au téléphone

Les conversations téléphoniques peuvent être déroutantes car on ne peut s'appuyer ni sur les expressions du visage, ni sur la gestuelle de son interlocuteur.

Apprenez ces expressions, elles vous permettront de ne pas être démuni(e) lors de vos échanges téléphoniques.

Introducing oneself

- *Hello, this is Keith.*
- *Jane **Le**wis **spea**king.*
- ***Sa**rah here…*

Asking for someone

- *I'd like to speak to Sam, please.*
- *Can / Could I speak to H**o**lly, please?*
- *Can / Could you put me through to P**o**ppy, please?*
- *Is Sam there, please?* → *Sorry, he isn't here right now.*

Connecting people

- *Hold on, please.*
- *Hold the line, please.*
- *S**o**rry to keep you w**ai**ting.*
- *Could you take / give him a m**e**ssage* /'mesɪdʒ/?
- *Could I leave a m**e**ssage?*
- *Can you ask him to call / ring me back?*
- *How can I get in touch* /tʌtʃ/ *with her?*
- *I'd like to make a rev**e**rse charge call, please* (téléphoner en PCV).
- *Hallo, I'd like to call long-d**i**stance* /ˌlɒŋ 'dɪstəns/ / *make an intern**a**tional* /ˌɪntə'næʃnəl/ *call.*

Asking for information

- *What's your m**o**bile* /'məʊbaɪl/ (GB) *n**u**mber / cell phone (US) n**u**mber?*
- *Could you spell your name, please?*
- *Can you send me a text m**e**ssage (SMS)? / Can you text me?*

Problems

- *The line is eng**a**ged* /ɪn'geɪdʒd/ *(GB) / b**u**sy (US).*
- *S**o**rry, wrong n**u**mber.*
- *I'm afr**ai**d you must have **e**ntered* /'entəd/ / *di**a**lled* /'daɪəld/ *the wrong n**u**mber.*
- *I get cut off **e**very time I phone.*
- *You're br**ea**king up / going faint…* (Je ne vous entends plus…)
- *We might be cut off. I don't have much m**o**ney left on my phone…*
- *Don't hang up / ring off* (raccrocher), *please!*

Saying goodbye

- *Thank you for c**a**lling.*
- *You've been very h**e**lpful.*
- *Nice t**a**lking to you.*
- *See you soon then / next week.*

C Interview

Est-il possible de prévoir intégralement le déroulement d'une interview ?

Le sujet de l'interview est connu des deux participants, donc certaines questions et certaines réponses peuvent être anticipées. Mais on ne peut pas tout prévoir ; il faut donc être prêt à s'adapter à la situation et à prendre des initiatives.

Variez la manière dont vous posez les questions : posez des questions directes et indirectes.

- *I w**o**nder if / wh**e**ther you could tell me…*
- *I'd like to know if…*
- *Is it true that…?*
- *Could you tell me if…?*
- *Would you say that…?*
- *Have you got any id**ea** how to…?*
- *Do you know **a**nything about…?*
- *Could you give me some inform**a**tion ab**ou**t…?*
- *How do you expl**ai**n the fact that…?*

D Discussion contradictoire

Vous voulez interrompre votre interlocuteur. Savez-vous le faire poliment ?

1 Écouter son interlocuteur

Lors d'une discussion, il est essentiel d'écouter les arguments de son interlocuteur et de ne pas l'interrompre systématiquement. Cependant, vous jugerez peut-être nécessaire d'intervenir ; sachez le faire de manière non agressive.

- *Sorry to interr**u**pt you but…*
- *You may be right, but…*
- *I supp**o**se it is true, how**e**ver…*
- *Exc**u**se me, but…*
- *Can I say s**o**mething?*

2 Demander des précisions

Il se peut que vous ne soyez pas sûrs d'avoir compris votre interlocuteur. N'hésitez pas à lui demander des éclaircissements.

- *Does that mean…?*
- *If I understand right.*
- *Can you repeat what you said, please?*
- *Sorry but I don't understand what you mean.*
- *I didn't get your point.*

3 Convaincre son interlocuteur

Il s'agit avant tout de convaincre son interlocuteur. Plusieurs stratégies peuvent vous y aider :

- donnez des exemples pour illustrer votre propos ;
- reformulez ou répétez si vous avez l'impression de ne pas avoir été compris ;
- utilisez les arguments de votre interlocuteur de façon à mieux les contrer ;
- utilisez des expressions qui expriment votre forte conviction.

- *Let's take an example.*
- *For instance / example…*
- *I must explain…*
- *In other words…*
- *Let's put it differently…*
- *I'll make myself clear…*
- *It is true to say… and yet…*
- *I'm quite sure that…*
- *I'm convinced that…*
- *I do believe that…*

4 Exprimer son désaccord

Pour exprimer votre désaccord, en plus des expressions appropriées, n'oubliez pas de bien utiliser votre voix, et rappelez-vous que la gestuelle est importante.

- *I don't think so.*
- *I don't agree with you.*
- *I don't see things that way.*
- *On the contrary…*
- *Definitely not! / Surely not!*
- *I totally disagree with you.*
- *You can't be serious!*
- *This is nonsense!*

E Débat

Vous avez à débattre du sujet suivant : *"Should cars be banned from city centres?"*
Comment vous organisez-vous ?

- La disposition spatiale du groupe est importante : tous les participants au débat doivent pouvoir se voir.
- Afin que chacun puisse préparer ses arguments, répartissez les rôles (pour, contre, sans opinion, animateur, etc.).
- Il est essentiel d'anticiper les arguments que vos contradicteurs vont vous opposer. Vous pourrez ainsi mieux les contrer.
- Lorsque c'est à votre tour d'argumenter, n'oubliez pas d'illustrer votre propos en donnant des exemples et en utilisant des expressions appropriées (voir « Discussion contradictoire », p. 158, et « Argumenter » p. 155).
- Chacun doit prendre la parole à son tour ; ce qui signifie écouter les autres sans les interrompre. De plus, on ne peut réfuter les arguments que si on les a entendus.
- Restez calmes… Vous n'avez aucune raison de vous emporter… Ce n'est qu'un débat après tout !
- Tous les participants au débat doivent absolument parler, ce qui signifie que la parole de chacun, quel que soit son niveau d'expression, doit être respectée.

Structures utiles pour s'exprimer à l'oral

Giving one's opinion

- To my mind / In my opinion…
- It seems to me that…
- I feel / believe that…
- I can't help thinking that…
- My feeling is that…
- As a matter of fact, I am convinced that…
- For my part, I consider that…

Expressing agreement

- I agree with…
- It is true to say that…
- So do I / Neither do I.
- That's exactly how I see it.
- I perfectly understand that…
- You / They are right to suggest that…
- I share your point of view…
- I see eye to eye with you…

Expressing disagreement

- I don't agree / disagree with you about that…
- Contrary to / Unlike…, I feel that…
- That's not how I see it.
- Instead of V-ING…
- I don't see things that way.

Expressing doubts, protest

- However, I am not really sure that…
- I am rather sceptical about…
- In theory, it sounds… but in practice…
- I object to / disapprove of *GN* / V-ING
- How can they…? / What right have they to…?

Suggesting and convincing

- How / What about V-ING
- Why don't you / Why not V
- Don't you think that…?
- I suggest V-ING / I suggest we (should) V
- We should definitely V…
- I'm convinced that…
- It seems to me that…
- I'm sure you will / won't V…

Expressing surprise

- I can't / couldn't believe it / my eyes!
- You can't imagine what I saw!
- How surprised I was!
- It was truly amazing!
- How fantastic it was!
- How astonishing to see such…!
- I was amazed by / stunned by / astounded by…
- It was just unbelievable!
- Just imagine!
- Fancy that!
- What a sight! / What strange things!…
- What I find the most incredible / unpleasant / shocking is that…

Expressing enthusiasm

- It must be great / terrific…
- How interesting / fantastic!
- I'd just love to…
- I was so impressed by…
- I can't wait to see that!

Expressing likes and dislikes

- I'm fond of / keen on *GN* / V-ING
- I fancy *GN* / V-ING
- I enjoy V-ING
- I love *GN* / V-ING
- I'm mad / crazy about…! *(informel)*
- I hate *GN* / V-ING
- I can't stand / bear *GN* / V-ING
- I can't put up with *GN* / V-ING
- I don't go for it. *(informel)*

Expressing preferences

- I prefer V-ing to V-ING
- I'd rather V than V
- I'd rather you V *(prétérit modal)*
- I feel more like V-ING than V-ING
- Instead of *GN* / V-ING *(Au lieu de)*
- I like it better / best

Being indifferent

- I don't mind (him / her) V-ING…
- As you like / wish.
- It doesn't matter. / Never mind.
- Why not?
- It doesn't matter to me whether… or…
- I don't care.

Expressing wishes and intentions

- I would like to V
- I'd love to V
- I feel like *GN* / V-ING
- I hope to V
- I wish you'd V
- If only I / you V *(prétérit modal)*
- I would appreciate it if…
- I am looking forward to V-ING
- I dream of *GN* / V-ING
- I'm dying for *GN* / to V
- I want to V
- I'm thinking of V-ING
- I'm about to V
- I plan / mean / intend / aim to V
- Whether you like it or not, I'll V
- I'm determined (not) to V

Expressing regret and reproach

- I regret V-ING
- I should (not) have V-EN
- If only / I wish I had (not) V-EN
- You shouldn't have V-EN
- Why didn't you V?
- How could you V?
- What a shame!
- How **awful** (of you)!
- Why on earth did / didn't you V?

Giving orders

- I want you to V
- You have / have got to V
- You must V
- Will you V!
- Stop shouting! / Do be quiet.
- Dont' V
- Stop V-ING
- I'll have / make *GN* / V

Compréhension de l'écrit

WORKBOOK → p. 69-72

CONSEILS

Avant de commencer à lire un texte, vous devez :

1. Identifier sa nature : article de presse, roman, pièce de théâtre, poème...

2. Identifier les éléments périphériques : l'auteur, la source, la date de publication, le titre...

Il vous faudra ensuite appliquer des stratégies de lecture qui vous permettront de vous appuyer sur le connu pour compenser l'inconnu afin de construire progressivement le sens du document.

LES STRATÉGIES

A Anticipation

De quoi parlera l'article de presse dont voici le titre et le sous-titre ?

Turning teenagers on to the benefits of being green

A new project aims to convince teenagers of the benefits of being environmentally friendly – by making it cool.

- Anticiper le contenu d'un texte vous permettra d'être plus efficace lors de votre lecture. Vous émettrez des hypothèses que vous vérifierez ensuite.
  - **L'illustration** fournit un indice immédiat sur le sujet probable du texte.
  - **Le titre** et **le sous-titre** (dans un article de presse) sont porteurs d'informations importantes.

B Compréhension globale

Lisez ce passage extrait de *The Octopus* (1901), de Frank Norris, et résumez la situation en français.

When Minna descended from the train, she found that the place was one of those suburban towns such as may be seen on the outskirts of any large American city. She found the house to which she had been directed. Her heart warmed at the sight of it. Oh, to find a home here, a refuge from those horrible city streets. How she would work, how she would endeavour to please.

Her heart beating, her breath failing, she rang the bell.

The lady of the house herself opened the door. Minna stated her errand.

"But I have already engaged a girl," the lady said.

- Dès la première lecture d'un texte, vous devez pouvoir **identifier les informations essentielles sans vous arrêter aux mots inconnus** : narrateur, période, lieux, personnages, faits principaux, problème soulevé...

C Compréhension détaillée

1 Mots de liaison et marqueurs de temps
(voir manuel p. 169)

Repérez un mot de liaison dans cette phrase. Ce mot exprime-t-il la cause ou le but ?

Tim decided not to go out as he was awfully tired after last night's party.

Les **articulations** structurent le discours. Il est important de bien les repérer car cela vous permettra d'émettre des hypothèses sur le sens du texte.

Ces articulations sont souvent des **marqueurs de temps** et des **mots de liaison** qui recouvrent de nombreuses notions (cause, conséquence, point de vue). Elles peuvent aussi indiquer un changement de lieu, de période, de sujet…

2 Référents des possessifs et des pronoms
PRÉCIS GRAMMATICAL → 20, 21

À qui ou à quoi se réfèrent les mots soulignés ci-dessous ?

Public schools get most of their money from state and local governments, which collect it from taxpayers. Yet, more and more of them are turning to companies that sell products to kids.

La compréhension est parfois rendue difficile par la présence de possessifs et pronoms (personnels, relatifs, réciproques, démonstratifs…). Repérer leurs **référents** (les personnes, choses ou idées auxquelles ils renvoient) vous permet de faire les liens à l'intérieur du texte et donc de mieux le comprendre.

3 Effacement de *THAT*
PRÉCIS GRAMMATICAL → 37, 38

Où pourriez-vous insérer *that* dans ces phrases ?

1. *She was speaking so softly I could hardly hear her.*
2. *The only thing he remembered was Jenny screaming.*

- Entraînez-vous à repérer la proposition principale et les propositions subordonnées. Par exemple, dans les subordonnées en *THAT*, *THAT* est souvent omis, ce qui rend parfois la compréhension difficile. De même, le pronom relatif complément est souvent le relatif *Ø*.

  → *If your mother said she'd come, she'll come.*
  → *There are lots of things I need to buy before the trip.*

- Repérez les groupes de sens, c'est-à-dire les unités de sens qui constituent un bloc dans lequel on ne marque pas de pause lors de la lecture.

4 Phrase minimale

Lisez l'extrait de presse suivant et trouvez la phrase minimale.

Many governments, their eyes focused on the impact that future pension claims will have on public finances, have embarked on reforms.

Il faut savoir repérer la phrase minimale : sujet, verbe, complément (direct ou indirect). Elle apporte l'information essentielle. Les adjectifs et adverbes ne font partie de la phrase minimale que s'ils sont absolument indispensables à la compréhension.

5 Groupe nominal complexe

Quel mot apporte l'information essentielle dans chaque groupe nominal souligné ?

Hollywood actor George Clooney has invested an undisclosed sum of money in a Las Vegas hotel resort.

Les groupes nominaux complexes sont fréquents dans les textes anglais, en particulier dans la presse. Il faut repérer le **nom principal** (toujours le dernier nom du groupe) et lire ensuite à l'envers. Les éléments qui le précèdent ne font qu'apporter des informations complémentaires.

D Particularités des articles de presse

Lisez ce premier paragraphe d'un article de presse. Est-ce une introduction générale ou un exemple précis ? Dites (en français) quel est le sujet de l'article.

People should have one meat-free day a week if they want to make a personal and effective sacrifice that would help tackle climate change, the world's leading authority on global warming, Dr Rajendra Pachauri, has told The Observer.

- **Le premier paragraphe** peut être une introduction générale du sujet ou un exemple précis illustrant le sujet. Comprendre le premier paragraphe vous permet donc d'avoir une information essentielle et facilite la compréhension de la suite de l'article.

- **La première phrase** de chaque paragraphe résume ce qui va être développé dans ce paragraphe. Comprendre cette première phrase vous permet donc de comprendre la suite du paragraphe, et de cerner la structure et les idées essentielles de tout l'article.

LES MOTS INCONNUS

A Formation

Les mots soulignés ci-dessous sont des mots dérivés ou composés. Donnez leur nature (voir page suivante), leur formation et traduisez-les.

1. *They noticed that the taxi driver was protected against gunshots by a safety screen.*

2. *In those days it was unthinkable for an unmarried woman to work outside the home.*

Trouver la façon dont un mot est formé vous aidera à en deviner le sens. Il existe en anglais deux principaux procédés de formation de mots : la composition et la dérivation.

1 Composition

PRÉCIS GRAMMATICAL → 26

- C'est la formation d'un mot à l'aide de plusieurs mots :
  → *hand* (main) + *brake* (frein) = *handbrake* (frein à main)
- Un mot composé peut également se former à partir d'un mot dérivé :
  → *bottle open**er**, sleep**ing** pill*
- Deux mots sont fréquents en composition : *self-* (soi-même) et *ill-* (mal) :
  → ***self**-analysis* / ***ill**-prepared*

2 Dérivation

C'est la formation d'un mot par ajout d'un préfixe et / ou d'un (ou plusieurs) suffixe(s) à une base.

→ *hopeless, undrinkable, joblessness*

A. Principaux préfixes

1. Idée de contraire

- *de- / dis- / il- / im- / in- / ir- / non- / un-*
  → ***de**code, **dis**agree, **il**legal, **im**patient, **in**justice, **ir**regular, **non**-smoker, **un**fair*

2. Sens péjoratif

- *mis-* → ***mis**judge*

3. Sens temporel ou spatial

- *pre-* (avant) / *post-* (après) / *sub-* (sous) / *super-* (au-dessus / sur) / *trans-* (à travers)
  → ***pre**arrange, **post**war, **sub**conscious, **super**human, **trans**atlantic*

4. Répétition

- *re-* (de nouveau) → ***re**open*

B. Principaux suffixes

1. Formation des verbes

- *-en* (transformation) / *-ize* (action)
  → *black**en**, American**ize***

2. Formation des adverbes

- adjectif + *-ly* → *fortunate**ly***

3. Formation des noms

- *-er / -or / -ess / -ist* (celui ou celle qui)
  → *teach**er**, collect**or**, actr**ess**, novel**ist***
- *-dom / -hood* (état, condition)
  → *free**dom**, brother**hood***
- *-age* / verbe + *-al* / *-ation* (fonction, condition, action)
  → *orphan**age**, rent**al**, demonstr**ation***
- verbe + *-ing* (profession, activité)
  → *advertis**ing**, swimm**ing***

PRÉCIS GRAMMATICAL → 34

- adjectif + *-ness* (état, caractéristique)
  → *happi**ness***
- *-ship / -ment* (état, action)
  → *friend**ship**, replace**ment***

4. Formation des adjectifs

- *-able / -ible* (pouvant être)
  → *wash**able**, elig**ible***
- *-al / -y / -ish* (comme, se rapportant à)
  → *music**al**, tast**y**, child**ish***
- verbe + *-ed* (participe passé = adjectif)
  → *fascinat**ed***

PRÉCIS GRAMMATICAL → 25

- verbe + *-ing* (participe présent = adjectif)
  → *lov**ing***

PRÉCIS GRAMMATICAL → 25

- nom + *-ful* (plein de) → *event**ful***
- nom + *-less* (sans) → *power**less***
- *-ch / -ish / -ese / -an* (nationalité)
  → *Fren**ch**, Swed**ish**, Japan**ese**, Americ**an***

B Nature

Lisez ce passage et trouvez la nature du mot manquant : nom, adjectif ou verbe ?

Our ..1... was three times bigger than my ..2... here. I was surprised because in Nepal my ..3... was made of bricks and stones but here, when I saw the ..4... I thought, "Is that a real ..5... ?" I thought it was fake. When you walk on the floors it makes noises.

Trouver la nature d'un mot inconnu est essentiel pour le comprendre. Ainsi le mot manquant ci-dessus est un nom puisqu'il est précédé chaque fois d'un possessif, d'un article ou d'un adjectif. Le contexte (voir « Contexte », ci-après) peut vous permettre de deviner ce mot : *house*.

C Contexte

Servez-vous du contexte pour deviner le sens des mots soulignés dans cette phrase.

On St Andrew's Street, they saw a girl who was sitting on the ground, on an old blanket, a dog stretched out at her side.

- Vous pouvez souvent deviner le sens d'un mot inconnu en vous fondant sur le contexte, c'est-à-dire partir du connu pour compenser l'inconnu. Ainsi, les mots *sitting on the ground*, *dog* et *at her side* dans la phrase ci-dessus vous donnent le sens de *stretched out* : « étendu ».
- Rappelez-vous qu'il n'est pas nécessaire de deviner le sens exact de tous les mots inconnus d'un texte pour comprendre le sens général. Il faut accepter les zones d'ombre.

D Transparence

Trouvez les mots transparents et traduisez ce passage.

A book by Linda Babcock called Women Don't Ask *recently drew attention to women's negotiating style. Ms Babcock noticed that male graduates with a master's degree from her university were paid starting salaries almost $4,000 above those of female students.*

- De nombreux mots anglais sont d'origine latine ou française. Servez-vous de cette ressemblance.
- Attention aux faux amis, ces mots anglais qui ressemblent à des mots français mais n'ont pas le même sens : *miserable* (très malheureux), *eventually* (finalement), *evidence* (preuve), *actually* (en fait, vraiment)... Le contexte (voir ci-dessus) vous permet souvent d'éviter les erreurs.

Expression écrite

WORKBOOK → p. 73-75

CONSEILS

Lorsque vous rédigez, pensez à :

1. conjuguer les verbes ;
2. accorder un verbe en fonction de l'auxiliaire qui le précède ;
3. introduire un auxiliaire aux formes négative et interrogative ;
4. ajouter un s à la 3e personne du singulier du présent simple (sauf pour les modaux) ;
5. placer l'adjectif épithète (invariable) avant le nom qu'il qualifie ;
6. ne pas mettre d'article défini devant un nom pris dans son sens général ;
7. ne pas séparer le verbe de son complément.

LA QUALITÉ DE L'EXPRESSION

A Rédiger des phrases correctes

Corrigez les erreurs dans ces phrases et expliquez (en français) vos corrections.

1. *They know each other for more than twenty years.*
2. *They have been to Australia ten years ago.*
3. *You think that she will come with us to the cinema?*
4. *This car is really more cheap than the one I saw yesterday.*
5. *We go always to New York City in April, because the weather is so nice!*

1 Groupe verbal

- Le verbe est le pivot de la phrase. Chaque phrase contient au moins un verbe qui doit être conjugué. Une phrase simple en contient un, une phrase complexe plusieurs, selon le nombre de propositions.
- Le verbe doit être conjugué. Réfléchissez au temps que vous allez utiliser sans vous inspirer des temps français. Méfiez-vous en particulier du passé composé français.

PRÉCIS GRAMMATICAL → 6

- Une phrase interrogative se construit avec un auxiliaire, sauf lorsque *WHO* ou *WHAT* sont sujets.

2 Groupe nominal

- L'article défini est beaucoup moins fréquent en anglais qu'en français.

PRÉCIS GRAMMATICAL → 21

- Attention aux adjectifs courts et longs lorsque vous formez des comparatifs et superlatifs.
- En anglais, l'adjectif possessif s'accorde toujours avec le possesseur.

3 Ordre des mots

L'ordre des mots dans les phrases anglaises diffère du français. Souvenez-vous des points suivants :

- L'adjectif épithète (invariable) se place avant le nom qu'il qualifie.
- On ne sépare pas le verbe de son COD. En particulier, les adverbes de fréquence (*always, often, never…*) se placent soit avant le verbe (sauf *be*), soit après le premier auxiliaire.
  → *They often go swimming on Saturdays.*
  → *She will never tell him the truth.*

- Au génitif, l'ordre des mots est : possesseur +'s ou ' + élément possédé. PRÉCIS GRAMMATICAL → 20
  - → *her friend's book*
  - → *their parents' car*

B Penser à la ponctuation

Quelle différence de sens y a-t-il entre ces deux phrases ?

1. *A woman, without her man, is nothing.*
2. *A woman: without her, man is nothing.*

Les signes de ponctuation ont pour la plupart le même rôle qu'en français. Ils facilitent la lecture, mais, selon la place qu'ils occupent, le sens de la phrase peut être radicalement différent…

C Enrichir sa production

Comment pouvez-vous améliorer les phrases suivantes ?

1. *The runner has won the 4x100 m relay. He is wearing a blue jersey.*
2. *Your computer is complex. Mine is very simple.*
3. *Martin kept laughing. It annoyed his sister!*

1 Les phrases complexes

Une phrase complexe est l'expression d'une pensée riche et structurée.

- Introduire une **proposition relative** permet d'identifier l'élément dont on parle ou d'apporter une précision supplémentaire. Le pronom *WHICH* permet également de reprendre la proposition précédente. PRÉCIS GRAMMATICAL → 38

- Les **mots de liaison** sont essentiels pour bien articuler et ordonner ses idées (voir manuel p. 169).

2 Mots passe-partout

Évitez les mots passe-partout ; utilisez des synonymes qui vous permettront d'enrichir votre expression en variant les possibilités.

- *good* → *excellent, interesting, thrilling, great, fine, pleasant…*
- *bad* → *serious, difficult, useless, awful, unpleasant, evil…*
- *important* → *major, crucial, significant, essential, serious…*
- *nice* → *friendly, lovely, delightful, pleasant, attractive, charming…*
- *interesting* → *appealing, entertaining, exciting, attractive, curious…*
- *problem* → *topic, issue, subject, question, matter, dilemma…*
- *speak* → *deal with, mention, refer to, focus on, point out, raise, tackle…*

LES DIFFÉRENTS TYPES DE SUJETS

Prenez le temps de lire attentivement un sujet d'expression écrite afin de savoir ce que l'on attend de vous.

A Écrire une lettre ou un courriel

Relevez les mots clés dans le sujet suivant. Dites (en français) quel sera le niveau de langue et pourquoi. Quelles formules de début et de fin de lettre faut-il utiliser ?

The next day, Danny, 16, writes to his parents about his plan to go to the United States.

1 Écrire une lettre

Il y a différentes façons de commencer et de finir une lettre selon la personne à laquelle vous écrivez.

Début

→ formel (demande de renseignements, du travail…) : *Dear Sir… Dear Madam… Dear Sir or Madam… Dear Mrs Johnson…*

→ informel (famille, amis…) : *Dear John… My dear(est) Jamie…*

Fin

→ formel : *Yours sincerely… Yours truly… Yours faithfully…*

→ informel : *All the best… Love from… I can't wait to see you / hear from you… See you soon… Take care… I look forward to hearing from you / seeing you…*

- Vous devez vous aider du contexte : période, lieux, événements, relations entre la personne qui écrit et le destinataire… Si la lettre est écrite par le personnage d'un texte, respectez le niveau de langue et le ton employés dans le texte.

2 Écrire un courriel

Les courriels, bien qu'ils soient plus courts, ne diffèrent pas vraiment de la rédaction d'une lettre.

- Les courriels destinés aux amis ou à la famille sont informels, écrits dans une langue proche de la langue orale. Ils incluent souvent :

- des abréviations (iow = *in other words* ; bfn = *bye for now* ; asap = *as soon as possible* ; fyi = *for your information* ; btw = *by the way* ; LOL = *lots of laughs or laughing out loud*...) ;
- des orthographes phonétiques (CU = see you ; L8R = *later* ; B4 = *before* ; GR8 = *great*...) ;
- des *smileys* ou *emoticons*, qui permettent de transmettre des sentiments à l'aide de symboles du clavier, comme :-) ou ;) par exemple.

● Si vous souhaitez envoyer une lettre à un employeur, un supérieur ou une personne officielle par courrier électronique, ne la rédigez pas directement dans le corps du courriel et mettez-la en pièce jointe. Comme les lettres, ces courriers sont écrits dans une langue soutenue, avec inclusion des formules de politesse citées plus haut. Mentionnez toujours l'objet du message.

B Écrire une page de journal intime ou un article sur un blog

1 Écrire une page de journal intime

Lorsque vous écrivez une page de journal intime *(diary)*, gardez à l'esprit que vous incarnez le personnage qui rédige son journal intime. Vous devez donc bien relire le texte afin de cerner sa personnalité et la situation.

- Les articles sont datés et écrits à la première personne du singulier.
- Les événements de la journée sont relatés au prétérit (récit de la journée / période passée) ou au *present perfect* (bilan de la journée / répercussion sur le présent).
- Utilisez des adjectifs et des adverbes qui vous permettront de décrire réactions et sentiments.
- Utilisez un registre de langue simple et concis.

2 Écrire un article sur un blog

La rédaction d'un article sur un blog (ou *web log*) nécessite de suivre quelques règles :

- La qualité et la clarté du contenu font la réputation d'un blog. Les visiteurs ont besoin d'informations facilement utilisables.
- Vos phrases doivent être courtes (moins de vingt mots).
- Placer les points importants en premier.
- Un article de blog ne doit pas dépasser une page.
- Découpez votre article en paragraphes courts de 3 ou 4 phrases.
- Utilisez des titres et sous-titres.

C Écrire une histoire ou continuer un récit

Mettez chaque verbe entre parenthèses au temps qui convient.

It (happen) in New York three years ago on January 26th. I (arrive) two days before, and I (be) in a hotel on 5th Avenue. When I first (see) her, she (stand) at the bar. I just (can – not) take my eyes off her. Then she (look) at me.

● Rédiger un récit demande de respecter un certain nombre de règles.

- Introduisez la situation de départ : lieu(x), époque, personnages principaux, relations entre les personnages...
- Utilisez les temps du récit :
  → prétérit simple pour décrire les actions / événements ponctuels ;
  → prétérit BE+ING pour décrire ou parler d'une action en déroulement ;
  → *pluperfect* (HAD -EN) pour parler de ce qui s'est passé avant l'événement au prétérit.
- Employez des **mots de liaison** permettant de rendre compte de la chronologie des événements (voir manuel p. 169).

● Certains sujets font appel à votre expérience personnelle. Illustrez votre récit à l'aide d'exemples précis.

● D'autres sujets vous demandent d'imaginer une histoire, une suite ou une fin : respectez le style et le ton du texte.

● Certains de ces sujets peuvent inclure des parties dialoguées qui répondent à des règles précises.

D Rédiger un dialogue

Étoffez les phrases suivantes en ajoutant chaque fois un verbe introducteur différent.

1. *"Is something wrong, darling?" he...*
2. *"Can't you help me? Just for once!" she...*
3. *"I'm so glad to see you!" he...*
4. *"Why don't we go and have a drink somewhere?" she...*

Lorsque vous rédigez un dialogue, vous devez :

- déterminer le niveau de langue demandé : est-ce une situation formelle ou plus familière ?
- mettre les paroles entre guillemets et aller à la ligne à chaque changement de locuteur ;
- varier les verbes introducteurs qui apportent de précieuses indications sur le ton utilisé, sur les expressions du visage ou les gestes :

→ *say, tell, ask, answer, explain, add, insist, reply, exclaim, agree, admit, declare, wonder, continue, announce, suggest...*

- enrichir les phrases à l'aide d'adverbes :
  → *angrily, kindly, lovingly, quietly, loudly, calmly, nervously, impatiently…*
- utiliser une langue orale :
  → réponses courtes : *I don't think so… I hope not… So do I…* PRÉCIS GRAMMATICAL → 30
  → formes contractées : *I can't wait… I've got to go…*
  → *tags* : *You'll help me, won't you?…* PRÉCIS GRAMMATICAL → 30
  → *gap fillers* : *Well… Er… You know…*

E Rédiger un essai

Expliquez (en français) la tâche à accomplir dans chacun des sujets suivants.

1. *"Where there's a will there's a way." Discuss.*

2. *More and more blogs on the Internet are dedicated to stars. How can you account for that phenomenon? Say what you think about it.*

3. *Do you think that women have the same chances of becoming managers as men?*

Dans un essai, on vous demande d'argumenter, de commenter une citation ou de formuler une opinion sur un sujet précis, dans une langue soutenue.

- L'essai répond à des règles précises.
  - L'introduction présente la problématique du sujet / l'idée générale.
  - L'organisation des idées doit apparaître clairement : vous devez structurer votre essai en exprimant une seule idée par paragraphe.
  - Les phrases doivent être liées de façon logique par des transitions et des mots de liaison.
  - La conclusion répond à la question posée / au sujet.
- Avant de composer, il est nécessaire d'écrire au brouillon autant de mots et phrases clés que possible.
- Veillez à illustrer votre propos à l'aide d'exemples précis empruntés à votre expérience et à vos connaissances ou culture personnelles.
- Le registre de langue doit être soutenu et vous devez prendre position si on vous le demande.

F Rédiger un article de presse

Un **article de presse** transmet de l'information et doit permettre au lecteur de se faire une opinion personnelle de l'événement décrit. Lorsque vous rédigez un article de presse :

- Efforcez-vous de rester objectifs / neutres. Si vous donnez votre opinion, précisez-le clairement.
- Mentionnez les circonstances, les faits, les causes et éventuellement les conséquences de l'événement à raconter.
- Le registre de langue doit être soutenu. Évitez les formes contractées, sauf pour reprendre des paroles rapportées.
- Les mots de liaison doivent faire apparaître la logique de votre propos.
- Donnez un titre concis à votre article après l'avoir rédigé.

G Résumer un article de presse

- Résumer un article de presse nécessite avant tout une bonne **compréhension** du texte. Vous devez être capables de distinguer l'essentiel de l'accessoire (voir « Compréhension de l'écrit », p. 161).

- Avant de rédiger votre résumé vous devrez :
  - dégager le thème général et les opinions ;
  - souligner l'idée essentielle de chaque paragraphe ;
  - souligner les mots qui expriment les liens logiques.

- Rédigez le résumé de façon personnelle en faisant attention à :
  - éviter les formules du type *"the journalist declares / says that…"* ;
  - conserver le point de vue, la personne et les temps des verbes du texte original ;
  - rapporter les propos des personnages en les résumant au discours indirect ;
  - suivre l'ordre des idées de l'article ;
  - respecter la fourchette de mots demandée (en général le tiers du texte de départ).

Expressions utiles pour comprendre et s'exprimer à l'écrit

Mots de liaison

Addition

- **besides** / **moreover** / **what's more**: *en outre*

I don't mind going out. **Besides**, the walk will do me good.

But

- **in order (not) to** / **so as (not) to**: *pour (ne pas)*

He drove at 50 mph **so as to** save petrol.

- **so (that)**: *pour que, de façon que*

He lowered his voice **so (that)** Tania couldn't hear.

Cause

- **as**: *comme*

As Philip knew the road, we asked him to come with us.

- **because of**: *à cause de*

I spent three hours waiting in the rain **because of** you!

- **since**: *puisque*

Since you are unable to answer, I'll ask someone else.

Concession

- **although** / **though**: *bien que*

Although he's 60, he still works more than 12 hours a day.

- **despite** / **in spite of** *(plus courant)*: *malgré, en dépit de*

Despite all our efforts to save the school, they closed it.

- **however**: *pourtant, cependant, toutefois*

This is a simple machine. **However** there are dangers.

- **still** / **yet**: *pourtant, cependant*

The hotel was terrible. **Still**, we were lucky with the weather.

Condition

- **or else** / **otherwise**: *sinon*

Hurry up **or else** we'll miss the train.

- **provided**: *à condition que, pourvu que*

He can come with us, **provided** he pays for his meal.

- **unless**: *à moins que*

He won't go to sleep **unless** you tell him a story.

Conséquence

- **consequently** / **therefore** / **as a result**: *par conséquent*

He didn't work; **as a result** he failed.

Opposition

- **unlike**: *contrairement à*

Unlike most people he knew, he never came to work by car.

- **whereas** / **while**: *alors que, tandis que*

His first book was a flop **whereas** this one is a bestseller.

Temps

- **as**: *comme, alors que, au moment où*

I saw Peter **as** I was getting off the bus.

- **as soon as**: *dès que, aussitôt que*

As soon as she entered the room, she saw him.

- **meanwhile**: *pendant ce temps*

The flight will be announced soon. **Meanwhile**, please remain seated.

- **once**: *une fois (que)*

Once they're in bed, the children usually stay there.

- **till** / **until**: *jusqu'à (ce que)*

He waited **until** she had finished speaking.

- **while**: *pendant que*

They arrived **while** we were having dinner.

Expressions utiles pour écrire un essai ou un article de presse

Présenter le sujet / l'idée générale

- This is a topical *(d'actualité)* subject…
- This is an essential question / issue *(problème)*…
- In most cases… *(Dans la plupart des cas)*
- It deals *(traite)* with…

Donner des exemples

- For example / For instance… *(Par exemple)*
- … that is to say… *(c'est-à-dire)*
- … such as… *(tel que)*

Ajouter une idée

- As regards / Concerning… *(En ce qui concerne)*
- Similarly… *(De la même façon)*
- As we have already seen / mentioned…

Résumer ses idées

- For all these reasons…
- In other words…
- To sum up…

Conclure

- To conclude… / To sum up…
- In short / brief…
- In a nutshell… *(En un mot)*
- On the whole… *(En définitive)*
- All in all… *(Tout bien pesé)*

Donner son opinion

- I think / feel / believe that…
- To my mind… *(Selon moi)*
- It seems to me that…
- According to X… *(Selon X – impossible avec me et us)*

Exprimer son accord / désaccord

- I (dis)agree with X about / that…
- On the contrary…
- Contrary to… *(Contrairement à)*
- Instead of V-ING… *(Au lieu de V)*

Exprimer le doute

- Anyway / Anyhow… *(De toute façon)*
- It is hard to believe that…
- I wonder whether… *(Je me demande si)*

1 Le présent simple

A Formes

● À la **forme affirmative**, on utilise la **base verbale** et on ajoute ***s*** à la 3e personne du singulier. Pour les **questions** et les **négations**, on emploie l'auxiliaire ***DO*** / ***DON'T*** (***DOES*** / ***DOESN'T*** à la 3e personne du singulier) suivi de la base verbale.

I know him and he knows me.
› Je le connais et il me connaît.

Does he know me? › Est-ce qu'il me connaît ?

● **Formes**

- **affirmative** : *I / You like him. – He / She like**s** you. – We / You / They like him.*
- **interrogative** : ***Do*** *I like him? –* ***Does*** *he / she like me? –* ***Do*** *we / you / they like them?*
- **négative** : *I* ***don't*** *like you. – He / She* ***doesn't*** *like you. – We / You / They* ***don't*** *like him.*

> **Le verbe *DO* (FAIRE)**
> Il se conjugue aussi avec l'auxiliaire ***DO***, aux formes interrogative et négative du présent simple.
> *Does he often do that?*
> › Est-ce qu'il fait cela souvent ?

B Emplois

● **On emploie le présent simple pour :**

- **définir** une personne ou un objet (métier, goûts, opinion, etc.).

He works on a farm. › Il travaille dans une ferme.

He likes animals. › Il aime les animaux.

- mentionner une **action habituelle** ou **fréquente**.

They always come back. › Ils reviennent toujours.

- exprimer une **vérité générale**.

The earth revolves around the sun.
› La terre tourne autour du soleil.

● **On utilise aussi le présent simple pour donner des informations lorsque :**

- on **raconte une histoire** (**présent de narration**).

Then he stops and looks at them.
› Puis il s'arrête et les regarde.

- on **s'informe sur ce qui va se passer**.

What happens after that? › Qu'est-ce qui se passe après ?

Who speaks next? › Qui parle ensuite ?

> ***HAVE*** **et *HAVE GOT* (POSSÉDER)**
> Le verbe ***HAVE*** se conjugue obligatoirement avec l'auxiliaire ***DO*** (aux formes interrogative et négative).
> *Do you have a car?* › Est-ce que tu as une voiture ?
> *Yes I do. / No, I don't.*
> *I have a motorbike.* › J'ai une moto.
>
> ***HAVE GOT*** **:** ***HAVE*** est un auxiliaire.
> *Have you got a computer?* › As-tu un ordinateur ?
> *Yes, I have. / No, I haven't.*
> *I have got (I've got) two computers.*
> › J'ai deux ordinateurs.

2 Le présent *BE+ING*

A Formes

● On utilise l'auxiliaire ***BE*** à toutes les formes.
On accole ***-ING*** au verbe.

● **Formes**

- **affirmative** : *I am sleeping. – You are sleeping. – He / She is sleeping. – We / You / They are sleeping.*
- **interrogative** : *Am I sleeping? – Are you sleeping? – Is he / she sleeping? – Are we / you / they sleeping?*
- **négative** : *I am not sleeping. – You are not sleeping. – He / She is not sleeping. – We / You / They are not sleeping.*

B Emplois

● **On emploie le présent *BE+ING* pour décrire :**

- une action **en cours de déroulement** dont on est **témoin**.

Listen! The phone is ringing!
› Écoute ! Il y a le téléphone qui sonne !

- la **position** de quelqu'un.

She is sitting on her bed. › Elle est assise sur son lit.

● **On emploie également le présent *BE+ING* pour :**

- faire un **commentaire** (positif ou négatif) **sur le sujet** de l'énoncé.

She's always nagging at me!
› Elle n'arrête pas de m'embêter !

- exprimer la **volonté du sujet** (intention ou refus).

I'm not talking to her. › Je refuse de lui parler.

3 Verbes d'état / verbes d'action et la forme BE+ING

● Les verbes suivants (verbes d'état) **ne peuvent normalement pas s'utiliser à la forme** *BE+ING* : ***be, have, agree, believe, belong, hate, know, like, look, mean, prefer, remember, see, seem, sound, think, understand, want.***

What do you want? » Qu'est-ce que tu veux ?

● Parmi ces verbes, certains peuvent changer de sens et être utilisés au **présent** *BE+ING* lorsque l'on parle d'une **situation particulière**.

S'emploient toujours au présent simple	Peuvent s'employer au présent *BE+ING*
THINK : lorsqu'il signifie CROIRE (opinion). *I think you're wrong.* » Je pense / crois que tu as tort. *SEE* : pour la **perception** ou une **faculté intellectuelle**. *I don't see what you're talking about.* » Je ne vois pas / comprends pas de quoi tu parles. *HAVE* : lorsqu'il signifie POSSÉDER et dans les expressions : ***have an idea, no idea, a problem, time, a headache.*** *Do you have any idea where he's been?* » Sais-tu où il est allé ?	*THINK* : lorsqu'il signifie PENSER À, RÉFLÉCHIR, ENVISAGER DE. *Who are you thinking of?* » À qui penses-tu ? *We're thinking of leaving London.* » Nous envisageons de quitter Londres. *SEE* : lorsqu'il signifie RENCONTRER. *Who are you seeing today?* » Qui vois-tu / Avec qui as-tu rendez-vous aujourd'hui ? *HAVE* : dans les expressions ***have dinner, lunch, an appointment, a bath, a rest, a good time.*** *Are you having a good time?* » Est-ce que tu t'amuses ?

4 Le prétérit

A Prétérit simple

● À la **forme affirmative**, il se forme avec *-ED* (sauf dans le cas des verbes irréguliers ; voir pages 206-207).

● Aux **formes interrogative** et **négative**, il se forme avec l'auxiliaire *DID* / *DIDN'T*. Les formes sont identiques à toutes les personnes.

- **affirmative** : *He laughed.*
- **interrogative** : *Did you laugh?*
- **négative** : *They didn't laugh.*

● Le prétérit est le **temps du récit** (de la narration). Les mots exprimant la **succession dans le temps** (*FIRST*, *AND THEN*, etc.) entraînent obligatoirement le prétérit.

He looked up and then smiled.
» Il leva les yeux, puis il sourit.

B *USED TO* et *WOULD*

● ***USED TO*** est une forme de prétérit qui exprime la rupture avec la situation présente : ce qui était vrai dans le passé ne l'est plus.

He used to wake up at night.
» Avant, il se réveillait la nuit. → Ce n'est plus le cas.

● ***WOULD*** (auxiliaire modal, suivi de la base verbale) peut exprimer l'habitude au passé.

As a child, he would wake up at night.
» Quand il était enfant, il se réveillait la nuit. → C'était une habitude.

C Prétérit *BE+ING*

● Il sert à la **description dans le passé**. On l'utilise souvent pour parler d'une **action en cours de déroulement dans le passé** et qui s'oppose à un événement ponctuel (au prétérit simple).

When I came in, they were watching TV.
» Lorsque je suis entré, ils regardaient la télévision.

5 Le *present perfect*

A *Present perfect* simple

● **L'auxiliaire** est *HAVE*. Le verbe est au **participe passé**. (La formule *HAVE -EN* symbolise le *present perfect.*)

● On utilise *HAVE* à toutes les personnes, sauf à la 3e personne du singulier → *HAS*.

● **Formes**

- **affirmative** : *I have finished. He has finished.*
- **interrogative** : *Have you finished?*
- **négative** : *He has not finished.*

- Le *present perfect* permet de présenter le **résultat présent** d'une action.

He's opened the door. › Il a ouvert la porte.
→ La porte est ouverte.

- Il permet de faire le **bilan** d'une situation dans le présent. On le trouve donc souvent associé à des verbes au présent ou à des adverbes établissant un lien avec le présent. (Voir **Gr. 6 B.**)

I've often talked to him lately. He doesn't agree with us.
› Je lui ai souvent parlé ces derniers temps. Il n'est pas d'accord avec nous.

B *Present perfect* BE+ING

- On associe la forme *BE+ING* au *present perfect.*

- Il exprime le **résultat d'une activité** qui a eu lieu, activité dont on voit souvent des traces dans le présent.

You've been crying. › Tu as pleuré.
→ J'en vois des traces (larmes, etc.).

C *Present perfect* simple ou *present perfect* BE+ING?

- Le *present perfect* simple met l'accent sur le **résultat** obtenu et le *present perfect BE+ING* sur **l'activité** qui a eu lieu.

You've painted the door. › Tu as peint la porte.
(On s'intéresse à la porte.)

You've been painting. › Tu as fait de la peinture.
(On s'intéresse à ce qu'a fait le sujet.)

- Avec une **mesure précise** (*three times, by 10%*, etc.), on utilise le *present perfect* simple et non pas *BE+ING.*

Prices have risen by 10%. › Les prix ont augmenté de 10 %.

- **Attention !** Le *present perfect BE+ING* à lui seul ne signifie **pas** que l'action dure encore ! Pour exprimer cette idée, il faut l'associer à ***for*** ou ***since***.

*Prices have been rising regularly **since** last year / **for** a few months.* › Les prix augmentent régulièrement depuis l'an dernier / depuis quelques mois.

6 *Present perfect* ou prétérit ?

A Choix de « l'éclairage »

- On peut répondre à une question au ***present perfect*** par un **prétérit**, lorsqu'on donne une information sur **le moment** ou **le lieu**. Comparez les deux réponses possibles à la question suivante :

Have you seen them lately? › Tu les a vus récemment ?

Réponse 1 :

Yes, I have. › Oui.

C'est le résultat présent qui compte. (Je sais qu'ils sont là.)
→ ***Present perfect.***

Réponse 2 :

Yes, I saw them in the park yesterday.
› Oui, je les ai vus hier dans le parc.

Information sur le lieu et le moment où s'est produit l'événement passé. → **Prétérit.**

B Adverbes et expressions de temps

- La présence d'**adverbes de temps** ou d'**expressions renvoyant au passé** (*AGO, LAST YEAR, WHEN*...) entraîne obligatoirement le **prétérit.**

He found a new job two months ago.
› Il a trouvé un nouvel emploi il y a deux mois.

- Certains adverbes et expressions de temps sont fréquemment associés au ***present perfect.*** C'est parce qu'ils peuvent exprimer un **lien avec le présent** : ***ALREADY, ALWAYS, BEFORE, EVER / NEVER, NOT YET*** (NE PAS... ENCORE), ***OVER THE PAST FEW MONTHS*** (CES DERNIERS MOIS), ***JUST, RECENTLY, SO FAR*** (JUSQU'À PRÉSENT), ***SINCE*** (DEPUIS).

We've just started. › Nous venons de commencer.

Have you ever been there? › Tu y es déjà allé ?

C Traduction du passé composé

- Si le passé composé renvoie à un **événement passé**, on le traduit par un **prétérit. C'est le cas le plus fréquent.**

Je les ai vus hier. › *I saw them yesterday.*

- On ne traduit le passé composé par un ***present perfect*** que s'il exprime un **résultat présent.**

Oui, je sais. Je les ai vus. › *Yes, I know. I've seen them.*

7 FOR - SINCE - AGO / PENDANT - DEPUIS - IL Y A

A FOR

FOR et le prétérit

Le **prétérit** indique que l'action n'a **aucun lien avec le présent**. On traduit *FOR* par PENDANT.

He stayed with them for two months last year.
› Il a vécu chez eux pendant deux mois l'année dernière.

FOR avec le *present perfect* simple et le *present perfect* BE+ING

Le ***present perfect*** met en évidence le **lien avec le présent**. On traduit FOR par DEPUIS et le verbe par un **présent**.

I've had this CD for years.
› J'ai ce CD depuis des années. / Cela fait des années que j'ai ce CD.

He's been sleeping for more than three hours now.
› Il dort depuis plus de trois heures. / Cela fait plus de trois heures qu'il dort.

B SINCE

SINCE est suivi d'une **date ou** d'une **expression indiquant le point de départ de l'action** : *since yesterday, since last year, since that time*, etc.

SINCE exprime un **lien entre le point de départ d'une action (dans le passé) et le présent**. C'est pourquoi le verbe principal est au *present perfect* : il peut s'agir du *present perfect simple* ou du *present perfect BE+ING*.

On traduit *SINCE* par DEPUIS et le verbe par un **présent**.

I've known him since Xmas.
› Je le connais depuis Noël.

She's been living in London since June.
› Elle vit à Londres depuis juin.

***FOR* ou *SINCE* ?**

- ***FOR*** : on additionne des moments : *for two weeks, for days*, etc. (Voir **Gr. 7 A.**)
- ***SINCE*** est suivi d'un élément qui a la valeur d'une **date**. Parfois, cet élément est un **verbe au prétérit**.

*She's been working here since **January** / **since she came back**.*
› Elle travaille ici depuis janvier / depuis qu'elle est revenue.

Le *present perfect* BE+ING avec *FOR* ou *SINCE* → DEPUIS

- La forme *BE+ING* du *present perfect* n'est possible qu'avec les **verbes d'action** qui sont compatibles avec l'idée de déroulement.
  I've been running for twenty minutes.
  › Je cours depuis vingt minutes.
- La forme *BE+ING*, qui souligne l'activité du sujet, est impossible avec les verbes d'état. (Voir **Gr. 3**.)

- Avec *FOR* ou *SINCE*, **on traduit** de la même manière le *present perfect* simple et le *present perfect BE+ING* → **présent en français**.

C AGO

AGO se place **après le complément de temps** et ne s'emploie qu'avec le **prétérit** car l'expression en AGO joue le rôle d'une date.

He sent me a message two days ago (on Sunday).
› Il m'a envoyé un message il y a deux jours (dimanche).

D « PENDANT » : *FOR* ou *DURING* ?

FOR, qui exprime la **durée**, répond à la question *HOW LONG?* (COMBIEN DE TEMPS ?). Il s'utilise :

- chaque fois que l'on **additionne** des jours, des semaines, etc. → *for **two** days, for **three** weeks, for **days**, for **weeks**, for **ages**, for **centuries***, etc.
- avec ***time***, ***long*** et ***ever*** → *for **a long time**, for **some time**, for **so long**, for **ever***, etc.

DURING est suivi d'un groupe nominal et répond à la question *WHEN?* (QUAND ?). Il renvoie à ***un moment précis***, situé à l'intérieur d'une période de temps. *DURING* signifie À UN MOMENT DONNÉ DE : *during the holidays, during that time, during the weekend*, etc.

Comparez les deux traductions de PENDANT.

Il l'a appelée **pendant la pause** et lui a parlé **pendant plus de vingt minutes**.
› *He called her **during the break** and talked to her **for more than twenty minutes**.*

E « DEPUIS »

Attention au temps ! À la différence du français, on n'emploie pas le présent en anglais lorsqu'on traduit un énoncé avec DEPUIS. On emploie le ***present perfect***.

J'ai cette voiture **depuis** un mois / **depuis** Janvier.
› ***I've had*** *this car* ***for*** *a month /* ***since*** *January.*

IL Y A ou DEPUIS ?

- **IL Y A** s'utilise pour un événement **passé**. On traduit par le **prétérit** + *AGO*.

Ils sont partis il y a une semaine. (partir : *leave*)
› *They left one week ago.*

- On peut parfois exprimer à peu près la même idée avec DEPUIS. Mais dans ce cas, on parle d'un état qui dure jusqu'au moment présent (et non plus d'un événement passé). On doit **changer de temps et de verbe**. On traduit par le ***present perfect*** + *FOR* ou *SINCE*.

Ils sont partis depuis une semaine / depuis lundi.
(être parti : *be away*)
› *They've been away for a week / since Monday.*

8 Le pluperfect

A *Pluperfect* simple

● Il se forme comme le *present perfect* avec l'auxiliaire ***HAVE*** et le **participe passé** du verbe. Cependant, à la différence du *present perfect*, **l'auxiliaire est au passé** : ***HAD***. (Pour parler du *pluperfect*, on utilise parfois la formule ***HAD -EN***, dans laquelle ***-EN*** symbolise le participe passé.)

He had finished. – Had he finished? – He had not finished.

● Il correspond souvent au *present perfect* dans un **contexte passé**. Ainsi il est souvent associé à des adverbes comme ***ALREADY, ALWAYS, BEFORE, EVER / NEVER***, etc.

I knew that he had already told her.
› Je savais qu'il le lui avait déjà dit.

● On l'utilise pour bouleverser l'ordre des événements (ordre chronologique) et faire des retours en arrière (flash-back).

She realized that he had left a few minutes before.
› Elle se rendit compte qu'il était parti quelques minutes auparavant.

Contractions de *HAD*

- À l'oral, on contracte souvent ***HAD*** en ***'D*** et ***HAD NOT*** en ***'D NOT*** ou ***HADN'T***.
  She'd not / hadn't eaten what I'd prepared.
  › Elle n'avait pas mangé ce que j'avais préparé.
- Ne pas confondre ***HAD*** et ***WOULD*** (auxiliaire du conditionnel) dans leur forme contractée ***'D*** :

– ***HAD*** est suivi du **participe passé** :
He'd told me. › Il me l'avait dit.
– ***WOULD*** est suivi de la **base verbale** :
I'd tell you if I knew. › Je te le dirais si je le savais.

B *Pluperfect* ***BE+ING***

● Comme le ***present perfect*** ***BE+ING***, il est formé avec ***HAVE -EN*** et ***BE+ING***. Mais à la différence du *present perfect*, l'auxiliaire ***HAVE*** est au passé : ***HAD***. Il correspond au *present perfect* ***BE+ING*** dans un **contexte passé**.

I could see that she had been crying.
› Je voyais bien qu'elle avait pleuré.

9 L'irréel

A Les deux valeurs du passé

● Un temps du passé (prétérit ou *pluperfect*) ne renvoie pas toujours à un événement qui s'est produit dans le passé. Il peut être utilisé pour des **faits irréels**, souhaités ou imaginés.

● **Comparez :**

- **événement passé : valeur temporelle du prétérit**
  He asked me long ago.
  › Il me l'a demandé il y a longtemps.
- **fait irréel : valeur modale (= prétérit modal)**
  If he asked me, I would help him.
  › S'il me le demandait, je l'aiderais.

B Hypothèse

● **Hypothèse simple :** ***IF*** **+ présent /** ***WILL*** **BV**

If she calls me, I will talk to her.
› Si elle m'appelle, je lui parlerai.

● **Hypothèse incertaine :** ***IF*** **+ prétérit modal /** ***WOULD*** **BV**

If she called me, I would talk to her.
› Si elle m'appelait, je lui parlerais.

● **Hypothèse non réalisée :** ***IF*** **+ *pluperfect* modal /** ***WOULD HAVE -EN***

If she had called me, I would have talked to her.
› Si elle m'avait appelé, je lui aurais parlé.

C Souhait – regret

On emploie le prétérit modal après :

● ***IF ONLY*** *If only she was / were with us!*
› Si seulement elle était avec nous !
WERE s'emploie à **toutes les personnes** dans une langue plus formelle.

● ***I'D RATHER*** *I'd rather you left / you didn't stay.*
› Je préfèrerais que tu partes / que tu ne restes pas.
Lorsque la phrase ne comporte qu'**un sujet**, on emploie l'**infinitif sans** ***TO***.
I'd rather do it myself.
› Je préfèrerais le faire moi-même.

● ***IT'S TIME*** *It's time you bought a new computer.*
› Il est temps que tu achètes un nouvel ordinateur.

● ***I WISH*** *I wish he was (were) younger.*
› J'aimerais qu'il soit plus jeune. / Je regrette qu'il ne soit pas plus jeune.

D Regret d'un fait passé

- Lorsqu'on veut exprimer le **regret à propos d'un fait passé**, on emploie le ***pluperfect* modal** après *WISH* et *I'D RATHER*.

I wish you had talked to him. » J'aurais aimé que tu lui parles. / Je regrette que tu ne lui aies pas parlé.
I'd rather you had told me.
» J'aurais préféré que tu me le dises.

Traduction de REGRETTER
WISH signifie SOUHAITER (qui est l'inverse de REGRETTER). On doit donc inverser le sens de la subordonnée lorsqu'on traduit en français : le négatif devient positif et inversement.

Je regrette qu'il soit si tard.
» *I wish it were **not** so late.*

Je regrette que tu ne sois pas mon frère.
» *I wish you were my brother.*

Je regrette que tu aies vu cela.
» *I wish you had **not** seen that.*

10 Expressions du futur

A *WILL* et *BE GOING TO*

- ***WILL*: on prévoit que l'action se réalisera dans l'avenir** (exemple : prévision météo).

It will snow tomorrow. » Il neigera demain.

- ***BE GOING TO***: l'action future est étroitement **liée à la situation présente** → « Étant donné ce que je sais du présent / ce que je vois, j'en conclus que… »

Careful! It's going to fall! » Attention ! Ça va tomber !

- **On emploie *WILL*:**

- avec un **repère de temps futur**, et donc avec une **subordonnée de temps**.

I'll ask her later / on Monday / when she comes back.
» Je le lui demanderai plus tard / lundi / quand elle reviendra.

Attention : *WILL* ne peut **pas** s'utiliser **dans la subordonnée**. (Voir **Gr. 10 C**.)

- avec une **subordonnée en *IF***.

If you ask me, I'll help you.
» Si tu me le demandes, je t'aiderai.

- **On emploie *BE GOING TO*:**

- lorsqu'il y a **observation de la situation présente**.

Look! It's going to rain. » Regarde ! Il va pleuvoir.

- généralement, lorsqu'il n'y a **pas de repère temporel**.

There's going to be a great change.
» Il va y avoir un grand changement.

B Autres expressions du futur

Comme *BE GOING TO*, elles sont construites avec *BE* et *TO*. ***To*** indique qu'il y a **projection dans l'avenir**.

- ***BE TO***

Indique que quelque chose est **prévu** ou **a été arrangé à l'avance**. On traduit souvent par DEVOIR.

*The meeting **is to** take place next week.*
» La réunion doit avoir lieu la semaine prochaine.

- ***BE ABOUT TO***

Indique que quelque chose est **sur le point de se produire**.

*He **is** just **about to** leave.* » Il est sur le point de partir.

- ***BE LIKELY TO***

Indique qu'il y a de **fortes chances pour que quelque chose se produise**.

*It **is likely to** happen again.*
» Il y a beaucoup de chances pour que cela se reproduise.

- ***BE SURE TO / BE BOUND TO***

Expriment la **certitude d'un événement futur**.

*She **is sure to** win.* » Il est certain qu'elle va gagner.

*They **are bound to** come back.*
» Il est certain qu'ils vont revenir.

C Subordonnées en *WHEN* et le futur

- **On n'emploie pas *WILL* dans une subordonnée de temps :** après *WHEN, AS SOON AS* (DÈS QUE), *WHILE* (PENDANT QUE), *AS LONG AS* (TANT QUE), *UNTIL* (JUSQU'À CE QUE / AVANT QUE). Pour exprimer l'idée d'avenir, on emploie le présent ou le *present perfect*.

*I'll get a new one **when** I have a little money.*
» J'en prendrai un autre lorsque j'aurai un peu d'argent.

*I won't go **until I have finished**.*
» Je ne partirai pas avant d'avoir fini.

Remarque : Si la subordonnée est remplaçable par *LATER*, c'est bien une subordonnée de temps.

Je lui écrirai quand j'aurai le temps / plus tard.
» *I'll write to him **when I have time** / **later**.*

- **On maintient *WILL* après *WHEN*** lorsqu'il s'agit d'une **interrogative** au style direct ou indirect.

Quand reviendra-t-elle ?
» *When will she come back?*

Je ne sais pas quand elle reviendra.
» *I don't know when she will come back.*

11 Les modaux : introduction

Les modaux ***CAN, COULD, MAY, MIGHT, WILL, WOULD, MUST, SHALL, SHOULD*** sont des **auxiliaires** qui ont un sens bien particulier : ils expriment **le possible**, **le certain**, **l'impossible**, **l'obligation**, **la permission**, etc.

She may call later. › Il se peut qu'elle appelle plus tard.

I must leave. › Il faut que je parte. / Je dois partir.

A Formes

- Ils ne prennent pas de ***S*** à la 3e personne et ne sont jamais suivis de ***TO***, ni de ***V-ING***.
- On utilise **un seul modal** par forme verbale. Par exemple, ***WILL*** n'est jamais suivi de ***CAN*** ou ***MUST***.
- Les modaux peuvent être suivis de :

▪ ***BE+ING*** pour une action vue sous l'angle du **déroulement**.

He may be sleeping. › Peut-être est-il en train de dormir.

▪ l'auxiliaire ***HAVE*** suivi du **participe passé** (***HAVE -EN***) pour **un fait accompli ou passé**.

She may have finished by now.
› Peut-être a-t-elle fini maintenant.

B Les deux sens des modaux

La modalité renvoie au domaine du **jugement**. Il y a deux types de jugement possibles. Selon le contexte, chaque modal peut avoir l'un ou l'autre sens :

▪ celui qui parle estime que **le sujet de la phrase a la capacité** / **l'obligation** / **la permission** / **la volonté** de faire quelque chose : on parle de **sens 1** du modal.

She must accept it! › Elle doit l'accepter !
→ Moi qui parle, j'affirme qu'il faut qu'elle l'accepte.

▪ celui qui parle dit qu'il est **plus ou moins certain** de quelque chose : on parle de **sens 2** du modal.

She must be very happy. › Elle doit être très heureuse.
→ Je suis certain qu'elle est très heureuse.

12 Les modaux : sens 1

A Capacité / incapacité : *CAN* / *CAN'T*

Can you help him? › Peux-tu l'aider ? → En es-tu capable ?

I can't stay much longer.
› Je ne peux pas rester beaucoup plus longtemps.

I can drive a lorry. › Je sais conduire un camion.

B Permission / absence de permission : *MAY* / *MAY NOT*

You may stay if you like. › Tu peux rester si tu veux.

Visitors may not feed the animals. › Les visiteurs ne sont pas autorisés à donner de la nourriture aux animaux.

Remarque : Dans la langue courante, la permission et l'interdiction sont souvent exprimées par ***CAN*** et ***CAN'T***.

You can stay, but you can't smoke.
› Tu peux rester, mais tu ne peux pas fumer.

C Obligation / interdiction : *MUST* / *MUSTN'T*

You must tell me everything. › Tu dois tout me dire.

You must not tell anyone. › Tu ne dois le dire à personne.

D Conseil : *SHOULD* / *SHOULD NOT*

You should ask him first. › Tu devrais lui demander d'abord.

You shouldn't say that. › Tu ne devrais pas dire ça.

E Volonté / refus : *WILL* / *WON'T*

Will you marry me? › Veux-tu m'épouser ?

He won't do it! › Il refuse de le faire !

Remarque : Dans la plupart des cas, le verbe VOULOIR se traduit par ***WANT***.

She wants to leave. He doesn't want to go.

F Nécessité / absence de nécessité : *NEED* / *NEEDN'T*

Need I tell you what I feel?
› Ai-je besoin de te dire ce que je ressens ?

You needn't tell me why you did it.
› Tu n'as pas besoin de me dire pourquoi tu l'as fait.

13 « Équivalents » des modaux (sens 1)

- ***HAVE TO*** (DEVOIR), ***BE ABLE TO*** (ÊTRE CAPABLE DE), ***BE ALLOWED TO*** (ÊTRE AUTORISÉ À), ***BE FORBIDDEN TO*** (ÊTRE INTERDIT / AVOIR L'INTERDICTION DE) expriment des notions proches de celles exprimées par les modaux de sens 1.
- Au passé et au futur, ils s'utilisent à la place des modaux.
- À la différence des modaux, ces verbes n'expriment **aucun jugement** de la part de celui qui parle. Ils présentent l'obligation, la permission, etc., sous l'angle de la **simple constatation**.

Notion	Forme non modale : simple constatation	Modal : jugement ou pression de celui qui parle
Obligation	**Présent :** *Sorry, **I have to** go now.* » Désolé, il faut que je parte maintenant. **Futur :** *He **will have to**…* **Passé :** ***Did** he **have to**…?*	*You **must** go now!* » Tu dois partir maintenant ! → C'est moi qui le veux.
Interdiction	**Présent :** *They're **forbidden to** go out.* » Il leur est interdit de sortir. **Futur :** *They **will be forbidden to**…* **Passé :** *They **were forbidden to**…*	*They **mustn't** go out!* » Ils ne doivent pas sortir ! → Je le leur interdis.
Absence d'obligation	**Présent :** *You **don't have to** answer.* » Tu n'es pas obligé de répondre. **Futur :** *You **won't have to**…* **Passé :** *You **didn't have to**…*	*You **needn't** shout!* » Tu n'es pas obligé de crier ! → Cette forme peut indiquer le reproche fait à l'autre.
Permission	**Présent :** *They**'re allowed to** leave now.* » Ils ont le droit de partir maintenant. **Futur :** *They**'ll be allowed to**…* **Passé :** *They **were allowed to**…*	*You **may** leave now.* » Vous pouvez partir maintenant. → Celui qui parle accorde la permission.
Ce qui n'est pas permis	**Présent :** *You**'re not allowed to** turn left.* » Tu n'as pas le droit de tourner à gauche. **Futur :** *You **won't be allowed to**…* **Passé :** *We **weren't allowed to**…*	*Visitors **may not** take photos.* » Il est interdit aux visiteurs de prendre des photos. → Ce sont les autorités qui le disent.
Volonté (refus)	**Présent :** *He **doesn't want to** answer.* » Il ne veut pas répondre. **Passé :** *He **didn't want to**…*	**Présent :** *He **won't** answer me!* » Il refuse de me répondre ! **Passé :** *I insisted but he **wouldn't** answer me.* » J'ai insisté, mais il a refusé de me répondre.
Conseil	***Why don't** you help them?* » Pourquoi ne les aides-tu pas ?	*You **should** help them.* » Tu devrais les aider. *You really **ought to** help them.* » Tu devrais vraiment les aider. → ***OUGHT TO*** exprime une **obligation morale** plus fortement que ***SHOULD***.
Reproche	***Why didn't** you ask them?* » Pourquoi ne le leur as-tu pas demandé ?	*You **should have** asked them.* » Tu aurais dû le leur demander.
(In)capacité	**Présent :** ***Is** he **able to** handle the situation?* » Est-il capable de faire face à la situation ? **Futur :** *He**'ll be able to**…* **Passé :** *He **was able to**…*	**Présent :** *I **can** stay with you.* » Je peux rester avec toi. **Passé :** *I **couldn't** stay with you.* » Je ne pouvais pas rester avec toi.

14 Les modaux (sens 2) : la probabilité

A Degrés de probabilité

On peut classer les modaux selon le **degré de probabilité** qu'ils expriment, **du moins certain au plus certain** :

It might rain tonight. » Il se pourrait qu'il pleuve ce soir.

It may rain tonight. » Il est possible qu'il pleuve ce soir.

It will rain tonight. » Il pleuvra ce soir.
→ J'affirme qu'il pleuvra ce soir.

He must be older than her. » Il doit être plus âgé qu'elle.
→ J'en suis à peu près sûr.

She can't be his daughter!
» Il est impossible que ce soit sa fille !
→ J'en suis certain.

B *MAY NOT* et *CAN'T*

- ***MAY NOT*** : « Il est possible que cela **ne soit pas**… »

She may not know that we're back.
» Peut-être ne sait-elle pas que nous sommes revenus.

- ***CAN'T*** : « Il est **impossible** que cela soit… »

He can't be that young!
» Il n'est pas possible qu'il soit si jeune !

B Probabilité d'un fait présent, passé, futur

On peut exprimer un jugement de probabilité sur un fait présent, passé ou futur : « Il est possible que cela se passe en ce moment / cela se soit passé / cela se produise dans l'avenir. » Le jugement est fait dans le présent par celui qui parle. **Ce n'est pas le modal qui exprime le passé, présent ou futur de l'action ; c'est la forme du verbe qui le suit et le contexte.**

Fait présent

- La **forme** *BE+ING* est possible avec les **verbes de processus** (actions) et impossible avec les verbes d'état (*BE, HAVE, KNOW, WANT*, etc.).

I must be dreaming! » Je dois rêver !

She may be sleeping.
» Il se peut qu'elle soit en train de dormir.

- Avec les **verbes d'état**, on emploie la **base verbale** pour indiquer que le fait est possible / probable dans le présent.

You must know her. » Tu dois la connaître.

He may not want to stay.
» Il se peut qu'il ne veuille pas rester.

Fait passé

On utilise le **modal suivi de l'auxiliaire *HAVE* et du participe passé** du verbe (modal + *HAVE -EN*).

You may have left it in the car.
» Il se peut que tu l'aies laissé dans la voiture.

He must have changed his mind.
» Il a dû changer d'avis.

Fait futur

La **base verbale** (infinitif sans *TO*) peut renvoyer à un **fait futur**.

You may get a promotion if you work hard enough.
» Il se peut que tu sois promu si tu travailles suffisamment.

D Forme passée du modal

COULD est le passé de *CAN* ; *MIGHT* est le passé de *MAY* ; *WOULD* le passé de *WILL*. La forme passée du modal exprime souvent l'**irréel**, c'est-à-dire ce qui est **moins certain**. Par exemple, *MIGHT* exprime une possibilité plus incertaine que *MAY*.

He may know the answer.
» Il se peut qu'il connaisse la réponse.

He might know the answer.
» Il pourrait qu'il connaisse la réponse.

15 Les modaux : *CAN, COULD, MAY, MIGHT*

A *CAN* / *COULD* : le possible

SENS 1	SENS 2
CAN : **capacité** *Can you see it?* » Tu le vois ? → Tu peux le voir ? *I can read Spanish.* » Je lis l'espagnol. → Je sais lire l'espagnol.	*CAN* : **possibilité** (seulement à la forme interrogative) *Can he be that stupid?* » Est-il possible qu'il soit aussi bête ?
CAN'T : **incapacité** *He can't explain it. He knows nothing about it.* » Il ne peut pas l'expliquer. Il n'en sait rien.	*CAN'T* : **l'impossible** *She can't be right!* Elle ne peut pas avoir raison. → C'est impossible.
CAN / *CAN'T* : **permission** / **interdiction** *Can I open the window? – No you can't.* » Puis-je ouvrir la fenêtre ? – Non.	

SENS 1	SENS 2
COULD / COULDN'T: capacité / incapacité – possibilité au passé ou au conditionnel ▪ **Passé :** *He couldn't sleep for weeks.* » Il n'a pas pu dormir pendant des semaines. ▪ **Possibilité irréelle :** *We could try and phone him.* » On pourrait essayer de lui téléphoner. ▪ **Possibilité non réalisée :** *He could have sold it.* » Il aurait pu le vendre. → Mais il ne l'a pas vendu.	**COULD : possibilité plus incertaine que *can*** *It could well be the last time.* » Il se pourrait bien que ce soit la dernière fois.

B *MAY*: le possible à 50 %

SENS 1	SENS 2
MAY : permission *May I have a look at your notebook?* » Puis-je jeter un coup d'œil à votre carnet?	**MAY : possibilité** *She may call you any minute.* » Il est possible qu'elle appelle d'une minute à l'autre. → Il y a autant de chances que cela arrive, que l'inverse.
MAY NOT : ce qui n'est pas permis *You may not use your mobile phone.* » Vous n'avez pas le droit d'utiliser votre portable.	**MAY NOT : il est possible que cela ne se passe pas / ne soit pas le cas** *Even if I invite him he may not come.* » Même si je l'invite, il est possible qu'il ne vienne pas.

C *MIGHT*: le possible très atténué

SENS 1	SENS 2
MIGHT : permission au style indirect *She asked if she might leave.* » Elle a demandé si elle pouvait partir.	**MIGHT : possibilité très incertaine** *The rumour might be true.* » Il se pourrait que la rumeur soit fondée.

16 Les modaux : *MUST, SHALL, SHOULD*

A *MUST*: la nécessité, ce qui doit être

SENS 1	SENS 2
MUST : obligation *You must believe me!* » Tu dois / Il faut me croire !	**MUST : certitude** *She must be his wife.* » Ce doit être sa femme. → C'est certainement vrai.
MUSTN'T : interdiction *You mustn't bother her.* » Tu ne dois pas l'embêter.	**CAN'T :** on est certain que cela n'est pas vrai *She can't be his sister!* » Cela ne peut être sa sœur ! → Ce n'est pas possible.

B *Shall / should*: la contrainte, ce qui doit être

SENS 1	SENS 2
SHALL: s'utilise pour faire une **suggestion** (presque toujours à la forme interrogative). *Shall I let them in?* » Je les fais entrer ?	*SHALL*: **sens futur** (à la première personne du singulier et du pluriel, mais beaucoup plus rarement que *WILL*) *When shall I see you again?* » Quand vous reverrai-je ?
SHOULD: **conseil** (forme atténuée de contrainte) *You should leave her alone.* » Tu devrais la laisser tranquille.	*SHOULD*: **probabilité forte** *It shouldn't be difficult to convince them.* » Cela ne devrait pas être difficile de les convaincre.
SHOULD HAVE -EN: **reproche** / **regret** (fait passé) *You should have told me before.* » Tu aurais dû me le dire plus tôt. *I should have told her.* » J'aurais dû le lui dire.	*SHOULD HAVE -EN*: **probabilité forte** (fait passé) *She should have found it by now.* » Elle a dû le trouver à l'heure qu'il est. → Elle doit l'avoir trouvé.

C Traduction de *devoir*

● **Devoir** / **ne pas devoir** peut exprimer **l'obligation**, **l'interdiction ou l'absence d'obligation**. Une erreur fréquente consiste à confondre ces notions lorsque l'on traduit « il ne doit pas », « il ne devait pas », « il n'a pas besoin de », « il n'a pas été obligé de ».

● **Devoir** peut également exprimer une **quasi-certitude**. On utilise *MUST* ou *CAN'T* lorsque l'on est certain que quelque chose est vrai ou n'est pas vrai.

● Avant de choisir la forme verbale en anglais, il faut **identifier la notion** exprimée.

Français	Notion	Anglais
Tu dois le leur dire.	Obligation au présent	*You must tell them. / You have to tell them. / You've got to tell them.*
Il ne doit pas le leur dire.	Interdiction au présent	*He mustn't tell them.*
Il ne devait pas sortir. (= Il n'en avait pas le droit.)	Interdiction au passé	*He wasn't allowed to go out.* → On n'utilise pas *MUST* au passé.
Tu n'as pas besoin de le leur dire.	Absence d'obligation au présent	*You needn't tell them. / You don't have to tell them.*
Il n'a pas eu besoin de le leur dire.	Absence d'obligation au passé	*He didn't have to tell them.*
Il doit être très jeune. Elle doit être en train de travailler. Ils ont dû être très contents.	Forte probabilité affirmative	*He must be very young.* *She must be working.* *They must have been very glad.*
Il ne doit pas faire très froid. Elle ne devait pas être très âgée.	Forte probabilité négative	*It can't be very cold.* *She can't have been very old.*

17 Les modaux : *will, would*

Will / would: projection vers la réalisation d'un acte

SENS 1	SENS 2
WILL: **volonté** *Stand up, will you?* » Lève-toi, veux-tu ? / Lève-toi, s'il te plaît.	*WILL*: **sens futur (prédiction)** *I will let you know.* » Je te tiendrai au courant.
WON'T: **refus** *I won't speak to him!* » Je refuse de lui parler !	*WON'T*: **sens futur** *The results won't be announced until Tuesday.* » Les résultats ne seront pas annoncés avant mardi.

SENS 1	SENS 2
WILL : **ce qui est prévisible et caractéristique du sujet** *He will talk all the time.* » Il ne peut pas s'empêcher de parler.	
WOULD : **volonté atténuée** *Do you know anyone who would do it?* » Connais-tu quelqu'un qui voudrait bien le faire ?	WOULD : **conditionnel** *It would be wonderful if they came.* » Ce serait merveilleux s'ils venaient. → Fait irréel, soumis à condition : conditionnel présent
WOULD : **habitude au passé** (ce qui caractérisait le sujet dans le passé) *The children would be up at dawn.* » Les enfants étaient toujours debout à l'aube.	*If we had left later we would have missed the train.* » Si nous étions partis plus tard, nous aurions manqué le train. → Fait non réalisé : conditionnel passé

18 Prépositions et particules adverbiales

Ce sont souvent les mêmes mots qui servent de préposition et de particule adverbiale (ou postposition).

*He goes **in**.* » Il entre. / *He goes **out**.* » Il sort.
→ ***In*** et ***out*** sont des particules adverbiales. **Chacune donne** au verbe GO un **sens particulier**.

*The money is **in** my bag.* » L'argent est dans mon sac.
→ ***In*** est ici une préposition. Elle a pour fonction **d'introduire un complément** (*in my bag* → complément de lieu).

A Verbes à particule

● Dans certains cas, la particule donne au verbe un sens immédiatement compréhensible.

ACROSS :	à travers	→ ***get across*** :	traverser
BACK :	idée de retour	→ ***get back*** :	revenir
DOWN :	vers le bas	→ ***look down*** :	regarder vers le bas
IN :	à l'intérieur	→ ***get in*** :	entrer
UP :	vers le haut	→ ***look up*** :	regarder vers le haut
OUT :	à l'extérieur	→ ***get out*** :	sortir

● Mais la particule ne permet pas toujours de comprendre le sens du verbe.

get by : se débrouiller — ***give in*** : céder
give up : renoncer, abandonner — ***look after*** : s'occuper de

● **Si le complément est un pronom**, il se place **entre le verbe et la particule**.

*He gave **it** up.* » Il l'abandonna.

B Verbes prépositionnels

● Certains verbes comme ***bring*** (apporter), ***give*** (donner), ***send*** (envoyer), ***write*** (écrire) ont **deux constructions** :

- **avec préposition** :

*I sent the book **to** her.* » Je lui ai envoyé le livre.
→ C'est à elle que j'ai envoyé le livre.

- **sans préposition** :

I sent her the book. » Je lui ai envoyé le livre.

● **Attention : À la différence du français**, on maintient la **préposition à droite du verbe** dans les cas suivants :

- **Questions**

*Who are you thinking **of**?*
» **À** qui penses-tu ?

- **Relatives**

*The lady we talked **to** is our new tenant.*
» La dame **à** qui nous avons parlé est notre nouvelle locataire.

- **Passives**

*That problem has never been dealt **with**.*
» On ne s'est jamais occupé **de** ce problème.

AS ou LIKE ?

- Les deux mots expriment la comparaison, mais LIKE indique que **les deux éléments sont différents**, alors que AS signifie que **les deux éléments sont identiques.**

As a father, *Charles will disagree.*
» En tant que père, Charles ne sera pas d'accord.
→ Charles est le père.

*Bill behaves **like** my father.*
» Bill se comporte comme mon père.
→ Ce n'est pas mon père, je le compare à mon père.

- On utilise LIKE après les verbes exprimant les cinq sens : **SOUND** (OUÏE), **SMELL** (ODORAT), **TASTE** (GOÛT), **FEEL** (TOUCHER), **LOOK** (VUE).

She sounds like my mother.
» Quand elle parle, on dirait ma mère.

It tastes like honey.
» Ça a un goût de miel.

Look at the sand. It looks like salt!
» Regarde le sable. On dirait du sel !

19 Les noms

A Dénombrables et indénombrables

- Le choix des déterminants, articles et quantifieurs par exemple, dépend de la nature des noms, qui peuvent être **dénombrables** ou **indénombrables**.

- Un **dénombrable** est un nom qui désigne un ou des éléments que l'on **peut compter**. On peut donc l'employer au **singulier** ou au **pluriel**, par exemple le nom *film*: *a film, one film, two films, several films*, etc.

- Un **indénombrable** est un mot qui désigne **un objet ou une activité vu(e) dans son ensemble, comme un tout qu'on ne peut pas compter, et qui est toujours au singulier en anglais**: ***luggage*** (des bagages), ***information*** (des informations / renseignements), ***advice*** (des conseils), etc.

B Indénombrables

- **Noms de matériaux et d'aliments**: ***silk*** (la soie), ***iron*** (le fer), ***steel*** (l'acier), ***wood*** (le bois), ***bread***, ***tea***, ***milk***, etc.

- **Noms renvoyant à un ensemble**:
  - **concret**: ***furniture*** (des meubles), ***hair*** (des cheveux), ***luggage*** (des bagages), ***rubbish*** / ***refuse*** (des détritus), ***trash*** (déchets), etc.
  - **abstrait**: ***accommodation*** (le logement), ***advice*** (des conseils), ***business*** (les affaires), ***damage*** (les dégâts), ***evidence*** (des preuves), ***growth*** (la croissance), ***information*** (des renseignements), ***knowledge*** (le savoir), ***luck*** (la chance), ***progress*** (des progrès), ***news*** (des nouvelles), ***nonsense*** (des absurdités), ***research*** (la [des] recherche[s]), ***trouble*** (des ennuis), ***work*** (l'emploi), etc.

- **Noms formés à partir de verbes**: ***swimming*** (la natation), ***housing*** (le logement), ***laughter*** (le rire), etc.

- **Noms formés à partir d'adjectifs**: ***homelessness*** (le fait d'être sans abri), ***joblessness*** (le chômage), ***optimism***, ***whiteness*** (la blancheur), ***youth*** (la jeunesse), etc.

- **Autres noms**: ***weather***, ***smoke***, ***thunder*** (le tonnerre), etc.

- Les indénombrables sont **incompatibles** avec:
  - **l'article indéfini** ***A*** / ***AN*** et ***ONE***.
  - **le pluriel**, donc avec ***A FEW***, ***FEW***, ***MANY***, ***SEVERAL***, ***TWO***, ***THREE***, etc.

- Le **verbe** est toujours au **singulier**.

  This news is good. › Les nouvelles sont bonnes.

C Dénombrables ou indénombrables ?

Certains mots peuvent être dénombrables dans un certain contexte et indénombrables dans un autre. Lorsqu'ils renvoient à une **notion**, ils sont **indénombrables**.

- **Indénombrable**:

  Time *is money.* › Le temps, c'est de l'argent.

- **Dénombrable**:

  We had ***a*** *wonderful* ***time*** *together.*
  › On a passé un très bon moment ensemble.

Certaines réalités peuvent être exprimées en anglais par deux mots, l'un dénombrable (article *a*), l'autre indénombrable (ø).

- **Dénombrable › Indénombrable**

  a house: une maison. › *housing:* le logement (en géneral).

  a job: un emploi. › *work / employment:* le travail / l'emploi.

- ***Pity*** et ***shame*** sont indénombrables. Mais dans les exclamations en ***WHAT*** et ***SUCH***, ces mots s'emploient avec l'article ***A***.

  What a pity! › Quel dommage !

  It's such a shame! › C'est une honte !

> ***A PIECE OF***
> En anglais, on peut, pour certains indénombrables, employer l'expression ***A PIECE OF*** qui signifie littéralement « un morceau de »: ***a piece of*** *furniture / information / luggage / news.*
> Mais ce n'est pas d'un emploi très courant.
> **L'article UN, UNE devant un mot qui est indénombrable en anglais, se traduit le plus souvent par l'absence d'article.**
> C'était **un** bon conseil. › *It was good advice.*

D Singuliers et pluriels particuliers

- **Toujours** suivis d'un verbe au **singulier**, malgré le ***s*** en fin de mot:
  - les noms de sciences en *-ics*: ***Economics*** / ***Mathematics*** ***is***…
  - autres: *The news* ***is*** *at eight… The United States* ***is***…

- **Toujours** suivis d'un verbe au **pluriel**: ***police***, ***clothes*** (des vêtements), ***cattle*** (le bétail).

- **Souvent** suivis d'un verbe au **pluriel**: ***government***, ***audience*** (le public), ***family***, ***crowd*** (la foule), ***sheep*** (les moutons).

> ***S*** **et le pluriel**
> - ***S*** n'est pas toujours la marque du pluriel, par exemple *news*, *mathematics*, etc.
> - Certains mots ont la même forme au singulier et au pluriel: *a series*, *series* (une série, des séries); *a means*, *means* (un moyen, des moyens).

20 Le génitif ou cas possessif ('s)

● Le **génitif** est un **déterminant du nom**. (Il se substitue par exemple à un article.) Il se forme avec ***'s***. Le premier élément permet d'identifier le deuxième.

It's my sister's computer. › C'est l'ordinateur de ma sœur.
→ Le génitif (*my sister's*) permet d'identifier l'ordinateur.

● Le **génitif** ou **cas possessif** peut exprimer la **possession**.

Lisa's father was out.
› Le père de Lisa était sorti.

James's /'dʒeɪmsɪz/ room is untidy.
› La chambre de James est en désordre.

● Les **pluriels en *s*** forment leur cas possessif par le simple **ajout d'une apostrophe**.

Where are the students' books?
› Où sont les livres des élèves?

● **Le génitif n'exprime pas toujours la possession**. On peut former le génitif avec un grand nombre de mots. Le premier élément doit être clairement reconnaissable ou avoir déjà été mentionné.

Le génitif peut exprimer:

- une **durée**:
  It's a few minutes' walk from the station.
  › C'est à quelques minutes à pied de la gare.
  After a hard day's work, he was exhausted.
  › Après une dure journée de travail, il était épuisé.
- un **repère dans le temps**: *today's TV programme* (le programme télé d'aujourd'hui), *last year's events* (les événements de l'année dernière), *yesterday's newspaper* (le journal d'hier).
- un **repère dans l'espace** (noms de villes ou de lieux connus ou déjà mentionnés): *London's museums* (les musées de Londres), *New York's national parks* (les parcs nationaux de New York).
- des **éléments du monde connus de tous** ou des **groupes humains**: *the government's decisions* (les décisions du gouvernement), *the world's biggest cities* (les plus grandes villes du monde).
- **magasins** ou **résidences**: *at the baker's, at Janet's* (chez le boulanger, chez Janet).

● Le **génitif générique**: certains génitifs ne désignent pas un objet particulier mais un type (ou genre) d'objet: *a woman's magazine* (un magazine féminin), *an officer's cap* (une casquette d'officier).

Attention !

- Pour former un génitif, **l'ordre des mots doit être inversé** par rapport au français; c'est le possesseur qui vient en premier en anglais.
  le téléphone portable **de Mike** › ***Mike's*** *mobile*
- Lorsque le **possesseur** est **sans article**, le **génitif** est également **sans article**. Par exemple, lorsque le possesseur est un **nom propre**:
  le bateau de Ben › *Ben's boat* (~~*the Ben's boat*~~ est impossible.)
- L'anglais est plus logique que le français: lorsqu'il y a **plusieurs possesseurs** et **plusieurs objets possédés**, les objets possédés sont au pluriel.
  la vie de nos enfants › *our children's* ***lives***

21 Les articles

A Un ou des éléments indéfinis

● Pour désigner **un** élément parmi d'autres, on emploie l'article ***A*** / ***AN***.

She's bought a new flat.
› Elle a acheté un nouvel appartement.

● On emploie ***A*** devant les consonnes (sauf « h » non-aspiré comme dans *hour, honest, honour, heir* [héritier]) ou devant les voyelles « fortes », comme par exemple celles qu'on prononce /j/ ou /juː/: *year* /jɪə/, *yellow* /'jeləʊ/, *European* /jʊərə'piːən/, *uniform* /'juːnɪfɔːm/, *useful* /'juːsfʊl/.

an *honest man,* ***a*** *quarter of* ***an*** *hour,* ***a*** *year ago,*
a *European country*

● On emploie ***AN*** devant les autres voyelles.

It is an interesting discovery.
› C'est une découverte intéressante.

● Pour désigner **des** éléments parmi d'autres, on emploie **l'article zéro** (**ø**), ce qui signifie qu'aucun article n'apparaît. Le nom est un **dénombrable au pluriel**.

I've often seen ***birds*** *on that tree.*
› J'ai souvent vu des oiseaux sur cet arbre.

B Le particulier

● Lorsqu'un ou des éléments sont **particuliers** et **bien définis**, on emploie l'article ***THE***, au singulier et au pluriel.

● **Le nom peut être défini par:**

- **ce qui le suit**: les **relatives** ou **compléments en *OF*** permettent souvent de particulariser un nom.
  The *baby* ***who's crying*** *is my nephew.*
  › Le bébé qui pleure est mon neveu.
  It was ***the*** *beginning* ***of a new story***.
  › C'était le début d'une nouvelle histoire.

- **la situation** dans laquelle on se trouve: le nom peut ainsi désigner un objet ou une personne **immédiatement reconnaissables ou connus de tous**.

  Open the door. › Ouvre la porte.
  → On sait de quelle porte il s'agit, elle est devant nous.

Sont censés être connus de tous:

- les éléments naturels: *the earth, the sky, the sea,* etc.
- les personnalités ou structures d'un pays: *the press, the president, the government,* etc.

C La généralité

La **généralité** s'exprime en anglais par **l'absence d'article** pour les **noms dénombrables au pluriel** et les **indénombrables**.

- **Dénombrables au pluriel**

  I don't like cats. › Je n'aime pas les chats.
  → Les chats en général.

- **Indénombrables:** ces mots ne se mettent pas au pluriel.

  Time does fly! › Comme **le** temps passe !

D Emplois particuliers de *A / AN*

À la différence du français, on emploie *A / AN*:

- **lorsqu'on définit une personne (ou un objet) à l'aide d'un nom et donc devant les noms de métiers.**

  *She is **a doctor**.* › Elle est médecin.

- **après les prépositions (sauf si le mot est indénombrable).**

  *He went out **without a coat**.* › Il est sorti sans manteau.

  *He talked **without enthusiasm**.* › Il parlait sans enthousiame.

- **devant les expressions de mesure ou de temps pour traduire** PAR.

  *It's 1.99 euro **a litre**.* › Cela vaut 1,99 euro le litre.

  *We see them once **a week**.*
  › On les voit une fois par semaine.

Attention !

- **Traduction de** LE, LA, LES

L'erreur la plus fréquente consiste à utiliser *THE* dans un contexte de généralité puisqu'en français on dit LE, LA, LES dans ce cas. En anglais, on utilise l'article ø (absence d'article).

Les jeunes enfants aiment **les** dessins animés.
› *Young children like cartoons.*

- *A / AN*

En français, on utilise l'article ø pour définir des personnes, ce qui est source d'erreur lorsqu'on traduit en anglais.

Lorsque j'étais **enfant**... › *When I was **a child**...*

E Emplois particuliers de *THE*

● **On emploie *THE*:**

- devant les superlatifs (*last, first, best*) et les adjectifs restrictifs (*only*), car ils désignent l'élément comme unique.

  She was the best writer and the only French girl in the contest. › C'était le meilleur écrivain et la seule Française en compétition.

- devant les instruments de musique après le verbe *PLAY*. Mais devant les noms de sports, on emploie **ø**.

  He plays the piano and she plays football.
  › Il joue du piano et elle joue au foot.

● **Noms de pays**

- **au singulier**, ils s'emploient généralement **sans article**: *England, France, Spain,* etc.
- **au pluriel**, ils sont précédés de *THE*:

  the United States (les États-Unis)
  the Netherlands (les Pays-Bas)
  the Canaries (les Canaries), etc.

F Noms propres et fonctions officielles

● Le **nom propre** s'emploie toujours avec l'**article ø**, même s'il est précédé d'un titre ou d'un grade, ce qui n'est pas le cas en français.

President Obama (**le** Président Obama)
Prime Minister Gordon Brown (**le** Premier ministre Gordon Brown)
Queen Elizabeth (**la** reine Elizabeth)
General Patton (**le** général Patton)
Admiral Nelson (**l'**amiral Nelson), etc.

● En revanche, lorsqu'aucun nom propre ne suit la fonction, on emploie l'article *THE*.

***the** French Prime Minister*
***the** President of the US*, etc.

G Groupes et individus

Certains adjectifs peuvent être utilisés avec des noms et des articles différents, selon qu'ils renvoient à **la totalité du groupe**, à **un ensemble** d'individus ou bien à **un individu**.

● **Le groupe dans sa totalité** › *THE* + adjectif au singulier.

the English (les Anglais)
the poor (les pauvres)
the homeless (les sans-abri)
the jobless (les personnes aux chômage)

● **Un ensemble d'individus** › Ø + adjectif + *people*.

homeless people: les / des sans-abri
jobless people: les / des gens au chômage

● **Un individu** › *A* + adjectif + *man / woman / person*.

a homeless man: un sans-abri
a jobless person: une personne au chômage

22 Les quantifieurs

La nature du nom (dénombrable ou indénombrable) permet de choisir le quantifieur qui convient.

A « Une certaine quantité de » : *SOME, ANY*

	Indénombrable	Dénombrable pluriel
Dans les affirmations : *SOME* ▪ *SOME* désigne « **une certaine quantité de…** », non précisée. ▪ L'article ø peut être employé à la place de *SOME* ou *ANY* lorsqu'il s'agit **d'opposer un élément à un autre**.	*Let's have some tea!* » Prenons du thé ! *Do you want milk or cream?* » Tu veux du lait ou de la crème ?	*There are some messages for you.* » Il y a des messages pour toi.
Dans les questions : *SOME* ou *ANY* ▪ On emploie *SOME* lorsqu'on attend une **réponse positive**, par exemple pour une offre. ▪ *ANY* dans la question implique qu'**on ne sait pas quelle réponse va être faite**.	*Would you like some water?* » Désirez-vous de l'eau ? *Is there any coffee?* » Est-ce qu'il y a du café ?	*Can you give me some biscuits?* » Pouvez-vous me donner des biscuits ? *Are there any people around?* » Est-ce qu'il y a des gens dans le coin ?
ANY peut également signifier N'IMPORTE LEQUEL. On le trouve alors aux trois formes (affirmative, interrogative et négative).	*Any student can do it.* » N'importe quel élève peut le faire. *Give me just any pencil.* » Donne-moi n'importe quel crayon.	

B Petite / grande quantité : *MUCH, MANY, LITTLE, FEW, A LOT OF, PLENTY OF*

	Indénombrable	Dénombrable pluriel
Grande quantité : BEAUCOUP DE	***a lot of*** *money,* ***plenty of*** *time*	***a lot of*** *books,* ***plenty of*** *friends*
(Pas) grande quantité : PAS BEAUCOUP DE	*There is* ***not much*** *time.*	*There are* ***not many*** *people.*
Petite quantité : (TRÈS / TROP / SI) PEU DE, UN PEU DE, QUELQUES	*(**very** / **too** / **so**)* ***little*** *time,* ***a little*** *money*	*(**very** / **too** / **so**)* ***few*** *people,* ***a few*** *people*
Plus grande quantité : PLUS DE	***more*** *money*	***more*** *people*
Plus petite quantité : MOINS DE	***less*** *money*	***fewer*** *people*

Traduction des quantifieurs

Pour **traduire** les quantifieurs, il faut se poser la question de la nature du nom : **dénombrable pluriel** (ex. *friends*) ou **indénombrable singulier** (ex. *money*).

PAS BEAUCOUP DE

- Dénombrable pluriel : Il n'a **pas beaucoup d'**amis.
  » *He has**n't** got **many** friends.*
- Indénombrable : Il n'a **pas beaucoup d'**argent.
  » *He has**n't** got **much** money.*

Remarque : *HOW MUCH* et *HOW MANY* signifient COMBIEN ?.

PEU DE

- Dénombrable pluriel : Il a **peu d'**amis.
  » *He's got **few** friends.*
- Indénombrable : Il a **peu** d'argent.
  » *He's got **little** money.*

Remarque : *LITTLE* et *FEW* peuvent être précédés de *VERY* ou *TOO* : *very / too little time* (très / trop peu de temps), *very / too few friends* (très / trop peu d'amis).

PEU DE / UN PEU DE

- ***LITTLE*** et ***FEW*** (**sans article**) expriment une **quantité insuffisante**. Ils ont les mêmes règles d'emploi que *much* et *many*.
  J'ai eu **peu** (= pas suffisamment) **de** temps.
  » *I had **little** time.*
  Il y avait **peu** (= pas assez) **d'**enfants.
  » *There were **few** children.*
- ***A LITTLE*** et ***A FEW*** (**avec article**) expriment seulement l'idée d'une **quantité faible** (UN PEU DE, QUELQUES).
  Nous avons encore **un peu** de temps.
  » *We still have **a little** time.*
  Il y avait **quelques** enfants. » *There were **a few** children.*

C Quantité nulle : *NO, NOT ANY, NONE*

	Indénombrable	Dénombrable pluriel
Avec un nom : *NOT ANY* ou *NO*	*There isn't any time / There's no time left.* ➤ Il ne reste plus de temps.	*There weren't any / There were no passengers on the platform.* ➤ Il n'y avait pas de voyageurs sur le quai.
À la place d'un nom : pronom ***NONE***	– *How many cars have they got?* ➤ Combien ont-ils de voitures ? – *None.* ➤ Aucune. **Ne pas confondre *NONE*** (en un mot → **AUCUN**) avec ***NO ONE*** (en deux mots → **PERSONNE**). *No one likes him.* ➤ Personne ne l'aime.	

***NOT ANY* ou *NOT A* ?**

Attention ! Avec un nom dénombrable singulier ***NOT ANY*** est impossible. On emploie ***NOT A***.

*I haven't got **a** car* ➤ Je n'ai pas de voiture.

D De l'unité à la totalité

Les quantifieurs suivants se construisent avec un **nom** (*all books, the whole bottle, etc.*) ou avec ***OF*** (*most of the kids, most of her friends, most of them, etc.*).

ONE : **UN (et un seul)**	*one child, one of the children*
BOTH : **LES DEUX**	*both children, both of the children*
EACH (toujours suivi du singulier ; le pluriel n'est possible qu'après ***OF***) : **CHAQUE**	*each child, each of the children*
EVERY (toujours suivi du singulier) : **CHAQUE, TOUS**	*every child* (pas de construction en ***OF***)
ALL : **TOUT, TOUS**	*all day, all that time, all his children, all those people, all of them*
THE WHOLE : **TOUT ENTIER / ENTIÈRE**	*the whole town, the whole of it*
EITHER (toujours suivi du singulier ; le pluriel n'est possible qu'après ***OF***) : **L'UN OU L'AUTRE**	*in either case, either of them*
NEITHER (toujours suivi du singulier ; le pluriel n'est possible qu'après ***OF***) : **NI L'UN NI L'AUTRE**	*neither dress fitted, neither of them*
MOST : **LA PLUPART DE**	*most people, most of the children I know* **Ne pas confondre *most* avec *the most* (superlatif).** *It's the most beautiful painting in the museum.* C'est le plus beau tableau du musée.

Traduction de TOUT, TOUS

- ***ALL*** exprime l'idée d'ensemble (TOUT, TOUS) : *all day* (toute la journée), *all the children* (tous les enfants).
- ***WHOLE*** exprime l'idée de totalité (TOUT ENTIER) : *the whole country* (tout le pays).
- À la différence de ***ALL***, ***WHOLE*** se place après ***THE, MY, YOUR***, etc.
  toute ma vie → ***all*** *my life / my* ***whole*** *life*
- ***EVERY*** (CHAQUE) peut s'utiliser pour traduire TOUS LES. On insiste alors sur **CHAQUE** élément. Le mot qui suit ***EVERY*** est au singulier.
  tous les enfants (= chaque enfant) ➤ *every child*

E Le nombre

Nombre précis

DOZEN, HUNDRED, THOUSAND, MILLION ne se mettent pas au pluriel lorsqu'ils sont précédés d'un nombre précis : *two dozen eggs* (deux douzaines d'œufs), *three hundred kilos* (trois cents kilos), *four thousand people* (quatre mille personnes), *five million dollars* (cinq millions de dollars).

DES CENTAINES / MILLIERS / MILLIONS DE

On emploie le pluriel lorsque le nombre est précédé de l'article **ø**.

There were hundreds of boats and thousands of people.
➤ Il y avait des centaines de bateaux et des milliers de gens.

23 Les pronoms

A Pronoms personnels

● **Pronoms personnels sujets et compléments**

- **Sujet :** *I, YOU, HE / SHE / IT, WE, YOU, THEY*
- **Complément :** *ME, YOU, HIM / HER / IT, US, YOU, THEM*

He never talks to me.
sujet complément

● ***HE*** (masculin) et ***SHE*** (féminin) s'emploient pour les êtres humains et les animaux familiers. ***IT*** s'emploie pour les objets et animaux.

B Possessifs

Déterminants possessifs
MY, YOUR, HIS / HER / ITS, OUR, YOUR, THEIR

● Ce sont des génitifs (Voir **Gr. 20.**) appliqués aux pronoms personnels. Ils sont **suivis de l'élément possédé**.

Where's your sister? › Où est ta sœur ?

● À la différence du français, les possessifs en anglais **s'accordent** en nombre (et en genre à la 3e personne du singulier) **avec le possesseur**.

La voiture de Paul › sa voiture › *his* car.

→ ***HIS*** est masculin comme le possesseur, Paul.

● Pour les parties du corps et les vêtements, on emploie le possessif en anglais (alors qu'en français, on emploie LE, LA, LES).

*He had **his** hands in **his** pockets.*
› Il avait les mains dans les poches.

● On peut renforcer le possessif par ***OWN***.

We have our own swimming pool.
› Nous avons notre propre piscine.

Pronoms possessifs
MINE, YOURS, HIS / HERS, OURS, YOURS, THEIRS

● On peut éviter la répétition de l'objet possédé grâce aux pronoms possessifs.

Is this bag yours (= your bag)? › Ce sac est-il à toi ?

● Pour dire « **un(e) de mes** / **tes** / **ses** / **nos** / **vos** / **leurs** + **groupe nominal** », on emploie : **groupe nominal** + *OF* + **pronom possessif**.

She is a cousin of mine. › C'est une de mes cousines.

I met a good friend of theirs.
› J'ai rencontré un de leurs bons amis.

THEY, THEIR, THEIRS, THERE'S

- ***THEY, THEIR, THEIRS*** renvoient à des **personnes** ou **objets**.

Tom and Lisa are gone. They're in Spain now.
→ *They* = *Tom et Lisa* → **pronom sujet**

*Sue is looking after **their** dog.*
→ *their* = appartenant à Tom et Lisa
→ **déterminant possessif**

*She is a friend of **theirs**.*
→ *of theirs* = parmi les amis de Tom et Lisa
→ **pronom possessif**

- ***THERE*** est un adverbe qui signifie LÀ. (***HERE*** signifie ICI.) L'expression *there's* (= *there is*) signifie donc littéralement « là est ». Par extension, ***THERE*** permet de dire « quelque chose existe (là) ». Au pluriel, on utilise ***THERE ARE***.

There's a new shop in Dawson Street.
› Il y a une nouvelle boutique rue Dawson.

There are huge difficulties.
› Il y a d'énormes difficultés.

C Pronoms réfléchis

Pronoms réfléchis
MYSELF, YOURSELF, HIMSELF / HERSELF / ITSELF, OURSELVES, YOURSELVES, THEMSELVES

● On emploie le pronom réfléchi lorsque **le sujet et l'objet sont la même personne**.

***He** looked at **himself** in the mirror.*
› Il se regarda dans la glace.

● Le pronom réfléchi peut également permettre d'**insister sur une personne ou un objet**.

*Why don't **you** do it **yourself**?*
› Pourquoi ne le fais-tu pas toi-même ?

● **Certains verbes français** se construisent avec un pronom réfléchi mais pas leur équivalent anglais. → se laver (*wash*), se sentir (*feel*), se raser (*shave*), se rencontrer (*meet*), s'excuser (*apologize*), se lever (*stand up*), se baigner (*have a bath*), etc.

Elle **s'**habille très bien. › *She dresses very well.*
*Comment **vous** sentez-vous ?* › *How do you feel?*

D Pronoms réciproques

On utilise ***EACH OTHER*** (deux éléments) et ***ONE ANOTHER*** (deux ou plusieurs éléments) pour exprimer l'idée d'un **échange entre deux ou plusieurs personnes**.

The two girls looked at each other / one another.
› Les deux filles échangèrent un regard.

E Pronoms indéfinis

● **Composés de *SOME, ANY, NO* et *EVERY***

	-BODY	*-ONE*	*-THING*	*-WHERE*
SOME	*somebody*	*someone*	*something*	*somewhere*
ANY	*anybody*	*anyone*	*anything*	*anywhere*
NO	*nobody*	*no one*	*nothing*	*nowhere*
EVERY	*everybody*	*everyone*	*everything*	*everywhere*

Remarque : ***No ONE*** (PERSONNE) s'écrit en deux mots. Ne pas confondre avec ***NONE*** (AUCUN). (Voir **Gr. 22.**)

● Les composés de ***SOME, ANY, NO*** et ***EVERY*** suivent les mêmes règles d'emploi que ***SOME, ANY, NO*** et ***EVERY***. (Voir **Gr. 22.**)

Someone has slept in my bed.
› Quelqu'un a dormi dans mon lit.

He has nowhere to go. › Il n'a nulle part où aller.

Everything is fine. › Tout va bien.

● Les composés de ***ANY*** peuvent avoir la valeur de N'IMPORTE LEQUEL. ***ANY*** est alors accentué à l'oral.

Any*body could have done it.*
› N'importe qui aurait pu le faire.

24 *THIS / THAT*

● ***THIS*** (pluriel : ***THESE***) désigne un objet qui est seulement **connu de celui qui parle** (d'où l'idée de « proximité »). ***THIS*** sert souvent par conséquent à présenter une personne ou un objet nouveau.

This is my brother. › Voici mon frère.
→ Je vous présente mon frère.

There are more and more homeless people these days.
› De nos jours, il y a de plus en plus de sans-abri.
→ De nos jours = dans le présent.

● ***THAT*** (pluriel : ***THOSE***) est utilisé pour tout objet ou fait qui est **éloigné de celui qui parle**, dans le temps ou l'espace.

People worked longer hours in those days.
› Les gens avaient des journées de travail plus longues en ce temps-là. → en ce temps-là = dans le passé.

● On emploie aussi ***THAT*** et non pas ***THIS*** lorsque celui qui parle et celui auquel il s'adresse savent tous deux de quel objet il s'agit.

Give me that, please. › Donne-moi ça, s'il te plaît.
→ Les interlocuteurs savent tous deux de quoi il s'agit car ils l'ont sous les yeux.

25 Les adjectifs

A Place et ordre des adjectifs

● Les adjectifs **épithètes** se placent toujours **devant le nom**, même s'il y en a plusieurs.

I just love your little black dress.
› J'adore ta petite robe noire.

● Certains adjectifs sont **toujours attributs**. Ils se placent après un verbe d'état comme ***BE***. Ce sont les adjectifs : ***alive*** (en vie), ***asleep*** (endormi), ***afraid*** (effrayé), ***awake*** (éveillé), ***cross*** (fâché), ***ill*** (malade), ***glad*** (joyeux).

● Lorsqu'il y a plusieurs adjectifs devant le nom, l'adjectif exprimant un jugement **subjectif** (*nice, good, bad, stupid, rich*, etc.) se place **en tête**. Les autre adjectifs se placent en général dans cet ordre : **taille** (forme, dimension), **âge**, **couleur**, **origine** (nationalité, religion, origine géographique ou politique), **matière**. (Formule : **S.T.A.C.O.M.**)

a huge old dark Italian wooden door
a small new red American car
a lovely tall young dark-haired Indian girl

B Comparatif des adjectifs (PLUS, MOINS)

● **Adjectifs courts :** adjectifs d'**une syllabe** ou de deux syllabes terminés par ***-ER, -Y, -OW*** et ***-LE*** : *big, old, small, tall, short, long, clever, happy, narrow, gentle*, etc.

● **Adjectifs longs :** adjectifs de **deux syllabes ou plus** (sauf ceux terminés par ***-ER, -Y, -OW*** et ***-LE***) : *stupid, expensive, interesting, intelligent, difficult*, etc.

	Adjectifs courts	Adjectifs longs
Supériorité (PLUS)	*-ER ... THAN* *She's younger than you.* › Elle est plus jeune que toi.	*MORE ... THAN* *It's more interesting than it used to be.* › C'est plus intéressant qu'avant.
Égalité ou inégalité (AUSSI / PAS AUSSI)	*AS ... AS / NOT SO (AS) ... AS* *He's as smart / intelligent as his mother.* › Il est aussi intelligent que sa mère. *It's not (so) as hard / difficult as I thought.* › Ce n'est pas aussi difficile que je le pensais.	

	Adjectifs courts	Adjectifs longs
Infériorité (MOINS)	LESS ... THAN *He is less dumb / stupid than I thought.* » Il est moins bête que je ne le pensais.	
DE PLUS EN PLUS	-ER AND -ER *It's getting smaller and smaller.* » Ça devient de plus en plus petit.	MORE AND MORE ... *It's more and more interesting.* » C'est de plus en plus intéressant.
DE MOINS EN MOINS	LESS AND LESS ... *His work is less and less satisfactory.* » Son travail est de moins en moins satisfaisant.	

C Superlatif des adjectifs (LE PLUS, LE MOINS)

	Adjectifs courts	Adjectifs longs
Supériorité (LE PLUS)	THE -EST *It's the biggest mistake you've ever made.* » C'est la plus grosse erreur que tu aies jamais faite.	THE MOST ... *It's the most difficult task we've ever had to do.* » C'est la tâche la plus difficile que nous ayons jamais eu à faire.
Infériorité (LE MOINS)	THE LEAST *She's the least clever of the three children.* » C'est la moins intelligente des trois enfants.	THE LEAST ... *We bought the least expensive of all.* » Nous avons acheté le moins cher de tous.

D Comparatifs et superlatifs irréguliers

	Comparatif	Superlatif
GOOD / WELL	*BETTER*	*THE BEST*
BAD	*WORSE*	*THE WORST*
FAR	*FURTHER*	*FARTHER*
	THE FURTHEST	*THE FARTHEST*

E Adjectifs en -*ED* et -*ING*

Ces adjectifs sont dérivés de verbes.

- Les adjectifs en -*ING* ont un sens **actif**.

I'm sure it's a fascinating / exciting job.
» Je suis sûr que c'est un travail passionnant.

- Les adjectifs en -*ED* ont un sens **passif**.

I'm not really interested.
» Ça ne m'intéresse pas vraiment.

I was shocked to hear these words.
» J'ai été abasourdi d'entendre ces mots.

F Adjectifs composés

À partir d'un verbe

- Comme les adjectifs simples en -*ING* (voir **Gr. 25 E**), les adjectifs composés en -*ING* ont un sens **actif**.

*a student who works hard → a hard-work**ing** student*

*a job that breaks your back → a back-break**ing** job*

- De même, les adjectifs composés en -*ED* ont un sens **passif** (sauf dans *well-behaved* : « qui se comporte bien »).

an institution controlled by the state
*→ a state-controll**ed** institution*

a machine operated by a battery
*→ a battery-operat**ed** machine*

À partir d'un adjectif et d'un nom + -*ED*

L'adjectif composé indique une **caractéristique** de la personne ou de l'objet.

*She has dark hair. → She's dark-hair**ed**.*

He's a man with a cold heart.
*→ He's a cold-heart**ed** man.*

It's a jacket with red stripes (rayures).
→ *It's a red-strip**ed*** jacket.

He's wearing a shirt with long sleeves (manches).
*→ He's wearing a long-sleev**ed** shirt.*

Expression de l'âge

- Après *BE*, on utilise la forme ... *YEARS OLD* :

*She is twenty **years old**.* » Elle a vingt ans.
→ *year* est au pluriel.

- Lorsque l'adjectif est placé **avant le nom** :

They have a twenty-year-old son.
» Ils ont un fils de vingt ans.
→ *year* est au singulier + trait d'union entre les trois mots.

26 Les noms composés

A Élément principal

Dans un nom composé, **le premier élément sert à préciser le sens du deuxième. C'est le deuxième élément qui est le mot principal**. Le premier élément ne se met jamais au pluriel (sauf exception).

*paper **bag**, hand**bag**, air **bag**, tea **bag**, sand**bag**, doggy **bag***

Les mots composés ne sont pas systématiquement soit séparés, soit attachés, soit reliés par un tiret. Il n'y a en fait pas de règle précise, sinon l'usage, donné par le dictionnaire : *dining room, schoolfriend, coffee-maker*, etc.

B Nom + nom

Le nom 1 indique…	Nom composé
… à quoi sert le nom 2	*teaspoon, breadknife, meat hook, fish fork*
… comment fonctionne le nom 2	*gas cooker, steamboat, petrol engine, atom bomb*
… la matière du nom 2	*silver chain, glass building, gold tooth, steel guitar*
… de quoi fait partie le nom 2	*doorknob, lampshade, chair back, table leg*
… le sexe du nom 2	*manservant, boy soprano, boyfriend, girl guide*
… le lieu du nom 2	*seabird, streetlamp, roadblock, village idiot*
… le moment du nom 2	*night train, morning paper, day nurse, afternoon tea*
… le métier, l'occupation du nom 2 (*man, woman, girl, boy*)	*newspaperman, businesswoman, schoolgirl, message-boy*
… la fonction du nom 2 et ce qu'il contient	*wine glass, teapot, butter dish, bookshelf*

C Nom + forme verbale

	La forme verbale désigne…	Mot composé
Nom + BV-*ER*	… la personne ou l'instrument qui fait l'action	*taxi driver, opera singer, coat hanger, bottle-opener*
Nom + BV-*ING*	… une profession ou une activité	*window cleaning, bungee jumping, sightseeing, bird-watching*
BV-*ING* + nom	… l'usage d'un objet ou d'un lieu	*driving licence, dining room, riding boots, looking-glass*

27 Énoncés affirmatifs

A Ordre des mots

À la différence du français, on ne sépare pas le **complément d'objet direct** (COD) du **verbe** en anglais.

Il y avait, dans la voiture, **un chien noir** (COD).
› ~~*There was in the car a black dog.*~~
› *There was **a black dog** in the car.*

Le **complément de manière** ou **d'intensité** (***well**, **very much***, etc.) se place **après le complément d'objet**. (Il se place avant en français.)

J'aime **beaucoup** ce livre.
› ~~*I like very much this book.*~~
› *I like this book **very much**.*

On place les **adverbes de fréquence** (***always**, **often**, **sometimes**, **usually***, etc.) :

- **avant le verbe** (sauf pour *BE*), alors qu'en français, on les place après.

  Je le vois **souvent**. › *I **often** see him.*

- **après le verbe** lorsque celui-ci est *BE*.

  *He **is often** angry.* › Il est souvent en colère.

- **après le premier auxiliaire**, s'il y en a un ou plusieurs.

  *I have **never** liked them.* › Je ne les ai jamais aimés.

Les **autres compléments de temps** (***last year**, **yesterday**, **in those days***, etc.) se placent **en fin d'énoncé**.

*We never visited them **in those days**.*
› On ne leur rendait jamais visite **à cette époque**.

B Do / did de reprise

- La présence de l'auxiliaire DO / DID dans les énoncés affirmatifs a un sens bien particulier car le présent simple et le prétérit simple ne font normalement pas apparaître d'auxiliaire à la forme affirmative.

- ***Do*** permet de **reprendre ce qui vient d'être dit pour confirmer ou contredire**. Le verbe peut rester sous-entendu.

*I thought that she would phone me and she **did** phone / and she **did**.*
› Je pensais qu'elle me téléphonerait et, effectivement, elle m'a téléphoné.

- *You don't like her very much.*
  › Tu ne l'aimes pas beaucoup.
- *That's not true. I **do** like her, but she hates me.*
  (L'auxiliaire est accentué à l'oral.)
  › Ce n'est pas vrai. Moi, je l'aime bien, mais c'est elle qui me déteste.

28 Énoncés négatifs

- La forme négative fait toujours apparaître un auxiliaire.

  *She **doesn't** know you. He **didn't** want to talk.*

- Avec un terme **négatif ou restrictif** comme ***NEVER, HARDLY EVER*** (PRESQUE JAMAIS), ***NOBODY, NOTHING***, **l'emploi de *NOT* est inutile** et le verbe reste à la forme affirmative.

  *He **never** wrote to me.* › Il ne m'a jamais écrit.

  *We **hardly ever** agree.*
  › Nous ne sommes presque jamais d'accord.

- On peut mettre en relief un terme **négatif ou restrictif** (***NEVER, NO SOONER … THAN***) en le plaçant en **tête de phrase**. Ceci entraîne une **inversion sujet / auxiliaire**. (Attention : **l'auxiliaire** est toujours nécessaire dans un cas d'inversion, y compris au présent simple et au prétérit simple.) Cette inversion se trouve dans un **anglais très soutenu.**

She never saw him again.
→ ***Never did she** see him again.*
› Elle ne l'a jamais revu.

He got in the car and fell asleep at once.
→ ***No sooner had he** got in the car **than** he fell asleep.*
› À peine était-il entré dans la voiture qu'il s'endormit.

Autres termes négatifs ou restrictifs pouvant être placés en tête de phrase : ***HARDLY / SCARCELY … WHEN*** (À PEINE), ***LITTLE, NOR, NOT ONLY, NOWHERE, SELDOM*** (RAREMENT).

Scarcely had the car stopped when the police surrounded it.
› À peine la voiture s'était-elle arrêtée que les policiers l'encerclèrent.

Little did she think that her novel would sell so well.
› Elle était loin de se douter que son roman se vendrait si bien.

29 Énoncés interrogatifs

A Questions

- En français, pour poser une question à l'oral, on utilise souvent la forme affirmative, avec une intonation montante : « Tu la connais ? » / « Elle est venue ? ».

En anglais, l'inversion sujet / auxiliaire est toujours nécessaire (sauf lorsque ***WHO*** ou ***WHAT*** est sujet de l'énoncé : voir ci-après).

Do you know her? / Did she come?

- Lorsqu'il y a une **préposition**, elle est maintenue **à droite du verbe**.

  À qui penses-tu ? › *Who are you thinking **of**?*

  De quoi parliez-vous ? › *What were you talking **about**?*

B Mots interrogatifs

- ***WHO*** s'emploie pour une **personne**, en fonction **sujet ou complément**.

  Who saw the murderer? › Qui a vu le meurtrier ?
  (***WHO*** est **sujet**.)

  Who did you see? › Qui as-tu vu ?
  (***WHO*** est **complément**.)

Remarque : Les auxiliaires ***DO*** (au présent) et ***DID*** (au passé) n'apparaissent pas lorsque ***WHO*** et ***WHAT*** sont sujet.

- ***WHOM*** s'emploie (rarement) en fonction **complément**, dans une langue plus formelle.

  Whom do you like best? › Qui préfères-tu ?

- ***WHAT*** s'emploie pour un **non-animé**, en fonction **sujet ou complément**.

  What happened? › Que s'est-il passé ?
  (***WHAT*** est **sujet**.)

  What did you find? › Qu'as-tu trouvé ?
  (***WHAT*** est **complément**.)

WHAT peut être suivi d'un **nom**.

What colour is it? › C'est de quelle couleur ?

What subjects did you choose?
› Quelles matières as-tu choisies ?

- ***Which*** **: choix entre plusieurs possibilités** (réduites).

  Which of the two brothers did he call?
  ➤ Lequel des deux frères a-t-il appelé ?

Which peut être suivi d'un **nom** ou de ***one***.

Which book is it? ➤ C'est quel livre ?

Which one is it? ➤ Lequel est-ce ?

- ***What ... like*** s'emploie pour une demande de **description**. ***Like*** se place en fin de phrase.

  – *What is her brother like?* ➤ Comment est son frère ?
  – *He's tall and thin.* ➤ Il est grand et maigre.

- ***Whose*** : question sur la **possession**. ***Whose*** **est suivi de l'élément possédé sans article**.

  – *Whose bike is it?* ➤ À qui est ce vélo ?
  – *It's Paul's.* ➤ À Paul.

- ***Where*** : question sur le **lieu**.

  Where is it? ➤ Où est-ce ?

- ***When*** : question sur le **moment**.

  When did he call? ➤ Quand a-t-il appelé ?

- ***Since when*** : question sur le **point de départ** d'une action ou d'un fait.

  Since when have you been here?
  ➤ Depuis quand es-tu là ?

- ***Why*** porte sur la **cause**. On trouve ***because*** dans la réponse.

  – *Why did she laugh at him?* ➤ Pourquoi s'est-elle moquée de lui ?
  – *Because she found him stupid.* ➤ Parce qu'elle a trouvé qu'il était idiot.

- ***What ... for*** porte sur le **but**. On répond souvent par **l'infinitif**. ***For*** se place en fin de phrase.

  – *What did you call him* ***for****?* ➤ Pourquoi l'as-tu appelé ?
  – ***To*** *tell him how sorry I was.* ➤ Pour lui dire combien j'étais désolé.

- ***How long*** : question sur la **durée**.

  – *How long has she known them?* ➤ Cela fait combien de temps qu'elle les connaît ?
  – *(For) two years.* ➤ Deux ans.

- ***How long ago*** : question sur la **date**.

  – *How long ago did she leave?* ➤ Il y a combien de temps qu'elle est partie ?
  – *Two hours ago.* ➤ Il y a deux heures.

- ***How often*** : question sur la **fréquence**.

  How often do you feed the cat?
  ➤ Tous les combien donnes-tu à manger au chat ?

- ***How*** **+ adjectif** permet d'évaluer le **degré d'un adjectif**.

  How big is his house?
  ➤ Quelle est la taille de sa maison ?
  → Quel est son « degré de grandeur » ?

  How old is she? ➤ Quel âge a-t-elle ?

- ***How far*** : question sur la **distance**.

  How far is it? ➤ C'est à combien / à quelle distance d'ici ?

- ***How much*** / ***how many*** : questions sur la **quantité**. ***How much*** s'emploie également pour **demander un prix**.

  How much money do you have?
  ➤ Combien d'argent as-tu ?

  How many children are there?
  ➤ Combien d'enfants y-a-t-il ?

  How much is it? ➤ C'est combien ?

Remarque : Lorsque ***how much*** est suivi d'un nom, celui-ci est nécessairement **indénombrable** et donc au **singulier**. ***How many*** est suivi d'un nom au **pluriel**.

- ***How*** : question sur le **moyen**, la **manière**.

  How did you get out of the car?
  ➤ Comment es-tu sorti de la voiture ?

How s'emploie aussi pour questionner sur l'**état de santé**.

How is he? ➤ Comment va-t-il ?

30 Les réponses courtes et les *tags*

A « Oui / non »

- **Oui** ou **non** suffisent en français pour faire une réponse courte. En anglais, **on utilise très souvent l'auxiliaire** (précédé du sujet) dans la réponse courte. On fait apparaître l'auxiliaire correspondant au premier énoncé.

  – Tu as fini ? ➤ *Have you finished?*
  – Non. ➤ *No,* ***I haven't****.*

- Au **présent simple** et au **prétérit simple**, l'auxiliaire ne figure pas dans l'énoncé affirmatif ; il faut le faire apparaître dans la réponse.

  – *You agree with me, I suppose.*
  ➤ Je suppose que vous êtes d'accord avec moi.
  – *Yes, I do. / No, I don't.* ➤ Oui. / Non.

B « Moi aussi / moi non plus »

On utilise ***so*** lorsque le premier énoncé est **affirmatif** et ***neither*** lorsque le premier énoncé est **négatif**. ***So*** et ***neither*** sont directement **suivis de l'auxiliaire**.

– *I often watch that TV show.* ➤ Je regarde souvent ce show télévisé.
– *So do I.* ➤ Moi aussi.

– *I didn't tell him about it.* ➤ Je ne lui en ai pas parlé.
– *Neither did I.* ➤ Moi non plus.

C « Moi si / pas moi »

La reprise courte permet de **s'opposer** à ce qui vient d'être dit. On utilise le même auxiliaire que dans la phrase de départ, à la forme affirmative ou négative selon le cas. Si l'auxiliaire ne figure pas dans la première phrase, il faut le faire apparaître dans la deuxième : ***do*** / ***did*** au **présent simple** et au **prétérit simple**. Le sujet est accentué.

– *She won't come.* › Elle ne viendra pas.
– ***I*** *will.* › Moi si.

– *They tried hard.* › Ils ont fait beaucoup d'efforts.
– *Well,* ***you*** *didn't.* › Pas toi.

D Réponses courtes en *so* et *not*

On utilise ***so*** après ***I think***, ***I don't think***, ***I hope***, ***I suppose*** et ***not*** après ***I'm afraid***, ***I hope***, ***I suppose*** et ***of course***. ***So*** et ***not*** ont pour fonction de reprendre ce qui précède. On n'utilise pas d'auxiliaire dans ce cas.

– *Did he understand what she said?*
› A-t-il compris ce qu'elle a dit ?

– *Yes, I think so. / No, I don't think so. / I suppose so.*
› Oui, je crois. / Non, je ne crois pas. / Je crois que oui.

– *Well, I hope not. / I'm afraid not. / Of course not.*
› Eh bien, j'espère que non. / Je crains que non. / Bien sûr que non.

E *Tags* interrogatifs

Ce sont de brèves formes interrogatives (sujet + auxiliaire) que l'on trouve à la fin d'énoncés affirmatifs ou négatifs. Souvent traduit par N'EST-CE PAS ?, le *tag* permet de **demander confirmation de ce qui a été déclaré**.

They have finished, haven't they?
› Ils ont fini, non / n'est-ce pas ?

● Il faut parfois faire apparaître dans le *tag* un auxiliaire qui ne figure pas dans la première partie de la phrase.

- **Au présent simple** et **au prétérit simple** : ***do*** / ***did***

She talks too much, doesn't she?
› Elle parle trop, n'est-ce pas ?

He gave up at once, didn't he?
› Il a tout de suite abandonné, n'est-ce pas ?

- **À l'impératif** : ***shall*** ou ***will***

Let's go out, shall we? › Sortons, voulez-vous ?

Stay there, will you? › Reste-là, s'il te plaît.

● Après un terme négatif ou restrictif comme ***never, hardly ever, nothing,*** le ***tag*** est **positif**.

She never complains, does she?
› Elle ne se plaint jamais, n'est-ce pas ?

● Les indéfinis ***everybody, nobody*** sont repris par ***they*** bien que le verbe soit au singulier.

Everybody was there, weren't they?
› Tout le monde était là, n'est-ce pas ?

Nobody knows him, do they?
› Personne ne le connaît, n'est-ce pas ?

Première forme verbale affirmative → *tag* interro-négatif	Première forme verbale négative → *tag* interrogatif
He ***is*** *swimming,* ***isn't*** *he?* *He* ***was*** *swimming,* ***wasn't*** *he?* *They'****ve*** *changed,* ***haven't*** *they?* *They* ***had*** *changed,* ***hadn't*** *they?* *He* ***will*** *change,* ***won't*** *he?*	*He* ***isn't*** *swimming,* ***is*** *he?* *He* ***wasn't*** *swimming,* ***was*** *he?* *They* ***haven't*** *changed,* ***have*** *they?* *They* ***hadn't*** *changed,* ***had*** *they?* *He* ***won't*** *change,* ***will*** *he?*

31 Énoncés exclamatifs

A L'exclamation sur un groupe nominal

● On emploie ***what*** avec l'article ***a, an*** ou le pluriel sans article si le nom est dénombrable.

What a nice trip! › Quel voyage agréable !

What fools we are! › Que nous sommes bêtes !

● On utilise ***what*** avec **ø** si le nom est indénombrable.

What awful weather! › Quel temps affreux !

● On peut formuler les exclamations en ***what*** avec ***such***.

What a nice boy he is! → *He's such a nice boy!*
› C'est un garçon si gentil !

B L'exclamation sur un adjectif

● On emploie ***how*** immédiatement suivi de l'adjectif.
How terrible! › Comme c'est affreux !

● On peut formuler les exclamations en ***how*** avec ***so***.

How disappointed I was!
→ *I was ever so disappointed!* › J'étais tellement déçu !
(***Ever*** renforce un adjectif précédé de ***so***.)

32 Énoncés à l'impératif

● **Ordre adressé à *YOU***

▪ **Forme affirmative**: *Try this one!* › Essaie celui-ci !

▪ **Forme négative**: *Don't get out!* › Ne sors pas !

● **Ordre adressé à *WE***

▪ **Forme affirmative**:

Let's go to bed! › Allons nous coucher !

▪ **Forme négative**:

Let's not forget to sign the book!
› N'oublions pas de signer le livre !

ou (plus formel): *Don't let's forget to sign the book!*

● L'auxiliaire *DO* **a une valeur de persuasion à l'impératif**.

Do try! › Mais essaie donc !

33 L'infinitif

A Infinitif complet

● C'est **l'infinitif précédé de *TO***. Il désigne généralement un **acte à venir** ou un **acte qu'on envisage de faire**.

*He intends **to go**.* › Il a l'intention de partir.

● **On trouve l'infinitif complet**:

▪ **après les verbes projetant l'action dans l'avenir.**

→ Verbes de **volonté** (**refus**) ou **désir**: ***decide***, ***plan***, ***refuse***, ***want***, etc.

We've decided to stay. › Nous avons décidé de rester.

→ ***allow***, ***can't afford***, ***ask***, ***expect***, ***force***, ***try***

You're not allowed to go out on your own.
› Tu n'as pas le droit de sortir tout seul.

▪ pour exprimer la **visée** (**action projetée dans l'avenir**) **après** *BE*.

The show is to start at 10 p.m.
› Le spectacle doit commencer à 10 heures.

▪ **en complément d'adjectif.**

This language is pleasant to hear but difficult to understand.
› Cette langue est agréable à entendre mais difficile à comprendre.

▪ **en complément de certains pronoms indéfinis** (*NOTHING*, *NOBODY*, *NOWHERE*).

We have nothing to do and nowhere to go.
› Nous n'avons rien à faire et nulle part où aller.

● La **négation** se place **avant** *TO*.

*We tried **not to** argue with him.*
› On a essayé de ne pas se disputer avec lui.

● L'infinitif complet peut exprimer le **but**.

I went to your room to get a clean T-shirt.
› Je suis allé dans ta chambre pour y prendre un T-shirt propre.

● **Formes de l'infinitif complet**

▪ **Forme simple**

Le verbe renvoie au **présent** ou à **l'avenir**. Cela dépend du verbe et du contexte.

*He seems **to know you**.* › On dirait qu'il te connaît.

▪ **Forme *BE+ING***

Le verbe renvoie souvent à une **action en cours**.

*He seems **to be waiting** for someone.*
› Il semble qu'il soit en train d'attendre quelqu'un.

▪ **Forme *HAVE -EN***

Le verbe renvoie à un **fait accompli ou passé**.

*He seems **to have given up**.* › Il semble qu'il ait abandonné.

B Proposition infinitive

● Lorsque **l'infinitif est précédé d'un sujet**, on parle de **proposition infinitive**. Si le **sujet** est un pronom, on utilise le **pronom complément**, car la proposition infinitive est complément du premier verbe.

*Would you like **Sarah** / **her** to help you?*
› Voudrais-tu que Sarah / qu'elle t'aide?
→ La proposition infinitive (*Sarah / her to help you*) est complément du premier verbe (*Would you like*).

● **Verbes acceptant la proposition infinitive**: ***allow***, ***advise***, ***ask***, ***expect***, ***force***, ***order***, ***prefer***, ***tell***, ***wait for***, ***want***.

*What do you expect **me to say**?*
› Qu'attends-tu que je dise?

*They advised **us not to buy** anything in that shop.*
› Ils nous ont conseillé de ne rien acheter dans cette boutique.

● La proposition infinitive peut exprimer le **but**. Le sujet est alors introduit par *FOR*.

*She turned round **for him to see** her new hairdo.*
› Elle se tourna pour qu'il voie sa nouvelle coiffure.

● La proposition infinitive peut **suivre un adjectif**. Le sujet est alors introduit par *FOR*.

*It was **difficult** / **impossible for me to admit** the truth.*
› Il m'a été difficile / impossible d'admettre la vérité.

*It is **necessary** / **important for him to do** this.*
› Il est nécessaire / important qu'il le fasse.

● ***IT*** **est nécessaire pour annoncer une proposition infinitive après *find*, *know*, *consider*.**

*I find **it** hard **to get an answer**.*
› Je trouve qu'il est difficile d'obtenir une réponse.

34 Le gérondif

On forme le gérondif en accolant la marque -ING au verbe (V-ING). Le gérondif désigne une **activité**, c'est-à-dire un ensemble d'actes ou un acte vu dans son déroulement.

*I hate stay**ing** indoors.*
» J'ai horreur de rester à l'intérieur.

A Gérondif utilisé comme un nom

On le trouve :

- **en fonction de sujet ou complément.**

  Reading is his favourite activity.
  » Lire (la lecture) est son activité préférée.

  He loves dancing. » Il adore danser (la danse).

- **après les prépositions** (OF, WITH, ABOUT, FOR, IN, etc.). Les prépositions sont normalement suivies de noms ; le gérondif étant proche d'un nom, on le trouve donc aussi après les prépositions.

  I'm no longer interested in doing this.
  » Je ne m'intéresse plus à cela.

B Prépositions TO et FOR

● ***To*** **est parfois préposition, donc suivi du gérondif.**

*I don't object **to** invit**ing** them.*
» Je ne suis pas contre le fait de les inviter.

● ***To*** est préposition avec les verbes suivants : ***be used to*** (être habitué à), ***be reduced to***, ***devote time to*** (consacrer du temps à), ***get used to*** (s'habituer à), ***look forward to*** (avoir hâte de / attendre avec impatience), ***limit oneself to*** (se limiter à), ***object to*** (avoir une objection contre), ***take to*** (se mettre à).

*I look forward **to** meet**ing** them.* » J'ai hâte de les rencontrer.

> ***BE / GET USED TO* et *USED TO***
>
> - Dans ***BE USED TO*** (ÊTRE HABITUÉ À) et ***GET USED TO*** (S'HABITUER À), ***TO*** est préposition et donc suivi du gérondif (V-ING).
>
>   *I'm **not used to** driv**ing** on the left.*
>   » Je ne suis pas habitué à conduire à gauche.
>   *I never **got used to** driv**ing** on the left.*
>   » Je ne me suis jamais habitué à la conduite à gauche.
>
> - ***USED TO*** est une forme de prétérit qui exprime la **rupture totale avec le présent** (voir **Gr. 4 B**). Le verbe qui suit ***USED*** est à **l'infinitif avec *TO***.
>
>   *I **used to drive** a smaller car.*
>   » Avant, je conduisais une voiture plus petite.

● ***For*** **suivi du gérondif exprime la cause**

*He blamed me **for letting** the cat out.*
» Il m'a reproché d'avoir laissé sortir le chat.

● En revanche, pour exprimer le **but**, on emploie ***FOR*** **+ GN** + infinitif complet, avec ***TO***. (Voir **Gr. 33 B**.)

*I brought it **for you to see**.*
» Je l'ai apporté pour que vous le voyiez.

C Gérondif désignant une activité

On le trouve :

- **après les verbes exprimant le goût :** ***like***, ***love***, ***enjoy***, ***fancy*** (avoir envie de), ***feel like*** (avoir envie de), ***resent*** (ne pas apprécier), ***hate***, ***can't stand*** / ***bear*** (ne pas supporter de), etc.

  I love going to the cinema but I can't stand queuing.
  » J'adore aller au cinéma mais je ne supporte pas de faire la queue.

Remarque : Certains de ces mêmes verbes peuvent exprimer le **désir** et sont alors suivis de **l'infinitif complet**. (Voir **Gr. 33 A**.)

- **après certains adjectifs ou verbes qui décrivent une action déjà en cours :** ***be busy*** (être occupé à), ***go on*** / ***keep on*** (continuer à), ***keep*** (ne pas cesser de), ***spend time*** (passer du temps à), ***can't help*** (ne pas pouvoir s'empêcher de), ***stop***.

  Why do they keep asking questions?
  » Pourquoi n'arrêtent-ils pas de poser des questions ?

- **après les verbes impliquant que l'action a été réalisée :** ***remember***, ***regret***.

  I regret speaking to her. » Je regrette de lui avoir parlé.

D Autres verbes et expressions suivis du gérondif

● ***acknowledge*** (reconnaître), ***avoid*** (éviter), ***consider*** (envisager de), ***delay*** (retarder), ***have difficulty*** (avoir du mal à), ***give up*** (cesser de, abandonner), ***I don't mind*** (ça ne me gêne pas / ça ne m'ennuie pas de), ***postpone*** (remettre à plus tard), ***resist***, ***risk***.

You should avoid driving and consider taking the train.
» Tu devrais éviter de conduire et envisager de prendre le train.

● ***It's no use*** / ***It's worth*** / ***There's no***

It's no use trying.
» Cela ne vaut pas la peine d'essayer.

It's worth going.
» Cela vaut la peine d'y aller.

There's no denying that she's a liar.
» On ne peut pas nier que c'est une menteuse.

35 Infinitif ou gérondif ?

A Verbes à deux constructions

Certains verbes peuvent être suivis soit de l'infinitif, soit du gérondif : ***like***, ***love***, ***hate***, ***begin***, ***start***, ***remember***, ***try***.

- **Action déjà réalisée ou en cours → gérondif**

  *I remember **talking** to him.*
  › Je me rappelle lui avoir parlé.

  *Stop **asking** silly questions!*
  › Arrête de poser des questions idiotes !

  *I tried **rock climbing** once.*
  › Une fois, j'ai essayé de faire de l'escalade.

- **Action non encore réalisée → infinitif**

  *Remember **to talk** to him.*
  › N'oublie pas de lui parler.

  *He stopped **to ask** a question.*
  › Il s'est arrêté pour poser une question.

  *I tried **to stop** but I couldn't.*
  › J'ai essayé de m'arrêter mais je n'ai pas pu.

B Propositions en -ING

● Le gérondif peut être **précédé d'un sujet** qui peut avoir la forme d'un possessif, d'un génitif, d'un pronom ou d'un nom.

*He objected to **their** going out (to **the children's** going out).*
*He objected to **them** going out (to **the children** going out).*
› Ça l'ennuyait qu'ils sortent (que les enfants sortent).
→ *TO* est ici préposition.

36 La base verbale

A Emplois de la base verbale

La base verbale est « l'infinitif sans *TO* ». On la trouve :

- **après les modaux.**

  She should stay. › Elle devrait rester.

- **après les expressions modales *YOU'D BETTER* et *I'D RATHER*.**

  You'd better ask them first.
  › Tu ferais mieux de leur demander avant.

  I'd rather stay on my own. › Je préférerais rester seul.

- **à l'impératif :**

  Stay back! › N'avancez pas !

- **après *WHY* / *WHY NOT* dans les questions sans sujet.**

  Why see her? Why not write to her?
  › Pourquoi la voir ? Pourquoi ne pas lui écrire ?

- **après les verbes de perception.**

  I heard him come in. › Je l'ai entendu entrer.

  I saw someone fall off the roof.
  › J'ai vu quelqu'un tomber du toit.

Remarque : Les verbes de perception peuvent être aussi suivis de la **forme en -*ING***. Dans ce cas, l'action est vue dans son **déroulement**.

I heard him singing. › Je l'ai entendu chanter.
→ Il était en train de chanter.

B « Faire faire »

● ***MAKE* ou *HAVE* + base verbale**

The police made the terrorist talk.
› La police a fait parler le terroriste.

Juliet had us talk all night.
› Juliet nous a fait parler toute la nuit.

→ ***MAKE*** exprime plus la contrainte que ***HAVE***.

● ***HAVE* + participe passé**

We've had the lock changed.
› Nous avons fait changer la serrure.
→ On ne nous dit pas qui a changé la serrure mais seulement que la serrure a été changée. Le participe passé a un sens passif. ***MAKE*** est impossible dans ce cas.

Remarque : *GET* + **participe passé** a le même sens.

I got my car serviced. › J'ai fait réviser ma voiture.

Traduction de FAIRE FAIRE

Il faut se demander si l'énoncé a un **sens passif** ou **actif**.

- **Sens passif : *HAVE* + participe passé**
  Elle s'est fait livrer de la nourriture.
  › De la nourriture a été livrée.
  › *She's had some food delivered.*
- **Sens actif (quelqu'un accomplit une action à la demande de quelqu'un d'autre) : *MAKE* ou *HAVE* + base verbale**
  Elle les a fait sortir de la pièce.
  › Ils sont sortis de la pièce.
  › *She made / had them go out of the room.*

C « Laisser faire »

On utilise *LET*, qui signifie DONNER LA POSSIBILITÉ DE. On utilise alors la base verbale pour le deuxième verbe.

He let us stay a little longer.
› Il nous a laissé rester un peu plus longtemps.

Remarque : Ne pas confondre *LET*, *LET'S* et *LEAVE*.

- ***LET'S*** sert à former **l'impératif** à la 1re personne du pluriel.

  Let's go! › Allons-y !

- ***LEAVE*** signifie généralement PARTIR ou LAISSER.

  He left Paris in 2002. › Il a quitté Paris en 2002.

  They left me alone. › Ils m'ont laissé tout seul.

37 Les subordonnées en *THAT* et *WHAT*

A Subordonnées en *THAT* (QUE)

On les trouve :

- **après les verbes exprimant un savoir ou une opinion : *believe, know, suppose, think*.**

  I think (that) it is too late. › Je pense qu'il est trop tard.

THAT est souvent effacé à l'oral dans ce cas.

- **après les verbes servant à rapporter des paroles : *answer, say, tell*.** (Voir **Gr. 42 D**.)

  He said (that) he didn't need any help.
  › Il a dit qu'il n'avait pas besoin d'aide.

- **après *suggest, demand, insist, recommend*.** Dans ce cas, *THAT* est souvent suivi de *SHOULD* ou de la **base verbale** (anglais soutenu, pas de *s* à la 3e personne du singulier).

  *Your brother has suggested that **she should stay** here / that **she stay** here.*
  › Ton frère a suggéré qu'elle reste ici.

TELL et SAY

- ***TELL* a deux constructions :**
  – Lorsque *TELL*, suivi d'une proposition, signifie DIRE QUE, il se construit avec une proposition en *THAT*.

    He told me that I was in danger.
    › Il m'a dit que j'étais en danger.

  – Lorsque *TELL* signifie DIRE DE (= ORDONNER), il se construit avec une **proposition infinitive**.

    *They told **me to** stop there.*
    › Ils m'ont dit (ordonné) de m'arrêter là.

  Remarque : Le verbe est à l'infinitif précédé de *TO*. Lorsque le sujet est un pronom, il se met au cas complément.

- *SAY*, qui signifie aussi DIRE, se construit généralement avec *THAT*.

  *He **said (to me) that** I was in danger.*
  › Il (m') a dit que j'étais en danger.

Traduction de QUE

- **On ne traduit pas toujours QUE par *THAT*.** Beaucoup de verbes se construisent en anglais avec la **proposition infinitive** (voir **Gr. 33 B**) et tout particulièrement les verbes exprimant le **désir** ou une **attente**.

  Je veux qu'ils m'écoutent.
  › *I want them to listen to me.*

  Je ne m'attends pas à ce qu'elle me comprenne.
  › *I don't expect her to understand me.*

- Certains QUE sont des **relatifs.** (Voir **Gr. 38**.)

  C'est le seul bateau que j'aie vu.
  › *It's the only boat (that) I have seen.*

B Subordonnées en *WHAT* (CE QUE)

On les trouve en position de **sujet** ou de **complément** de la phrase. *WHAT* se traduit alors par CE QUE.

***What happened** was unpredictable.* (sujet)
› Ce qui s'est passé n'était pas prévisible.

*I'll do **what I can**.* (complément)
› Je ferai ce que je pourrai.

Traduction de TOUT CE QUE

TOUT CE QUE se traduit par *ALL THAT* et non par ~~*ALL WHAT*~~. *THAT* peut être effacé.

C'est tout ce que j'ai. › *This is all (that) I have.*

38 Les subordonnées relatives

A Qu'est-ce qu'une relative ?

● C'est une proposition subordonnée qui apporte une information sur un nom.

Voici le livre **que tu voulais**. → La relative (en gras) apporte une précision concernant le nom « livre » que l'on vient de mentionner. On appelle ce nom **l'antécédent**.

● Les subordonnées relatives sont introduites par des **pronoms relatifs**. En anglais, les **pronoms relatifs** expriment la **distinction entre « humain » et « non-humain »** :

- Pronoms relatifs pour un **humain** : *WHO, THAT, WHOM.*
- Pronoms relatifs pour un **non-humain** : *THAT, WHICH.*

B Fonction du pronom relatif

Outre la différence entre « humain » et « non-humain », il faut déterminer si le pronom relatif est **sujet** de la relative ou bien **complément**.

- **Pronom sujet** : il est placé juste **avant le verbe de la subordonnée**. On emploie *WHO* pour un **humain**, et *THAT* ou *WHICH* pour un **non-humain**.

  *The man **who**'s painting the front door is the caretaker.*
  › L'homme qui est en train de peindre la porte d'entrée est le gardien.

  *You'll have to clean the couch **that** / **which** is in your study.*
  › Il va falloir que tu nettoies le canapé qui est dans ton bureau.

- **Pronom complément :** on emploie *THAT* ou *WHO(M)* pour un **humain** et *THAT* ou *WHICH* pour un **non-humain**.

Remarque : *WHOM* est de moins en moins fréquemment utilisé. *THAT* **est souvent effacé**.

Here is the lady that / whom / ø I've told you about.
› Voici la dame dont je t'ai parlé.

The CD that / which / ø you've lent me is in the drawer.
› Le CD que tu m'as prêté est dans le tiroir.

C Absence du pronom relatif

● Dans un grand nombre de cas, la relative suit directement le nom, **sans aucun pronom relatif**.

*You can use the new computer **I've bought**.*
› Tu peux te servir du nouvel ordinateur **que j'ai acheté**.

● On pourrait introduire *THAT* devant la relative.

*You can use the new computer **that I've bought**.*

● **Dans quel cas peut-on « effacer »** *THAT* **? Uniquement lorsque** *THAT* **est complément.** Dans l'exemple ci-dessus, *THAT* peut être effacé car il est complément du verbe ***I've bought***.

En revanche lorsque *THAT* est **sujet**, **on ne peut pas l'effacer**.

It's the tallest skyscraper that was ever built.
› C'est le plus grand gratte-ciel qui ait jamais été construit.

● **On efface le plus souvent** *THAT* **après :**

- *ALL, THE ONLY, THE FIRST, THE LAST* et les **superlatifs** (*THE MOST*…, *THE BEST*…, etc.).

All I need is a little rest.
› Tout ce dont j'ai besoin, c'est d'un peu de repos.

He's the funniest man I know.
› C'est l'homme le plus drôle que je connaisse.

- **les prépositions :** si le verbe est construit avec une préposition (***look at***, ***laugh at***, ***look for***, etc.), la **préposition** est maintenue **à droite du verbe** et *THAT* **peut être effacé**.

*This is the baby **she's been looking after**.*
› C'est le bébé dont elle s'est occupée.

D Les deux types de relatives

● Si la relative est **essentielle au sens**, c'est-à-dire qu'elle **permet d'identifier l'élément dont on parle**, on dit qu'elle est « **déterminative** » ou « **restrictive** ». Ces relatives sont **les plus fréquentes**. On emploie le plus souvent les pronoms *THAT* et *WHO*.

*This is the car **that I'd like to buy**.*
› C'est la voiture que j'aimerais acheter.
→ Cette voiture-là et pas une autre.

*Here is the journalist **who wrote the article you liked so much**.*
› C'est le journaliste qui a écrit l'article que tu as tant apprécié. (*THAT* est possible.)

● Si la relative apporte une **précision accessoire**, un **détail supplémentaire** qui n'est pas essentiel au sens, on dit que la relative est « **non-déterminative** ». Ces relatives se placent généralement **entre virgules**. On emploie les pronoms *WHICH* et *WHO* (ou, plus rarement, *WHOM* en fonction complément).

*Her house, **which was built by a famous architect**, overlooks the bay.*
› Sa maison, qui a été construite par un architecte célèbre, domine la baie.
→ On comprend de quelle maison il s'agit, même si l'on supprime la relative.

*His father, **who used to work in publishing**, is now retired.*
› Son père, qui travaillait dans l'édition, est maintenant à la retraite.

E « Ce que / ce qui »

● On utilise *WHAT* pour **annoncer quelque chose qui va être précisé**.

What you did was sheer madness.
› Ce que tu as fait était de la folie pure.

● On utilise *WHICH* lorsqu'on **reprend la proposition qui précède**.

I didn't ask him why he'd done that, which was a mistake.
› Je ne lui ai pas demandé pourquoi il avait fait cela, ce qui était une erreur.

Rappel : Tout ce que se traduit par *ALL THAT*. On n'utilise pas *WHAT* dans ce cas. (*THAT* est souvent effacé.)

Donne-moi tout ce que tu as.
› *Give me all (that) you have.*

Elle m'a dit tout ce qu'elle savait.
› *She told me all (that) she knew.*

F « Dont »

● Lorsque dont exprime la **possession**, on utilise le pronom *WHOSE*.

C'est la fille **dont** les parents travaillent dans un hôpital.
› *This is the girl **whose** parents work in a hospital.*

C'est un pays **dont** j'aime le climat.
› *It's a country **whose** climate I like.*

● Lorsque dont n'exprime pas la possession, il correspond souvent en français à un verbe suivi de la préposition de. Il faut donc trouver le verbe correspondant en anglais. La préposition, en anglais, est placée **à droite du verbe**. (Le pronom complément *THAT* peut être effacé.)

Les enfants **dont** elle s'occupe ne parlent qu'allemand.
› *The children (that) she's looking after only speak German.*

G « Où »

En anglais, on utilise *WHERE* pour le lieu et *WHEN* pour le temps.

C'est l'endroit **où** cela s'est passé.
› *This is the place **where** it happened.*

Il fut un temps où tu avais besoin de lui.
› *There was a time **when** you needed him.*

39 Les subordonnées de condition et de temps

A Condition

- ***If***

▪ **Condition simple**

If *you help me, I* ***will*** *succeed.* › Si tu m'aides, je réussirai.

▪ **Condition incertaine**

If *you helped me, I* ***would*** *succeed.*
› Si tu m'aidais, je réussirais.

▪ **Condition non-réalisée**

If *you had helped me, I* ***would have*** *succeeded.*
› Si tu m'avais aidé, j'aurais réussi.

- ***Provided*** : À CONDITION QUE / POURVU QUE

I will do the job ***provided*** *I get a reward.*
› Je ferai le travail à condition que j'obtienne une récompense.

- ***Unless*** : À MOINS QUE

I won't do it ***unless*** *they offer to help me.*
› Je ne le ferai pas, à moins qu'ils ne proposent de m'aider.

- ***Whether*** correspond à une **interrogation** et présente toujours **deux possibilités**.

I still wonder ***whether*** *it's true (or not).*
› Je me demande encore si c'est vrai.
→ « Est-ce vrai ? Oui ou non ? »

Ne pas confondre ***whether*** avec ***if***, qui exprime la **condition**.

B Temps

- ***When*** : QUAND

When *you're older, you'll understand.*
› Quand tu seras plus grand, tu comprendras.

> **Les subordonnées de temps et le futur**
> En anglais, les subordonnées de temps, **comme les subordonnées en *if***, ne sont pas compatibles avec ***will***. Pour exprimer le futur, on emploie le présent ou le *present perfect* dans la subordonnée. (Voir **Gr. 10 C.**)
> Je lui parlerai **si** je le vois / **quand** je le **verrai**.
> › *I'll talk to him* ***if I see him*** */* ***when I see*** *him.*

- ***Whenever*** : CHAQUE FOIS QUE

He calls me ***whenever*** *he feels low.*
› Il m'appelle **chaque fois qu'**il se sent déprimé.

- ***As soon as*** : DÈS QUE / AUSSITÔT QUE

Let me know ***as soon as*** *you've finished.*
› Prévenez-moi **dès que** / **aussitôt que** vous aurez fini.

- ***Before*** : AVANT QUE

Try to find him ***before*** *it's too late.*
› Essaie de le retrouver **avant qu'**il ne soit trop tard.

- ***Until*** : JUSQU'À CE QUE / AVANT QUE

I'll stay ***until*** *you tell me he's safe.*
› Je resterai **jusqu'à ce que** tu me dises qu'il est en sécurité.

Avec une forme négative, on traduit ***until*** par **AVANT QUE**.

I won't move ***until*** *you tell me we're safe.*
› Je ne m'en irai pas **avant que** tu ne me dises que nous sommes en sécurité.

- ***While*** : PENDANT QUE

He slept ***while*** *I was working.*
› Il a dormi **pendant que (tout le temps que)** je travaillais.

- ***As*** : ALORS QUE / TANDIS QUE / COMME

As *she got on the bus, she saw him cross the street.*
› **Alors** / **Tandis qu'**elle montait dans le bus, elle le vit traverser la rue.

40 Les subordonnées de cause et de but

A Cause

- ***Because*** (PARCE QUE) **répond à la question *why?***

– ***Why*** *did you turn down his offer?* › Pourquoi as-tu refusé sa proposition ?
– ***Because*** *it wasn't very sensible.* › Parce qu'elle n'était pas très raisonnable.

- ***As*** / ***since*** : COMME / PUISQUE

As *it was getting late, we decided to pack up.*
› **Comme** il se faisait tard, nous avons décidé de faire nos bagages.

Since *it's over, we can leave.*
› **Puisque** c'est fini, nous pouvons partir.

- ***For*** + ***-ing*** ou **GN**

He was blamed ***for smoking*** *too much.*
› On lui a reproché **de trop fumer.**

B But

- ***To*** / ***in order to*** / ***so as to*** (POUR / AFIN DE) répondent à la question ***what … for?***

– ***What*** *did you do that* ***for****?* › **Dans quel but** as-tu fait cela ?
– *I did it* ***to*** *help you /* ***in order to*** *help you /* ***so as to*** *help you.* › Je l'ai fait **pour** t'aider.

- ***For*** + **GN** + ***to*** (POUR QUE / AFIN QUE)

We bought a piano ***for him to*** *practise at home.*
› Nous avons acheté un piano **pour qu'**il puisse faire ses exercices à la maison.

41 Subordonnées d'opposition, de concession, de manière

A Opposition

- **WHEREAS / WHILE : ALORS QUE**

*She's never been to New York, **whereas / while** most of her friends have been there several times.*
› Elle n'est jamais allée à New York **alors que** la plupart de ses amis y sont allés plusieurs fois.

B Concession

- **ALTHOUGH / THOUGH : BIEN QUE / QUOIQUE**

Ils sont proches par le sens de ***AND YET*** (ET POURTANT).

*I'll stay **although** I don't feel like it.*
› Je vais rester, **bien que / quoique** je n'en aie pas envie.

*I'll stay **and yet** I don't feel like it.*
› Je vais rester, **et pourtant** je n'en ai pas envie.

Ne pas confondre ***ALTHOUGH*** (conjonction, suivie d'une phrase) et ***DESPITE / IN SPITE OF*** (MALGRÉ), qui sont des prépositions (suivies d'un **GN**).

***Despite / In spite of** his despondency, he went on working.*
› **Malgré** son abattement, il continua à travailler.

***Although** he felt despondent, he went on working.*
› **Bien qu**'il se sentît abattu, il continua à travailler.

- **HOWEVER : BIEN QUE / QUOIQUE**

Dans ce sens, ***HOWEVER*** est suivi d'un adjectif ou d'un adverbe.

***However sweet** she may be now, I can't forgive her.*
› **Bien qu'elle soit gentille** maintenant (pour aussi gentille qu'elle puisse être maintenant), je ne peux lui pardonner.

HOWEVER signifie aussi **CEPENDANT**.

*We've been asked to wait. **However**, we've decided to leave as soon as possible.*
› On nous a demandé d'attendre ; **cependant**, nous allons partir dès que possible.

C Manière

- ***How*** **introduisant une subordonnée signifie LA MANIÈRE DE / COMMENT.**

I wonder how she managed to do it.
› Je me demande comment (de quelle manière) elle a réussi à le faire.

- ***How*** **peut aussi exprimer le degré :**

▪ **d'un adjectif.**

Ask them how big / deep / wide it is.
› Demande-leur quelle est sa taille / quelle est sa profondeur / quelle est sa largeur.

▪ **d'un adverbe** (***HOW MUCH, HOW OFTEN***).

Do you have any idea how much they need you?
› Sais-tu combien / à quel point ils ont besoin de toi ?

42 Le style indirect

On peut transformer un énoncé au style direct (phrase d'un dialogue, par exemple) en un énoncé introduit par un verbe comme ***SAY*** ou ***TELL*** au passé (DIRE QUE), ou bien ***ASK*** (DEMANDER SI), etc. On a alors un énoncé au style indirect. Cette transformation entraîne des modifications **dans les formes verbales, les pronoms, les possessifs, l'ordre des mots et les repères de lieu et de temps**.

A Formes verbales

Style direct	Style indirect passé
*"**I'm watching TV**," said Paul.*	*Paul said (that) **he was watching TV**.*
*"**I don't believe you**," he said to them.*	*He said (that) **he didn't believe them**.*
*"**I have never talked to her**," she said.*	*She said (that) **she had never talked to her**.*
*"**He's been crying**," she said.*	*She said that **he had been crying**.*
*"**I saw them yesterday**," he said.*	*He said (that) **he had seen them the day before**.*
Modaux	
*"**I will help you**," he said.*	*He said (that) **he would help her**.*
*"**I can't** drive," she said.*	*She said that **she couldn't** drive.*
*"**May I** sit next to **you**?" asked Paul.*	*Paul asked whether **he might** sit next to **her**.*
*"You **must** wait for him," I said.*	*I said that they **were to** wait for him (that they **must** wait for him).* On peut conserver ***MUST***, mais on emploie souvent ***WAS / WERE TO*** (forme non-modale) qui exprime la contrainte.

● ***Could, could have, might, should*** **et** ***should have*** **restent inchangés au style indirect.**

"You ***should*** *see this film," he said.*
› « Tu devrais voir ce film, » dit-il.

→ *He said that I* ***should*** *see this film.*
› Il a dit que je devrais voir ce film.

● **Le prétérit devient** ***pluperfect*** lorsque le verbe désigne un **événement unique** qui est **antérieur** au moment où on en parle.

"I ***didn't eat*** *much last night," he said.*
› « Je n'ai pas beaucoup mangé hier soir, » dit-il.

→ *He said that he* ***had not eaten*** *much the night before.*
› Il a dit qu'il n'avait pas beaucoup mangé la veille au soir.

● **On maintient le prétérit** lorsque l'énoncé décrit une **habitude** et lorsque le verbe est un **verbe d'état**, comme par exemple *be, have, hate, know, like, want.*

"When Helen ***was*** *in Chester, we sometimes* ***went out*** *for a drink."*
› « Lorsqu'Helen était à Chester, nous sortions parfois boire un verre ensemble. »

→ *He said that when Helen* ***was*** *in Chester, they sometimes* ***went out*** *for a drink.*
› Il a dit que lorsqu'Helen était à Chester, ils sortaient parfois boire un verre ensemble.

B Questions : ordre des mots

Au style indirect, on n'inverse jamais le sujet et le verbe.

"Where's your car?" › « Où est ta voiture ? »

→ *She asked me where* ***my car was****.*
› Elle m'a demandé où **était ma voiture**.

C Expressions de temps et de lieu

Au style indirect passé, certains repères de temps et de lieu sont modifiés :

- *yesterday* → *the day before*
- *two days ago* → *two days before*
- *last year* → *the year before*
- *tomorrow* → *the following day / the day after*
- *next week* → *the following week / the week after*
- *here* → *there*

"I'll buy my ticket tomorrow," he said.
› « J'achèterai mon billet demain, » dit-il.

→ *He said (that) he would buy his ticket* ***the following day****.*
› Il a dit qu'il achèterait son billet le lendemain.

D Verbes introducteurs du style indirect

● **Dire que :** ***say*** **ou** ***tell*** **?**

▪ Pour rapporter des paroles, on peut utiliser *say* ou *tell* suivis de *that*. La différence est que *say* peut se construire sans complément, alors que ce n'est pas le cas de *tell*.

She said that he was silly. / She told ***him*** *that he was silly.*
› Elle (lui) a dit qu'il était idiot.

▪ *Say* peut aussi se construire avec un complément, bien que ce ne soit pas obligatoire. Dans ce cas, on utilise la **préposition** *to* (alors qu'on place le complément directement après *tell*, sans préposition).

She said ***to John*** *that he was silly.*
› Elle a dit à John qu'il était idiot.

Remarque : *Tell* peut signifier ordonner (= dire à quelqu'un **de** faire quelque chose). Dans ce cas la **proposition infinitive** est obligatoire.

She told ***me to*** *do it.* › Elle m'a dit (ordonné) de le faire.

● ***Ask*** **: demander /** ***wonder*** **: se demander**

"When are they coming?" she asked him.
› « Quand arrivent-ils ? »

→ *She asked him when they were coming.*
› Elle lui a demandé quand ils arrivaient.

On utilise *whether* (si) pour transformer une **question attendant une réponse en** ***yes / no*****.**

"Will they like it?" › « Est-ce que ça leur plaira ? »

→ *She wondered whether (if) they would like it.*
› Elle se demanda si ça leur plaisait.

● ***Order / tell*** **: expression de l'ordre**

"Close your eyes! Don't laugh!" he said to her.
› « Ferme les yeux ! Ne ris pas ! »

→ *He ordered her / told her* ***to close her eyes*** *and* ***not to laugh****.*
› Il lui a ordonné / dit de fermer les yeux et de ne pas rire.

● ***Advise*** **: conseiller**

"Why don't you buy a new one?"
› « Pourquoi n'en achètes-tu pas un neuf ? »

→ *She advised him to buy a new one.*
› Elle lui a conseillé d'en acheter un neuf.

● ***Blame for / reproach for*** **: expression du reproche**

"You shouldn't have laughed at her."
› « Tu n'aurais pas dû te moquer d'elle. »

→ *He reproached him* ***for*** */ blamed him* ***for laughing*** *at her.*
› Il lui reprocha de s'être moqué d'elle.

● ***Apologize for*** **: s'excuser**

"I'm sorry I'm late," he said.
› « Je suis désolé d'être en retard », dit-il.

→ *He apologized* ***for being*** *late.*
› Il s'excusa d'être en retard.

● ***Suggest*** **: suggérer que**

On utilise la **base verbale simple après** ***suggest*****,** quelle que soit la personne (anglais soutenu).

"Why don't you try another one?"
› « Pourquoi n'en essaies-tu pas un autre ? »

→ *He suggested that she* ***try*** *the other one.*
› Il proposa / suggéra qu'elle en essaie un autre.

43 La voix passive

A Formes

La voix passive met l'**objet** sur lequel porte l'action en **tête de l'énoncé**. L'auxiliaire de la voix passive est *BE*. Le verbe est au **participe passé**.

- **Voix active :**

They built the new museum in 2009.
› Ils ont construit le nouveau musée en 2009.

- **Voix passive :**

The new museum was built in 2009.
› Le nouveau musée a été construit en 2009.

Formes verbales	Voix active	Voix passive
Présent simple	*They never **discuss** our plans.*	*Our plans **are** never **discussed**.*
Prétérit	*They **discussed** it.*	*It **was discussed**.*
Présent *BE+ING*	*They **are discussing** it.*	*It **is being discussed**.*
Prétérit *BE+ING*	*They **were discussing** it.*	*It **was being discussed**.*
Present perfect	*They **have discussed** it.*	*It **has been discussed**.*
Pluperfect	*They **had discussed** it.*	*It **had been discussed**.*
Modal	*They **will discuss** it. / They **can't discuss** it.*	*It **will be discussed**. / It **can't be discussed**.*

B Sens

● **Pourquoi la forme passive ?**

- Si l'on parle de l'**événement lui-même**, on utilise la **voix active**.

*The authorities **cancelled** the performance.*
› Les autorités ont annulé la représentation.

- Si l'on parle de l'**objet sur lequel porte l'action** (la « victime », la personne ou l'objet qui subissent l'action), on utilise la **voix passive**.

*The performance **was cancelled** by the authorities.*
› La représentation a été annulée par les autorités.

● **Traduction de ON**

On utilise très fréquemment la voix passive en anglais lorsque l'agent (celui qui fait l'action) n'est pas identifié. En français, on utilise souvent **ON** dans ce cas-là.

On a créé **deux mille nouveaux sites Internet** la semaine dernière.
› ***Two thousand new websites*** *were created last week.*

On **m'**a donné le code d'accès. › ***I*** *was given the passcode.*

On ne **les** a jamais revus. › ***They*** *were never seen again.*

● **Complément d'agent (celui qui fait l'action)**

On ne le mentionne que si celui-ci a une importance particulière. Il est introduit par *BY*.

*The dress was offered to her **by a British designer**.*
› La robe lui a été offerte par un grand couturier britannique.

C Verbes à deux compléments

● **Il y a deux façons en anglais de former la voix passive** à partir de la phrase suivante :

Someone gave me the key. › Quelqu'un m'a donné la clé.

- **Le complément d'attribution** (ME) devient **sujet**.

I *was given the key.* › On m'a donné la clé.

C'est la forme du passif **la plus fréquente en anglais avec ce type de verbe**, car c'est un être humain qui est placé en tête d'énoncé. Cette forme est impossible en français : on traduit par **ON**.

- **Le complément d'objet direct** (*the key*) devient **sujet**.

The key *was given to me.* › La clé m'a été donnée.

● Les verbes ***ASK, SHOW, TELL, TEACH, OFFER, SEND, LEND*** peuvent se construire à la voix passive de la même manière que ***GIVE***.

I was asked / told to keep silent.
› On m'a demandé de me taire.

She was lent / offered / shown a new car.
› On lui a prêté / offert / montré une nouvelle voiture.

D Les verbes prépositionnels

● On maintient la **préposition à droite du verbe** à la voix passive.

- **Voix active :**

*Somebody **will look after** him.*
› Quelqu'un s'occupera de lui.

- **Voix passive :**

*He **will be looked after**.*
› On s'occupera de lui.

● Cette forme passive est impossible en français : on traduit par **ON**.

E -ING après NEED et WANT

WANT peut signifier **AVOIR BESOIN DE**, comme **NEED**.

The flowers need / want ***watering****.*
› Les fleurs ont besoin d'être arrosées.

-ING a ici un sens **passif**.

F Construction passive de certaines phrases complexes

Les trois phrases complexes suivantes se passivent de la même façon. On fait apparaître *TO* à la voix passive.

Rapporter des paroles ou une opinion

- On utilise ***BELIEVE, CONSIDER, DECLARE, HEAR, KNOW, REPORT, SAY, THINK*** au passif, suivis de *TO*.

They are said to... › On dit qu'ils...

She is believed to... › On pense qu'elle...

He is thought to... › On pense qu'il...

- S'il n'y a pas de décalage temporel entre les deux propositions, on utilise l'infinitif simple.

They say that she is a secret agent.
→ *She is said* ***to be*** *a secret agent.*
› On dit qu'elle est agent secret.

They believe he has a chance of succeeding.
→ *He is believed* ***to have*** *a chance of succeeding.*
› On pense qu'il a des chances de succès.

- Si le fait dont on parle est antérieur à ***SAY, THINK,*** etc., on utilise l'infinitif à la forme ***HAVE -EN***.

They think that he died in Africa.
→ *He is thought* ***to have died*** *in Africa.*
› On pense qu'il est mort en Afrique.

It is reported that a prisoner has escaped.
→ *A prisoner is reported* ***to have escaped****.*
› Un détenu se serait évadé.

Propositions infinitives exprimant la pression (*ASK, EXPECT, TELL, ORDER*)

They told him to hang up the phone.
→ *He was told to hang up the phone.*
› On lui a dit de raccrocher le téléphone.

Structures causatives en *MAKE* (voir **Gr. 36 B**)

She made us unpack at once.
→ *We were made to unpack at once.*
› On nous a immédiatement fait défaire nos affaires.

Index du Précis grammatical

Les points de grammaire sont référencés par rapport aux fiches.

Verbes irréguliers

	Base verbale	Prétérit	Participe passé	Traduction
	Trois formes identiques			
C	cut /ʌ/	cut /ʌ/	cut /ʌ/	*couper*
H	hurt /ɜː/	hurt /ɜː/	hurt /ɜː/	*blesser*
L	let /e/	let /e/	let /e/	*permettre, louer*
P	put /ʊ/	put /ʊ/	put /ʊ/	*mettre, poser*
R	read /iː/	read /e/	read /e/	*lire*
S	set /e/	set /e/	set /e/	*fixer*
	shut /ʌ/	shut /ʌ/	shut /ʌ/	*fermer*
	Prétérit et participe passé identiques			
B	bend /e/	bent /e/	bent /e/	*(se) courber*
	bring /ɪ/	brought /ɔː/	brought /ɔː/	*apporter*
	build /ɪ/	built /ɪ/	built /ɪ/	*construire*
	burn /ɜː/	burnt /ɜː/	burnt /ɜː/	*brûler*
	buy /aɪ/	bought /ɔː/	bought /ɔː/	*acheter*
C	catch /æ/	caught /ɔː/	caught /ɔː/	*attraper*
D	dream /iː/	dreamt /e/	dreamt /e/	*rêver*
F	feel /iː/	felt /e/	felt /e/	*(se) sentir, éprouver*
	fight /aɪ/	fought /ɔː/	fought /ɔː/	*se battre, combattre*
	find /aɪ/	found /aʊ/	found /aʊ/	*trouver*
G	get /e/	got /ɒ/	got /ɒ/	*obtenir*
H	have /æ/	had /æ/	had /æ/	*avoir*
	hear /ɪə/	heard /ɜː/	heard /ɜː/	*entendre*
	hold /əʊ/	held /e/	held /e/	*tenir*
K	keep /iː/	kept /e/	kept /e/	*garder*
L	lead /iː/	led /e/	led /e/	*mener, guider*
	learn /ɜː/	learnt /ɜː/	learnt /ɜː/	*apprendre*
	leave /iː/	left /e/	left /e/	*laisser, quitter*
	lend /e/	lent /e/	lent /e/	*prêter*
	light /aɪ/	lit /ɪ/	lit /ɪ/	*allumer*
	lose /uː/	lost /ɒ/	lost /ɒ/	*perdre*
M	make /eɪ/	made /eɪ/	made /eɪ/	*faire, fabriquer*
	mean /iː/	meant /e/	meant /e/	*signifier, vouloir dire*
	meet /iː/	met /e/	met /e/	*(se) rencontrer*
P	pay /eɪ/	paid /eɪ/	paid /eɪ/	*payer*
S	say /eɪ/	said /e/	said /e/	*dire*
	sell /e/	sold /əʊ/	sold /əʊ/	*vendre*
	send /e/	sent /e/	sent /e/	*envoyer*
	shoot /uː/	shot /ɒ/	shot /ɒ/	*tirer*
	sit /ɪ/	sat /æ/	sat /æ/	*être assis*
	sleep /iː/	slept /e/	slept /e/	*dormir*
	smell /e/	smelt /e/	smelt /e/	*sentir (odorat)*
	spend /e/	spent /e/	spent /e/	*dépenser, passer (le temps)*
	stand /æ/	stood /ʊ/	stood /ʊ/	*être debout*
	stick /ɪ/	stuck /ʌ/	stuck /ʌ/	*coller*
	strike /aɪ/	struck /ʌ/	struck /ʌ/	*frapper*
T	teach /iː/	taught /ɔː/	taught /ɔː/	*enseigner*
	tell /e/	told /əʊ/	told /əʊ/	*dire, raconter*
	think /ɪ/	thought /ɔː/	thought /ɔː/	*penser*
U	understand /ʌ/ə/æ/	understood /ʌ/ə/ʊ/	understood /ʌ/ə/ʊ/	*comprendre*
W	win /ɪ/	won /ʌ/	won /ʌ/	*gagner*

	Base verbale	Prétérit	Participe passé	Traduction
	Deux formes identiques			
B	beat /iː/	beat /iː/	beaten /iː/ə/	*battre*
	become /ɪ/ʌ/	became /ɪ/eɪ/	become /ɪ/ʌ/	*devenir*
C	come /ʌ/	came /eɪ/	come /ʌ/	*venir*
R	run /ʌ/	ran /æ/	run /ʌ/	*courir*
	Trois formes différentes			
A	awake /ə/eɪ/	awoke /ə/əʊ/	awoken /ə/əʊ/ə/	*(se) réveiller*
B	be /iː/	was /ɒ/ / were /ɜː/	been /iː/	*être*
	bear /ɛə/	bore /ɔː/	borne /ɔː/	*supporter*
	begin /ɪ/ɪ/	began /ɪ/æ/	begun /ɪ/ʌ/	*commencer*
	bite /aɪ/	bit /ɪ/	bitten /ɪ/ə/	*mordre*
	blow /əʊ/	blew /uː/	blown /əʊ/	*souffler*
	break /eɪ/	broke /əʊ/	broken /əʊ/ə/	*casser*
C	choose /uː/	chose /əʊ/	chosen /əʊ/ə/	*choisir*
D	do /uː/	did /ɪ/	done /ʌ/	*faire*
	draw /ɔː/	drew /uː/	drawn /ɔː/	*dessiner*
	drink /ɪ/	drank /æ/	drunk /ʌ/	*boire*
	drive /aɪ/	drove /əʊ/	driven /ɪ/ə/	*conduire*
E	eat /iː/	ate /e/	eaten /iː/ə/	*manger*
F	fall /ɔː/	fell /e/	fallen /ɔː/ə/	*tomber*
	fly /aɪ/	flew /uː/	flown /əʊ/	*voler*
	forbid /ə/ɪ/	forbade /ə/eɪ/	forbidden /ə/ɪ/ə/	*interdire*
	foresee /ɔː/iː/	foresaw /ɔː/ɔː/	foreseen /ɔː/iː/	*prévoir*
	forget /ə/e/	forgot /ə/ɒ/	forgotten /ə/ɒ/ə/	*oublier*
	forgive /ə/ɪ/	forgave /ə/eɪ/	forgiven /ə/ɪ/ə/	*pardonner*
	freeze /iː/	froze /əʊ/	frozen /əʊ/ə/	*geler*
G	give /ɪ/	gave /eɪ/	given /ɪ/ə/	*donner*
	go /əʊ/	went /e/	gone /ɒ/	*aller*
	grow /əʊ/	grew /uː/	grown /əʊ/	*grandir, faire pousser*
H	hide /aɪ/	hid /ɪ/	hidden /ɪ/ə/	*(se) cacher*
K	know /nəʊ/	knew /njuː/	known /nəʊn/	*savoir, connaître*
L	lie /aɪ/	lay /eɪ/	lain /eɪ/	*être étendu*
R	ride /aɪ/	rode /əʊ/	ridden /ɪ/ə/	*aller (à cheval / vélo)*
	ring /ɪ/	rang /æ/	rung /ʌ/	*sonner*
	rise /aɪ/	rose /əʊ/	risen /ɪ/ə/	*s'élever, se lever*
S	see /iː/	saw /ɔː/	seen /iː/	*voir*
	shake /eɪ/	shook /ʊ/	shaken /eɪ/ə/	*secouer*
	show /əʊ/	showed /əʊ/	shown /əʊ/	*montrer*
	sing /ɪ/	sang /æ/	sung /ʌ/	*chanter*
	speak /iː/	spoke /əʊ/	spoken /əʊ/ə/	*parler*
	steal /iː/	stole /əʊ/	stolen /əʊ/ə/	*voler, dérober*
	swear /ɛə/	swore /ɔː/	sworn /ɔː/	*jurer*
	swim /ɪ/	swam /æ/	swum /ʌ/	*nager*
T	take /eɪ/	took /ʊ/	taken /eɪ/ə/	*prendre*
	tear /ɛə/	tore /ɔː/	torn /ɔː/	*déchirer*
	throw /əʊ/	threw /uː/	thrown /əʊ/	*jeter*
U	undergo /ʌ/ə/əʊ/	underwent /ʌ/ə/e/	undergone /ʌ/ə/ɒ/	*subir*
W	wake (up) /eɪ/ʌ/	woke (up) /əʊ/ʌ/	woken (up) /əʊ/ə/ʌ/	*(se) réveiller*
	wear /ɛə/	wore /ɔː/	worn /ɔː/	*porter (des vêtements)*
	write /aɪ/	wrote /əʊ/	written /ɪ/ə/	*écrire*

Crédits photographiques

p. 12 h : © collection Christophel ; **p. 12 b** : © Rue des Archives/BCA ; **p. 13 bg** : © Paul/Kharbine-Tapabor ; **p. 13 bd** : © Rem/Shutterstock ; **p. 14-15** : © Getty Images ; **p. 17 hg** : © Agostino Pacciani ; **p. 17 hm** : © www.campsinternational.com ; **p. 17 hd** : © www.travellersworldwide.com ; **p. 17 b** : © Reinhard Eisele/Corbis ; **p. 18** : © Masha Hamilton ; **p. 19** : © Masha Hamilton ; **p. 20 h** : © Photo12.com/Alamy ; **p. 20** : © Cross-Cultural Solutions ; **p. 21 h** : © Comenius ; **p. 21 mg** : © Pixel Memoirs/ShutterStock ; **p. 21 m** : © Photo12.com/Alamy ; **p. 21 md** : © Photo12.com/Alamy ; **p. 22** : © www.stillwildstillthreatened.org ; **p. 23** : © Matthew Newton ; **p. 25** : © Photolibrary.com ; **p. 26** : © Gautam/AP/Sipa ; **p. 27** : © Gautam/APPhoto/Sipa ; **p. 28** : © Fotosearch/age fotostock ; **p. 29** : © Helene Bamberger/Cosmos ; **p. 30-31** : © collection Christophel ; **p. 32 h** : © Costa/Leemage ; **p. 32 m** : © Photo12.com/Alamy ; **p. 32 b** : © Don Cravens/Time Life Pictures/Getty Images ; **p. 33 h** : © Bettmann/Corbis ; **p. 33 b** : © Walden Media/Bristol Bay/The Kobal Collection ; **p. 34** : © www.superheroesanonymous.com ; **p. 36 hg** : © Getty Images/AFP Photo ; **p. 36 hd** : © Dean Lewins/Epa/Corbis ; **p. 36 b** : © The Andy Warhol Foundation for the Visual Arts, Inc/Corbis/ADAGP, Paris 2011 ; **p. 37** : © TM & 2010 Marvel Entertainment LLC and its subsidiaries. Used with permission ; **p. 38 g** : © Stevent Forster/AP/Sipa ; **p. 38 d** : © Jim Goldberg/Magnum Photos ; **p. 42 h** : © collection Christophel ; **p. 42 m** : © collection Christophel ; **p. 42 b** : © collection Christophel ; **p. 43 g** : © TM & 2010 Marvel Entertainment LLC and its subsidiaries. Used with permission ; **p. 43 m** : photo The Advertising Archives © DC Comics ; **p. 43 d** : © TM & 2010 Marvel Entertainment LLC and its subsidiaries. Used with permission ; p. **44 g** : © Sadia/Fotolia ; **p. 44 d** : © Mark Wilson/AP Photo/Sipa ; **p. 45 h** : © Rob Kim/Retna Ltd./Corbis ; **p. 45 b** : © Frank Siteman – Doctor Stock/Science Faction/Corbis ; **p. 46 h** : © Dorothea Lange – Image by © Corbis ; **p. 46 b** : © Dennis Stock/Magnum Photos ; p. **47 h** : © Oscar Graubner/Time Life Pictures/Getty Images ; **p. 47 b** : © Leonard Freed/Magnum Photos ; **p. 48-49** : © Walter Bibikow/The Image Bank/Getty Images ; **p. 50 h** : © Hulton/Getty ; **p. 50 b** : © Corbis ; **p. 51** : © collection Christophel ; **p. 52 g** : ©Elliott Erwitt/Magnum Photos (détail) ; **p. 52 d** : © Sanna Lindberg/ès Photography/Corbis ; **p. 53** : © www.thecompanycar.ca ; **p. 54 hg** : © collection Christophel ; **p. 54 hd** : © Photolibrary ; **p. 54 bd** : © Imago/Rue des Archives ; **p. 55** : © National Parks Conservation Association ; **p. 56** : © Photolibrary ; **p. 59** : © Shutterstock ; **p. 60 h** : © SuperStock/Leemage ; **p. 60 b** : © collection Christophel ; **p. 61 h** : © Bruce Davidson/Magnum Photos ; **p. 61 b** : © collection Christophel ; **p. 62 g** : © Simon Krzic/Shutterstock ; **p. 62 d** : © Maga/Shutterstock ; **p. 63** : © Corbis ; **p. 64-65** : © Bo Zaunders/Corbis ; **p. 66 h** : d'après l'affiche *Made in USA : Mythes et rêves américains* – © D. Balitran – Perspectives ; **p. 66 b** : © collection Christophel ; **p. 67** : © The Rocky Mountains News/Dist. by United Features Syndicate, Inc ; **p. 68 g** : © Basso Cannarsa/Opale ; **p. 68 d** : © The Granger Collection NYC/Rue des Archives ; **p. 70 g** : © www.CartoonStock.com ; **p. 70 d** : © Curtis Publishing/The Saturday Evening Post ; **p. 71 g** : © Yuri Acurs/Shutterstock ; **p. 71 d** : © Yuri Acurs/Shutterstock ; **p. 72** : © Paramount/The Kobal Collection ; **p. 75** : © S.O. Carroll/Altopress/Andia ; **p. 76** : © Bettmann/Corbis ; **p. 77** : © Burstein Collection/Corbis ; **p. 78** : © Mirisch-7 Arts/United Artist/The Kobal Collection ; **p. 79** : © Lewis W. Hine/George Eastman House/Getty Image ; **p. 80 h** : Museum of Modern Art, NY, Scala ©Jasper Johns/Adagp, Paris 2011 ; **p. 80 bg** : Wadsworth Atheneum Museum of Art/Art Resource/Scala © Robert Rauschenberg/Adagp, Paris 2011 ; p. **80 bd** : © SuperStock/Leemage – Adagp, Paris 2011 ; **p. 81 h** : Smithsonian American Art Museum/Art Resource/Scala, Copyright Parasol Press, S.A., New © Richard Estes ; **p. 81 m** © The Estate of Jean-Michel Basquiat/ADAGP, BI, Paris 2011 ; **p. 81 b** : © The Estate of Jean-Michel Basquiat/ADAGP Paris 2011-The Andy Warhol Foundation for the Visual Arts, Inc/ADAGP, Paris 2011 ; **p. 82-83** : © Catherine Shepard/Rue des Archives ; **p. 84 h** : © Contemporary African Art Collection Limited/Corbis ; **p. 84 m** : © STR New/Reuters ; **p. 84 b** : © www.madamandeve.co.za **p. 85 h** : © David Turnley/Corbis ; **p. 85 m** : © Per-Anders Pettersson/Getty Images ; **p. 85 b** : © collection Christophel ; **p. 86 g** : © BooKphotoSA ; **p. 86 d** © Peter Turnley/Corbis ; **p. 88 g** : © Peter Andrews/Reuters ; **p. 88 d** : © Elwyn Tait/Time Life Pictures/Getty Images ; **p. 89** : © Matthew McKee; Eye Ubiquitous/Corbis ; **p. 90** : © Rue des Archives/BCA ; **p. 93** : © Boris/Shutterstock ; **p. 94 h** © Oliver Strewe/Lonely Planet Images/Getty Images ; **p. 94 b** : © Heritage images/Leemage ; **p. 95 h** : © Warlukurlangu artists of yuendumu/ph Gérard Blot/RMN ; **p. 95 m** : © Christine Osborne/Corbis ; **p. 95 b** : © Circle of blue **p. 96 h** : © Siphiwe Sibeko/Reuters ; **p. 96 b** : © Alan Porritt/Epa/Corbis ; **p. 97** © Cartoon by Nicholson from The Australian www.nicholsoncartoons.com.au **p. 98-99** : © Bruno Fert/Picturetank ; **p. 100 h** : © D.A. Khan/UNHCR ; **p. 100 m** © Photo12/Alamy ; **p. 100 b** : © Philippe Huguen/AFP photo ; **p. 101 h** © Photo12/Alamy ; **p. 101 b** : © collection Christophel ; **p. 102 g** : © Isabelle Simon/Sipa ; **p. 102 d** : © Reid Lincoln Ashton/Masterfile ; **p. 103** : © Bried Shutterstock ; **p. 104 h** : © UNHRC Argentina Young & Rubicam Advertisement Agency in Buenos Aires ; **p. 104 b** : © With thanks to UNHCR for the use of this poster ; **p. 105** : © Sandra Calligaro/Picturetank ; **p. 106** : © Photo12/Alamy **p. 109** : © Chris Futcher/Age fotostock ; **p. 110 b** : © Maja Suslin/Epa/Corbis **p. 111 h** : © Wavebreakmedia Ltd/Shutterstock ; **p. 111 m** : © Fly Fernandez Corbis ; **p. 111 b** : © Corbis ; **p. 112** : © Deborah Gray Mitchell, Asyati Center Marc Joseph – www.artsouthhomestead.org ; **p. 113 h** : © Karen Kasmauski Corbis ; **p. 113 b** : © collection Christophel ; **p. 114 h** : © collection Christophel **p. 114 b** : © collection Christophel ; **p. 115 h** : © collection Christophel ; **p. 114** **115 b** : © collection Christophel ; **p. 116-117** : © Sherborne Learning Centre **p. 118 h** : © Getty Images/Time & Life Pictures Creative ; **p. 119 h** : © Corbis **p.119 b** : © ARP Selection ; **p. 120** : © Heritage Images/Leemage ; **p. 121** © Gary Hershorn/Reuters ; **p. 122** : © Mark Ralston/AFP Photo ; **p. 123** : © Bran Shutterstock ; **p. 124 g** : © BIS – archives Labor ; **p. 124 d** : © 1995 Ralph Steadman ; **p. 128** : © Photo12/Alamy ; **p. 129 hg** : © Images.com/Corbis **p. 129 hd** : © Tony Avelar/Bloomberg/Getty Images ; **p. 129 b** : © Ramerez/INF Starface ; **p. 130** : © europa-eu ; **p. 134** : © British Library ; **p. 136** : © Photo Re-Pubblic/leemage ; **p. 137** : © Paramount/The Kobal Collection ; **p. 138** © Paramount/The Kobal Collection ; **p. 139 h** : © Christine et Michel Denis Huot/Jacana ; **p. 139 b** : © Dave Watts/Biosphoto ; **p. 140 hd** : © Suddeutsche Zeitung/Rue des Archives ; **p. 140 hg** : © Rue des Archives/RDA ; **p. 140 b** © Mary Evans/Rue des Archives ; **p. 141 hg** : © photolibrary.com ; **p. 141 hd** © The Granger Collection NYC/Rue des Archives ; **p. 142 g** : © Photo12.com/Alamy ; **p. 142 d** : © Rue des Archives/BCA ; **p. 143 hg** : © Animals Animals/Sunset ; **p. 143 bg** : © Jon Hrusa/Epa/Corbis ; **p. 143 bd** : © Torsten Blackwood/AFP Photo ; **p. 144** : © Werner Forman Archive/Courtesy Entwistle Gallery, London ; **p. 145** : © Rue des Archives/BCA ; **p. 146** : © Helder Almeida Shutterstock ; **p. 148** : © Elinapas/Shutterstock ; **p. 150** : © Kacso Sandor Shutterstock ; **p. 153** : © Inobjective/Shutterstock ; **p. 155** : © Rawalpind MAXPPP ; **p. 156** : © The Advertising Archives ; **p. 157** : © William Perugini Shutterstock ; **p. 159** : © Andresr/Shutterstock ; **p. 161** : © William Perugini Shutterstock ; **p. 165** : © Yuri Arcurs/Shutterstock.

Crédits textes

p. 18 : © 2007 by Masha Hamilton, Reprinted by permission of HarperCollins Publishers ; **p. 26-27** : Seth Mydans, from *The New York Times*, © April 9th 2007, *The New York Times*. All rights reserved. Used by permission and protected by the Copyright Laws of the United States. The printing, copying, redistribution, or retransmission of the Material without express written permission is prohibited. **p. 29** : Copyright *Guardian* News & Media Ltd 2010 ; **p. 34** : Trymaine Lee, from *The New York Times*, © October 29th 2007, *The New York Times*. All rights reserved. Used by permission and protected by the Copyright Laws of the United States. The printing, copying, redistribution, or retransmission of the Material without express written permission is prohibited ; **p. 56** : © Ben Macintyre, September 18th 2008, *The Times* ; **p. 72** : Copyright *Guardian* News & Media Ltd 2010 ; **p. 78** : Copyright 1956, 1957, 1958, 1959 by Amberson Holdings LLC and Stephen Sondheim. Copyright renewed. Leonard Bernstein Music Publishing Company LLC, publisher. International copyright secured. Reproduced by permission of Boosey & Hawkes Music Publishers Ltd ; **p. 86** : *Dog Eat Dog* by Niq Mhlongo reproduced by permission of Kwela Books ; **p. 90** : © 1996, Doris Pilkington, *Rabbit Proof Fence*, Hyperion Buenas Vista Books ; **p. 97** : © AFP ; **p. 102** : © 2008, Chri Cleave, *Little Bee*. Originally published as *The Other Hand* in Great Britain in 200 by Sceptre, an imprint of Hodder & Stoughton ; **p. 106** : Copyright 2010, E& Publishing, LLC. Republished with permission ; **p. 107** : © Viewpoint by Cecili Tacoli, September 29th 2009 ; **p. 123** : Copyright *Guardian* News & Media Lt 2010 ; **p. 124** : *Animal Farm* by George Orwell. Copyright © George Orwel 1945 by permission of Bill Hamilton as the Literary Executor of the Estate of th Late Sonia Brownell Orwell and Secker & Warburg Ltd ; **p. 131** : Photo and tex Minnesota Public Radio, Sasha Aslanian, © 2010. Used with permission. All right reserved ; **p. 134** : © 2005 by James Baldwin, *Fifty famous stories retold*.

Nous avons recherché en vain les éditeurs ou les ayants droit de certains texte dans ce livre. Leurs droits sont réservés aux Éditions Nathan.

Crédits sonores

Piste 14 : © VOA ; **pistes 15, 53** : © NPR ; **piste 16** : © CBS ; **piste 35** : © Ten/D.R. ; **piste 41** : © 5th & Ocean Productions ; **piste 42** : © RT News Channel ; **piste 47** : © Cross-Cultural Solutions ; **piste 48** : © The MY HERO Project http://myhero.com ; **piste 49** : © Podcast.com / D.R. ; **piste 50** : © CBS ; **piste 51** © ABC ; **piste 52** : © Kids Company.

N° d'éditeur 10233338 - Dépôt légal Février 2017 - Imprimé en Italie par BONA